Logion Press Books

Stanley M. Horton, Th.D.

General Editor

OUR DESTINY

Stanley M. Horton

OUR DESTINY

Biblical Teachings on the Last Things

LOGION
P R E S S
Springfield, Missouri
02-0322

Logion Press books are published by Gospel Publishing House.

Library of Congress Cataloging-in-Publication Data
Horton, Stanley M.
Our destiny : biblical teachings on the last things / Stanley M. Horton.
p. cm.
Includes bibliographical references and indexes.
ISBN 0-88243-322-9
1. Eschatology. 2. Eschatology—Biblical teaching. I. Title.
BT821.2.H67 1995
236—dc20   95-31343

Printed in the United States of America

Contents

Preface

Teaching about the prophesied last things and the blessed hope of the believer in Christ has been my privilege and joy over a period of forty-six years. Faith in Christ involves trust, obedience, and expectation. These have been made more and more important to me as the Holy Spirit continues to work in my life and ministry. It is with my students in mind, who are serving God all over the world, that I write. May they and the ones to whom they minister be encouraged as they read and study what the Bible says about the last things.

In line with the usage of both the KJV and the NIV, "Lord" is used in capitals and small capitals where the Hebrew of the Old Testament has the personal, divine name of God, Yahweh.[1]

In quoted Scripture, words I wish to emphasize are highlighted with italics.

For easier reading, Hebrew, Aramaic, and Greek words are all transliterated with English letters.

A few abbreviations have been used:

Gk.: Greek
Heb.: Hebrew
Lat.: Latin
KJV: King James Version
RSV: Revised Standard Version

---

[1] The Hebrew wrote only the consonants YHWH, Later traditions followed the New Latin JHVH and added vowels from the Hebrew for "Lord" to remind them to read *Lord* instead of the divine name. This was never intended, however, to be read "Jehovah."

Preface

LXX: The Septuagint, a Greek translation of the Old Testament made in Alexandria, Egypt, during the two centuries before Christ.

Williams: *The New Testament in the Language of the People* (Charles B. Williams)

My special thanks go to Dr. Zenas Bicket, Dr. Edgar Lee, and Dr. Jesse Moon for reading the manuscript and making valuable suggestions. Special thanks also to Glen Ellard and his editing staff at Gospel Publishing House and to all who assisted in preparing this book.

Introduction: Good News

The word "gospel" means "good news." The central fact of this good news Peter gave on the Day of Pentecost: "God has raised this Jesus to life, and we are all witnesses of the fact. Exalted to the right hand of God, he has received from the Father the promised Holy Spirit and has poured out what you now see and hear. For David did not ascend to heaven, and yet he said, 'The Lord said to my Lord: "Sit at my right hand until I make your enemies a footstool for your feet"'" (Acts 2:32-35). It is good news not only that Jesus rose from the dead, but also that He is at God the Father's right hand in the place of authority, interceding for us: He "speaks to the Father in our defense" (1 John 2:1). From the throne He keeps pouring out the Holy Spirit upon believers to give us help and power. He is also waiting for the time when God will say it is enough and send Him back victorious over all His enemies (Heb. 10:13).

Peter gave the further good news that the promise of the Holy Spirit's outpouring was not just for the Day of Pentecost, but for all who repent and are baptized, "'You will receive the gift of the Holy Spirit. The promise is for you and your children and for all who are far off—for all whom the Lord our God will call'" (Acts 2:38-39).

The call, however, is not just to come to Christ and receive forgiveness and power. Peter pleaded, "'Save yourselves from this corrupt generation'" (Acts 2:40).

11

That plea is even more necessary today. We live in a world where the future seems to be more and more uncertain. The great scientist Albert Einstein, after World War II, pointed out that fear among nations was increasing, as were starvation, injustice, territorial conflicts, and power politics.[1] In spite of all the current peace efforts, this is still true. Fallen human nature has not changed. John the Baptist called unrepentant unbelievers a "brood of vipers" (Matt. 3:7). Jesus called them hypocrites, dogs, pigs, blind guides, full of greed and self-indulgence, belonging to their father, the devil (Matt. 7:5-6; 23:24-25,28; John 8:44). He sent His apostles out "like sheep among wolves" (Matt. 10:16). Peter wrote of

those who follow the corrupt desire of the sinful nature and despise authority. Bold and arrogant, these men are not afraid to slander celestial beings; yet even angels, although they are stronger and more powerful, do not bring slanderous accusations against such beings in the presence of the Lord. But these men blaspheme in matters they do not understand. They are like brute beasts, creatures of instinct, born only to be caught and destroyed, and like beasts they too will perish. . . . Their idea of pleasure is to carouse in broad daylight. . . . With eyes full of adultery, they never stop sinning; they seduce the unstable; they are experts in greed—an accursed brood! (2 Pet. 2:10-14).

Jude adds that they "are grumblers and faultfinders; they follow their own evil desires; they boast about themselves and flatter others for their own advantage . . . ; scoffers who will follow their own ungodly desires . . . who follow mere natural instincts and do not have the Spirit" (Jude 16,18-19). As Pastor Guy Duty wrote, "The diseased moral mind sinks lower and lower in the moral scale."[2]

---

[1]Otto Nathan and Heinz Norden, eds., *Einstein on Peace* (New York: Harper & Row, Publishers, 1980), 355-56.

[2]See Guy Duty, *Christ's Coming and the World Church* (Minneapolis: Bethany Fellowship, 1971), 119.

THE ONLY GOOD NEWS LEFT

Nevertheless, most people of the world still want to hope for the best, even though today's media give us very little hope, very little good news. In fact, the gospel, God's "good news," is about the only really good news left. This good news looks to the past, the present, and the future. It is good news that God, who created all things through Jesus Christ (John 1:3), loves everyone in the world and desires to share His blessings and fellowship with each of us. It is good news that Jesus died for all, and His death put into effect a new covenant that offers not only salvation and fellowship with God through Jesus, but also the gift of the Holy Spirit and the sure hope of Christ's return and our sharing in eternal glory (Rom. 8:9-10,23-24; 15:13; 2 Cor. 3:8,11-12; Eph. 3:16-19; Col. 1:17; 1 Pet. 4:14). It is good news, too, that in spite of the corruption in this world, whenever people repent and turn to God their sins will be wiped out and times of refreshing will come from the Lord. The Greek indicates that we can have these seasons of refreshing, these times of mighty spiritual revival, right up to the time Jesus comes back to earth again.

This good news gives meaning to life today. We can still affect our world for Christ. We can still expect to see Pentecostal outpourings and thousands saved and added to the Church, as is actually happening in many parts of the world even now. We can and must be "the salt of the earth," having a seasoning and preserving effect on those around us. We can and must be "the light of the world," letting our "light shine before men, that they may see [our] good deeds and praise [our] Father in heaven," as Jesus commanded (Matt. 5:13-16). Withdrawing from the corruption of the world does not mean turning our backs on the world and its needs. It does not mean taking no part in the political process or in community efforts to improve our situation. Our good deeds involve not only imparting spiritual blessings, but also helping the poor and doing whatever else we can to lessen the corruption and violence that affect our world and its environment.

Long ago, humankind as a whole did turn away from God (Rom. 1:18–23). But God did not turn away from us. He came down into the stream of human life and history to reveal himself and to prepare the way for the gift of His Son. The death and resurrection of Jesus guarantees that all who believe in Him will not perish but have eternal life (John 3:16). This life is available in the present through the ministry of the Holy Spirit. Then we have the further promise that "this same Jesus . . . will come back in the same way" the disciples saw Him "go into heaven" (Acts 1:11). A cloud received Him. He will return in clouds, just as He himself indicated when He referred to the prophecy of Daniel 7:13 at His trial before the Sanhedrin (see Matt. 26:64).

ESCHATOLOGY: REALITY NOT ESCAPE

Though we should avoid unscriptural speculation, we neglect at our peril what the Bible says about the future fulfillment of God's eternal plan and purpose.[3] The technical term for this study is "eschatology," from the Greek *eschatos,* "last," and *logos,* "word," "message," "knowledge." Pentecostals, along with most Bible believers, have always recognized that eschatology "forms the central and essential framework of New Testament theology."[4] It draws attention to the truth that God is a personal God who has a purpose and a plan for the future as well as for the present, and He can be counted on to carry out His plan. It lets us know that the world is wrong in seeking a better future through evolutionism and mere human

---

[3]W. A. Whitehouse, "The Modern Discussion of Eschatology," in *Eschatology,* William Manson, G. W. H. Lampe, T. F. Torrance, W. A. Whitehouse (Edinburgh, Scotland: Oliver & Boyd, 1953), 66–67, 77, 79, 89.

[4]Eldin Villafañe, *The Liberating Spirit* (Grand Rapids: William B. Eerdmans Publishing Co., 1993), 184.

effort. It "reminds us that the redemption of history must ultimately be a miracle of grace."[5] It lets us know, too, that God is concerned about individuals. For the evolutionist, the individual has little importance. The New Testament offers salvation and a blessed future, not to humankind in general but to individuals, to "whoever believes" (John 3:16-18).

As Alf Corell pointed out, "Eschatology is not a flight away from reality. . . . On the contrary it carries with it a deepening perception of the meaning of reality. It is founded on revelation given in the past, . . . experienced here in the present," and gives assurance of future fulfillment.[6] God sent His Son "when the time had fully come" (Gal. 4:4). This implies fulfillment of a plan. But that plan did not end with the first coming of Christ. Because Jesus came we are redeemed so that we "might receive the full rights of sons" (Gal. 4:5). Thus we become heirs of God with a future inheritance that will be fully ours when Jesus comes again and we share in His glory (Rom. 8:17; Gal. 4:7). Then He "must reign until he has put all his enemies under his feet . . . so that God may be all in all" (1 Cor. 15:25-28). From this perspective it can be said that all theology is ultimately eschatology.

Eschatology is definitely not "an appendix left over from the major concerns of the present life," but "is the confidence that 'he who began a good work in [us] will bring it to completion at the day of Jesus Christ' (Phil. 1:6, RSV). It assures us that '[w]hen Christ, who is [our] life, appears, then [we] also will appear with him in glory' (Col. 3:4)."[7] He is our hope

---

[5]James M. Childs, Jr., *Christian Anthropology and Ethics* (Philadelphia: Fortress Press, 1978), 126.

[6]Alf Corell, *Consummatum est: Eschatology and the Church in the Gospel of St. John,* trans. Order of the Holy Paraclete, Whitby (London: Society for the Promotion of Christian Knowledge, 1958), 7.

[7]Dale Moody, *The Hope of Glory* (Grand Rapids: William B. Eerdmans Publishing Co., 1964), 15.

(Col. 1:27), and the hope of His return gives meaning to life. He is victor, and the future ultimately belongs to Him.[8] Consequently, "the future is not a minor category." The Bible in all its teaching clearly points to the coming consummation. "All the vital energies of the prophets, apostles, and martyrs focus on events yet to come that will illumine all present life."[9]

SUBSTITUTES FOR TRUTH

The world outside of Christ has lost its way. Many reject the light the Bible sheds on life's pathway. They do not yet know what a wonderful, dependable guide the Holy Spirit is. As a result, the world does not know where the rapid changes in world relationships and world history are leading us. Stephen Travis pointed out that to unbelievers "it is as though the human race were passengers in an accelerating jet airliner—with no one on the flight deck."[10] The uncertainty of modern life has caused a spirit of despair to envelop some to the point that they believe the world will self-destruct.[11] If a nuclear bomb doesn't destroy us, pollution will.

Some blind their eyes to this by wishful thinking. Others try to forget by immersing themselves in self-

---

[8]Jürgen Moltmann, *Theology of Hope: On the Ground and the Implications of a Christian Eschatology,* trans. James W. Leitch from the 5th German ed. (New York: Harper & Row, Publishers, 1967), 16–17, recognized this, though his theology separates hope from history and, along with that of the Roman Catholic John Baptist Metz, inspired a liberation theology that sees the kingdom of God as a metaphor and seeks to make radical political and social changes in the present. Cf. Stanley M. Horton, ed., *Systematic Theology* (Springfield, Mo.: Gospel Publishing House, 1994), 617; Donald G. Bloesch, *A Theology of Word and Spirit* (Downers Grove, Ill.: InterVarsity Press, 1992), 106.

[9]Thomas C. Oden, *Life in the Spirit,* vol. 3, Systematic Theology (San Francisco: Harper, HarperCollins Publications, 1992), 368, 371, 373.

[10]Stephen Travis, *The Jesus Hope* (Downers Grove, Ill.: InterVarsity Press, 1974), 10.

[11]See Oden, *Life in the Spirit,* 375.

indulgence and entertainment. Multitudes try to escape by turning to humanistic, mystical, or pagan philosophies, or they are caught up in occult practices in a vain attempt to try to control the future or at least find hope for it. They ignore the biblical warnings against astrology, fortune-telling, spiritist mediums, witchcraft, satanism, and pagan worship. All these things are not only foolish and futile (Isa. 44:25), they also defile people and are detestable to the one true God (Lev. 19:31; Deut. 18:9–12).[12] They are part of the devil's territory and can only lead down the broad road to destruction (Matt. 7:13). They also have a wrong view of history that comes from satanic deception.

PAGAN PHILOSOPHIES

Most of the old pagan philosophies looked at history as cyclical, with no beginning and no end, no goal. Archaeological discoveries at Ugarit, north of Tyre and Sidon, show that the people there were afraid that "aging gods, destructive powers, realms of death" were working to blow out "the lamp of civilized order," thus bringing "a universal return to the beginning of the cycle, and . . . chaos."[13]

Canaanites saw in the gods Baal and Mot "a seasonal rhythm between life and death" that "did not provide much incentive for any long-range planning. . . . [T]he Greek view of life [also] was utterly pessimistic."[14] Many pagans taught reincarnation. That is, one life was supposed to follow another in an endless cycle. Hindus, however, do not consid-

---

[12]G. C. Berkouwer, *The Return of Christ,* trans. James Van Oosterom (Grand Rapids: William B. Eerdmans Publishing Co., 1972), 11.

[13]Ulrich E. Simon, *The End Is Not Yet* (Digswell Place, Welwyn, England: James Nisbet & Co., 1964), 4.

[14]Hans Schwarz, *On the Way to the Future: A Christian View of Eschatology in the Light of Current Trends in Religion, Philosophy, and Science,* rev. ed. (Minneapolis: Augsburg Publishing House, 1979), 17.

er reincarnation a benefit. They seek to deny the craving for life, hope to get off the wheel of life, lose their identity, and be swallowed up in a Brahman or Atman, a supposed "great soul" of the universe.[15] This "great soul," however, turns out to be something their philosophers claim cannot be said to exist and cannot be said not to exist. People who are influenced by these philosophies usually do not realize the emptiness and meaninglessness such teachings bring into human lives. This cyclical view of history has no real answer for the problems of human life. Neither does a linear view of history that is divorced from its biblical roots, as is the case with many modern ideas of progress.

Since René Descartes (1637) secular philosophers have made humanity the center of everything. Immanuel Kant (1783) made human reason the sole authority. Today human efforts are still attempting to lead the world to democracy, freedom, and a new order. But instead, "they lead to new slavery and potential self-destruction."[16] Modern existential philosophy also focuses on the human "and ignores the cosmic dimensions of the Scriptures."[17]

---

[15]See Swami Adiswarananda, "Hinduism," in *How Different Religions View Death and Afterlife,* ed. Christopher J. Johnson and Marsha G. McGee (Philadelphia: Charles Press, Publishers, 1991), 159–62, 175.

[16]Schwarz, *On the Way to the Future,* 25; cf. 125, 127, 158.

[17]Zachary Hayes, *What Are They Saying about the End of the World?* (New York: Paulist Press, 1983), 7. He points out that Rudolph Bultmann used the philosophy of Martin Heidegger to interpret the symbols of Scripture as mythical and to separate eschatology completely from chronology, denying any Kingdom to come. Much modern Roman Catholic thought has been influenced in this direction by comparing R. Bultmann, J. Moltmann, W. Pannenberg, J. Jeremias, and O. Cullmann. See Zachary Hayes, *Visions of the Future: A Study of Christian Eschatology* (Wilmington, Del.: Michael Glazier, 1985), 13.

BIBLICAL RESPONSE

The Bible, on the other hand, stands in judgment against all such humanistic ideas and imaginations. It gives us "a hope and a promise that we are unable to attain through our own efforts." It reveals what is primarily a linear view of history that has God as Creator and Redeemer.[18] There was a real beginning. God had a plan in creation that showed His concern for those created in His image. He had a plan in redemption that focused on the outpouring of His love for humanity on the cross (John 3:16). He will be faithful to carry out His plan to its grand fulfillment, not in a return to the beginning, but in something far better: a consummation that will bring the millennial kingdom, and ultimately the new heavens and the new earth and the New Jerusalem that He is preparing.

Because of sin, "this world in its present form is passing away" (1 Cor. 7:31). It must do so, for the future Kingdom can come in its fullness and perfection only through judgment (Dan. 2:44–45). Yet, because Jesus came, the Kingdom power, rule, and salvation of God has entered in a new way into history and prepares us to share in God's "eternal purpose which he accomplished in Christ Jesus our Lord" (Eph. 3:11).

That eternal purpose was already a part of God's plan before the creation of the universe. His plan had a real beginning and will have a real consummation. The Hebrew of Genesis 1:1 puts the chief emphasis on the phrase "in the beginning."[19] Ancient pagan religions usually avoided the idea of a beginning. If they talked about creation, it was usually creation from something that was already there, such as earth, air,

---

[18]Oscar Cullmann, *Christ and Time*, rev. ed., trans. Floyd V. Filson (Philadelphia: Westminster Press, 1964), 105.

[19]The Hebrew sentence normally begins with the verb, but anything can be put first for the sake of emphasis, as in Gen. 1:1.

fire, and water; slime; or a giant's body.[20] They pictured their gods as fighting each other, with no one god truly sovereign of the universe. They did not even imagine there could be a God who is big enough, powerful enough, and wise enough to create something out of nothing. Baal, for example, was seen not "as the one who made the fertile world, but rather as the one who makes [their part of] the world fertile . . . he becomes the means by which we gain things . . . a god to be used," rather than truly worshiped.[21] But the Bible keeps pointing to God as Creator. In fact, He alone can create. The Old Testament Hebrew never uses the word for "create" *(bara')* with anyone but God as the subject.

And the same God who created us loves us enough to redeem us. The Bible is a record of the unfolding of His great plan of redemption, a plan that gives us a sure hope. As believers in Jesus we are a new creation spiritually, and we look forward to a resurrection with a new body and ultimately to an eternity with a new heavens and a new earth, a whole new creation. Therefore, eschatology is not only the study of the last things; it is related to everything that the Bible teaches. Above all, it deals with the faithfulness of God and gives us assurance that the ultimate victory is His—not Satan's.[22]

As believers in Jesus we also have the Holy Spirit as "another Counselor" *(paraklētos,* "helper," John 14:16), who enables us to serve God and one another as He prepares us for the life to come. As an experience of empowerment the promised baptism in the Holy Spirit bestows gifts and ministries. But it also

[20]James B. Pritchard, ed., *The Ancient Near East: An Anthology of Texts and Pictures,* vol. 1 (Princeton, N.J.: Princeton University Press, 1973), 35.

[21]A. J. Conyers, *The Eclipse of Heaven: Rediscovering the Hope of a World Beyond* (Downers Grove, Ill.: InterVarsity Press, 1992), 131.

[22]Joseph Papin, ed., *The Eschaton: A Community of Love* (Villanova, Pa.: Villanova University Press, 1971), 59.

does more. The power of the Holy Spirit brings an upsurge and overflow of hope, a hope fixed in the God of hope, a hope of eternal rewards reserved for us in heaven, a resurrection hope, a hope of Christ's return and His millennial reign, a hope of eternal glory that far outweighs all the "light and momentary troubles" that we now experience (2 Cor. 4:17). We can in this age taste "the goodness of the word of God and the powers of the coming age" (Heb. 6:5).

THE GOD OF HOPE

The apostle Paul prayed, "May the God of hope fill you with all joy and peace as you trust in him, so that you may overflow with hope by the power of the Holy Spirit" (Rom. 15:13). The "power" (Gk. *dunamei*) is the powerful actions and gifts of the Spirit in the present.[23] When these are evident, as in the Pentecostal revival, there is always an overflow of hope that the Lord will surely come and that the glory and blessings of the millennial age are real.[24]

A SURE HOPE

Because our hope comes from the God of hope who confirmed His promise with an oath, both "unchangeable things in which it is impossible for God to lie" (Heb. 6:17-18), it has no sense of uncertainty connected with it. It is called a hope only because we do not have it yet (Rom. 8:24-25). Therefore it is a sure hope, "an anchor for the soul, firm and secure" (Heb. 6:19). We know it will never disappoint us "because God has poured out his love into our hearts by the Holy Spirit, whom he has given us" (Rom. 5:5).

---

[23]Neill Quinn Hamilton, *The Holy Spirit and Eschatology in Paul,* Scottish Journal of Theology Occasional Papers, no. 6 (Edinburgh, Scotland: Oliver & Boyd, 1957), 35.

[24]This was certainly true in the Azusa Street revival in Los Angeles (1906-8), as my mother and her parents experienced it. The Holy Spirit created in them an intense desire to see the soon coming of Jesus.

The Holy Spirit makes the love of God real in our experience. That means that the God who loved us enough to send Jesus to die on Calvary for our sins, loves us enough to make every provision to see us all the way through to glory (Rom. 5:9–10; 8:17–20) and makes the Christian hope live. It is no wonder then that the very beginning of the twentieth-century Pentecostal revival was marked by an intense anticipation of the return of our Lord Jesus Christ to earth.[25]

God has always been the God of hope. An analysis of the first chapter of Genesis shows that in creation there was a step-by-step sequence; correspondence between days one and four, two and five, three and six; balance with one distinct creative act each on days one, two, four, and five, with two distinct creative acts on day three and again on day six. Finally there was climax with the creation of the man and the woman in the image of God. These facts all indicate God created by a plan. Before the plan was put into effect, there was anticipation, or hope, indicated by the continual hovering of the Spirit of God over the primeval ocean. That hope found initial fulfillment in the fellowship God enjoyed with Adam and Eve in the cool of the day (Gen. 3:8).

A CONTINUING HOPE

Even when that fellowship was broken by sin, God did not give up His hope for humankind. Though Adam and Eve and the serpent who tempted her were punished, in the midst of the judgment on the serpent, God offered hope by promising that the offspring of the woman would crush the head of the serpent (Gen. 3:15). Then He provided Adam and Eve with garments of skin from slain animals, which anticipated the covering of sins by the shedding of sacrificial blood, ultimately by the blood of Jesus. From that

---

[25]James R. Goff, Jr., "Closing Out the Church Age: Pentecostals Face the Twenty-first Century," *Pneuma* 14:1 (Spring 1992): 12.

point on God began a plan of redemption which would offer salvation to all who would turn to Him in faith. Again, the very fact that we can see the unfolding of this plan in the Bible shows that there was hope.[26]

In the time of Enosh, a few did turn to God and call on Him for blessing (Gen. 4:26). But by the time of Noah the world had become so corrupt and so full of violence that God "was grieved that he had made man on the earth, and his heart was filled with pain," so He determined to bring judgment on the human race (Gen. 6:5-7,11-13). But even then there was hope, for Noah walked with God and found favor (Gen. 6:8-9). God graciously gave directions for an ark that meant salvation for Noah and his family.

A new start did not solve the world's problems, however. By the time of the tower of Babel (Gen. 11:1-9), the world had again turned away from God and was consumed with a passion for self-preservation and self-exaltation in a unified world order. Not only did God scatter them, He quit dealing with the world as a whole and gave them over to their sins (Rom. 1:24,26) so that their sins would bring part of their judgment on them and prepare them to see their need for a Savior.

But God did not give up His plan for humankind. He found a man, Abraham, who would respond in faith. To him God gave an unconditional fourfold promise of blessing—for himself, for his descendants, for the land, and for all nations—through one unique descendant who was to come (Gen. 12:1-3). God

---

[26]This is a profound hope which links "the destiny of all the Gentiles ["nations"] to the victory of the gentle Jesus" (Isa. 42:1-4; Matt. 12:18,20-21). The Greek word *(elpis)* is always found in the singular in the Bible, never in the plural; there is only one hope humankind can truly live by. Paul Sevier Minear, *The Christian Hope and the Second Coming* (Philadelphia: Westminster Press, 1954), 19, 23.

was in this way revealed as the God of promise, and from Abraham on, the Bible has a forward look.[27]

THE COVENANTING GOD

The promise to Abraham was confirmed by God's covenant and His oath, two things "in which it is impossible for God to lie" (Heb. 6:17-18). God further confirmed the promise to Isaac (Gen. 26:3-4) and to Jacob (Gen. 28:13-14) and then, at the Exodus, to the nation of Israel (Exod. 6:8).[28] God would fulfill it in His own way, and this assurance was intensified both by the later prophets and by the New Testament.[29]

THE COVENANT OF THE LAW

At Mount Sinai God brought Israel into a covenant relationship with himself by giving them the Law through Moses. That Law was not God's final purpose, however. God still had in view blessing for all the peoples of the world. Israel was a chosen nation, chosen as a servant to help bring about that purpose. They were chosen in much the same sense that the commandos of World War II were a chosen group— chosen to go into enemy territory and make a beachhead so others could follow. The whole world had become Satan's territory; Israel in the Promised Land was to become a beachhead to prepare the way for the blessings of God to be spread to the nations through the promised One to come.

The world was not ready for Christ and the Cross, however. Nor was Israel the witness that was needed as preparation for the spread of the gospel. Consequently, the Law was given as a temporary tutor (Gk.

---

[27]William J. Dalton, *Aspects of New Testament Eschatology* (Nedlands, Australia: University of Western Australia Press, 1968), 4.

[28]T. V. Farris, *Mighty to Save: A Study in Old Testament Soteriology* (Nashville: Broadman Press, 1993), 72-73.

[29]Dalton, *Aspects of New Testament Eschatology,* 5.

paidagōgos, Gal. 3:24) to bring Israel down through the centuries until "the time had fully come" and "God sent his Son" (Gal. 4:4).

Though God "made known his ways to Moses, his deeds to the people of Israel," and was "compassionate and gracious" (Ps. 103:7-8), Israel kept falling back into sin and idolatry. Yet, in spite of Israel's failures, God sent the prophets to reinforce the covenant and to encourage them with the hope of future restoration and blessing. That hope included a step-by-step revelation of the promised Messiah, God's anointed Prophet, Priest, and King. Some critics, saying that hopeful passages are later additions, have seen the prophets as proclaimers of nothing but doom and despair. But it is impossible to "discredit the surge of prophetic hopefulness that looks . . . to restoration . . . in which God reigns himself in the hearts of men and especially through the Son of David."[30]

Nathan's prophecy to David assured him that God would see to it that there would always be a man for the throne. This specifically looked ahead to the One who will make David's throne eternal. The prophecy also made clear that if David's descendants sinned, they would be punished "with the rod of men" (2 Sam. 7:14). Therefore, since Israel did fall again and again into idolatry, God brought an end to the Davidic kingdom and sent the people into exile.

The prophets show, however, that God's purpose in sending His people to Babylon was to get rid of their idolatry (Jer. 29:8-13). This did take place. In exile they began to realize who the true prophets were and through the study of the prophets saw the foolishness of idolatry.[31] When they returned, their purpose was to rebuild the temple and restore pure worship of the Lord. By the time Jesus was born in

---

[30]Simon, *The End Is Not Yet,* 14.

[31]Note the tremendous irony in the descriptions of idolatry (Isa. 40:18-20; 44:9-20; Hos. 4:12; 13:2; Amos 5:26).

Bethlehem, Jews and their synagogues were scattered over the known world and they were recognized as a people who served one God and held high moral standards.

Unfortunately, their view of the Messiah focused only on the earthly aspects of His kingdom (or rule). They were looking for one who was just a man, and their hope was more temporal and political than religious;[32] they wanted someone who would overthrow the Roman Empire and make the Jews rulers of the world. Yet, because they did have the Scriptures, their synagogues became a base for the rapid spread of the gospel in the first century.

With the coming of Jesus and His death on the cross, the Law's work was done and it was no longer needed. Actually, the Law had become a barrier separating the Jews from the rest of the nations (the Gentiles). But Jesus "himself is our peace, who has made the two one and has destroyed the barrier, the dividing wall of hostility, by abolishing in his flesh the law with its commandments and regulations. His purpose was to create in himself one new man out of the two, thus making peace, and in this one body to reconcile both of them to God through the cross" (Eph. 2:14–16).

THE NEW COVENANT

The covenant of the Law having been abolished, Christ's death and the shedding of His blood put a brand-new covenant into effect (Heb. 8:13; 9:15 through 10:18). This covenant promises "an eternal inheritance" (Heb. 9:15), and assures us that Jesus "will appear a second time, not to bear sin, but to

---

[32]George Raymond Beasley-Murray, *Jesus and the Future: An Examination of the Criticism of the Eschatological Discourse, Mark 13 with Special Reference to the Little Apocalypse Theory* (London: Macmillan & Co., 1954), 14–15.

bring salvation to those who are waiting for him"
(Heb. 9:28).[33]

Then, as always, the Bible makes a practical application for the present.

Since we have confidence to enter the Most Holy Place
by the blood of Jesus, by a new and living way opened
for us through the curtain, that is, his body, and since we
have a great priest over the house of God, let us draw
near to God with a sincere heart in full assurance of faith,
having our hearts sprinkled to cleanse us from a guilty
conscience and having our bodies washed with pure water. Let us hold unswervingly to the hope we profess, for
he who promised is faithful. And let us consider how we
may spur one another on toward love and good deeds.
Let us not give up meeting together, as some are in the
habit of doing, but let us encourage one another—and all
the more as you see the Day approaching (Heb. 10:19–
25).[34]

In this passage too we see, very forcefully presented, that the "Second Coming is the inevitable historical
sequence of the first coming. The two are indissolubly
bound together."[35]

The apostle Paul had a similar practical application
in mind when he told the Thessalonian believers:
"We continually remember before our God and Father your work produced by faith, your labor prompt-
ed by love, and your endurance inspired by hope in
our Lord Jesus Christ." This faith, hope, and love was
the result of the gospel coming to them "not simply
with words, but also with power, with the Holy Spirit
and with deep conviction." They "welcomed the mes-

---

[33]Heb. 9:28 gives grounds for referring to Christ's return as
the "second coming." Cf. Travis, *The Jesus Hope,* 51.

[34]The "Day" is not referring to a period of twenty-four hours
but rather to a period of God's activity, however long it might
be. See J. E. Fison, *The Christian Hope: The Presence and the
Parousia* (London: Longmans, Green & Co., 1954), 94.

[35]Edgar Young Mullins, *The Christian Religion in Its Doctrinal Expression* (Valley Forge, Pa.: Judson Press, 1917), 451.

sage with the joy given by the Holy Spirit," and they became a model because they "turned to God from idols to serve the living and true God, and to wait for his Son from heaven, whom he raised from the dead—Jesus, who rescues us from the coming wrath" (1 Thess. 1:2-10).

Peter also, in view of the final fiery judgments of the Day of the Lord, says, "Since everything will be destroyed in this way, what kind of people ought you to be? You ought to live holy and godly lives as you look forward to the day of God and speed its coming" (2 Pet. 3:11-12). Then, in view of the new heavens and new earth to come, he adds, "Make every effort to be found spotless, blameless and at peace with him" (2 Pet. 3:14).

A Blessed Hope

We have seen that there was a God-directed progression of history that led to Christ's first coming. As Galatians 4:4-5 says, "When the time had fully come, God sent his Son, born of a woman, born under law, to redeem those under law, that we might receive the full rights of sons." But the fullness of those rights is not yet ours, for the Scripture passage goes on to say, "Because you are sons, God sent the Spirit of his Son into [your] hearts, the Spirit who calls out, '*Abba,* Father.' So you are no longer a slave, but a son; and since you are a son, God has made you also an heir" (Gal. 4:6-7). The word "heir" looks forward here to a future inheritance, thus tying the first coming to the promise of the Second Coming and implying we can expect a God-ordered progression toward its fulfillment.[36]

The first coming is tied to the Second Coming also when the Bible speaks of the grace of God that brings salvation. That saving grace "teaches us to say 'No' to ungodliness and worldly passions, and to live

---

[36]Geerhardus Vos, *The Pauline Eschatology* (Grand Rapids: William B. Eerdmans Publishing Co., 1972), 83.

self-controlled, upright and godly lives in this present age, while we wait for *the blessed hope*—the glorious appearing of our great God and Savior, Jesus Christ, who gave himself for us to redeem us from all wickedness and to purify for himself a people that are his very own, eager to do what is good" (Titus 2:11–14). "Blessed" (Gk. *makarian*) implies a fullness of blessing, happiness, and joy through the gracious, unmerited favor of God. Though we, as believers, are blessed now, there is much more to come.

Christ Jesus is our hope now (1 Tim. 1:1), and Christ in us is the hope of glory to come (Col. 1:27), for "when Christ, who is [our] life, appears, then [we] also will appear with him in glory" (Col. 3:4). As Paul Minear points out, "Life in Christ without hope is unthinkable. Wherever there is life in Christ there is a living hope."[37] Minear notes also that the word "hope" (Gk. *elpis*) is never found in the plural in the New Testament. There is only one hope that is real, that is consistent with reality and the will of God, and that is worth living by.[38]

EXPECTATIONS OF THE EARLY CHURCH

It is obvious that the New Testament considers the Kingdom, in the sense of the reign of God,[39] already present in Jesus during His ministry on earth. Through Him believers could "live under the dominion of God's righteousness as a gift of God's gra-

---

[37]Minear, *Christian Hope,* 28.

[38]Ibid., 22, 26.

[39]Jesus gave new meaning to the phrases "kingdom of God" and "kingdom of heaven," which appear only rarely in Jewish literature (including the Dead Sea sectarian scrolls) outside of the Gospels. Most of the phrases Jesus used in connection with the Kingdom "have no parallels (not even secular ones) in the language of Jesus' contemporaries." Joachim Jeremias, *New Testament Theology,* trans. John Bowden (New York: Charles Scribner's Sons, 1971), 32.

ciousness" (Matt. 6:33; 13:44-46).[40] In Him "the future had already begun."[41] The Kingdom was a present reality, as His driving out demons by the Spirit of God powerfully demonstrated (Matt. 12:28). It was a treasure, a fine pearl of great value (Matt. 13:44-46), immediately available to the childlike (Matt. 18:3-4; 19:14). It was near those who would repent (Matt. 4:17). Yet the fullness of the Kingdom will not come until Jesus returns (Matt. 26:29), a time when believers will enter into the fullness of eternal life and share their Master's happiness (Matt. 25:21,23,46). Through Jesus, God's power and presence were breaking into the human scene in a new way, and the future would be but "the unfolding and completion of that which already exists in Christ and the Spirit and which he carried through triumphantly in spite of . . . suffering and death."[42]

Then, when the Holy Spirit came as another Helper at Pentecost, Peter interpreted Joel's "afterward" as "in the last days" (Joel 2:28; Acts 2:17).[43] In other words, he recognized that the Church Age, the age of the Holy Spirit, is the last age before the Kingdom Age, "the age to come."[44] Peter's concern, however, was not the time of Christ's return. His concern was getting the people to repent and take advantage of God's promise of the forgiveness of sins and the gift of the Holy Spirit in order to save themselves "from this corrupt generation" (Acts 2:38-40). The people

---

[40]William David Kirkpatrick, "Christian Hope," *Southwestern Journal of Theology* 36:2 (Spring 1994): 39.

[41]Hendrikus Berkhof, *Well-Founded Hope* (Richmond, Va.: John Knox Press, 1969), 11.

[42]Ibid., 19.

[43]This was not Peter's idea. Peter was inspired by the same Holy Spirit who inspired Joel.

[44]See R. P. C. Hanson, *The Attractiveness of God: Essays in Christian Doctrine* (Richmond, Va: John Knox Press, 1973), 190-91. He points out that the phrase "'Second Coming' is not used in the New Testament because the First Coming was so eschatological that the Second Coming cannot be more than a consummation, rather than an introduction, of eschatology."

of that generation were headed in the wrong direction and were trying to drag others down with them (Rom. 1:32). Those who turned to Christ could make a difference by the holiness of their lives and by their influence on their communities.

There is no doubt that the Early Church did expect Jesus to return very soon, even within their own lifetime. The Thessalonians were waiting for Him with such expectation that when some of them died, those who remained were afraid that those who had died might have missed the joys of Jesus' return. Paul had to assure them that the dead in Christ would miss nothing, for they would rise first, and together with them, the living believers would be caught up for a meeting with Christ in the air (1 Thess. 4:13-18).

That hope continued to be a living hope to Paul and a powerful incentive for godly living. It was toward the end of his life that he wrote of waiting "for the blessed hope—the glorious appearing of our great God and Savior, Jesus Christ" (Titus 2:11-14).

That hope was still alive in Paul's heart even when he knew he was about to be martyred. In his last letter he proclaimed his hope once more: "Now there is in store for me the crown of righteousness, which the Lord, the righteous Judge, will award to me on that day—and not only to me, but also to all who have longed for his appearing" (2 Tim. 4:8). He was sure also of his safe arrival in the Lord's heavenly kingdom (2 Tim. 4:18).

The Book of Revelation shows that the hope of Christ's return was still strong near the end of the first century, the last recorded words of the risen and ascended Jesus being "Yes, I am coming soon" and the Church's response being "Amen. Come, Lord Jesus" (Rev. 22:20). Thus, the God of hope revealed in Jesus focused attention on the fact that Jesus will indeed come. This puts an urgency on the invitation to come to Jesus, a sense of imminency He wants us to keep. We need to make the same response John did on Patmos and pray for Jesus to come soon. He is indeed coming in triumph, to reign as King of kings and Lord of lords (Rev. 19:16).

Jesus himself emphasized that "this gospel of the kingdom will be preached in the whole world as a testimony to all nations, and then the end will come" (Matt. 24:14). There will be an end, but not just a cutting off, not just a dead end. The word "end" here implies a bringing together and a consummation. God will bring together whatever is necessary to fulfill His glorious plan.

Some of what will take place God has revealed in the prophecies of the Bible. However, Revelation 10:3-4 tells how the apostle John heard seven thunders utter their voices. They had a message. But when John was about to write it down, a voice from heaven stopped him. This means some things are going to happen that God has chosen not to let us know about in advance. There are surprises ahead that are just as much a part of His plan as those things He has revealed.

THE IMPACT OF THE FUTURE ON THE PRESENT

Actually, as we go through the Bible we see that God is much more interested in telling us about His will for the present life than He is in giving us all the details about the future. The inspired Scriptures that God has given us are "useful for teaching, rebuking, correcting, and training in righteousness, so that the man of God may be thoroughly equipped for every good work" (2 Tim. 3:16-17). The "great and precious promises" of the Bible are given that we "through them . . . may participate in the divine nature and escape the corruption in the world caused by evil desires [or lusts]" (2 Pet. 1:4).

For example, when Isaiah foretold how all nations will someday seek the Lord, desiring His instruction, he went on to say, "Come, O house of Jacob, let us walk in the light of the LORD" (Isa. 2:2-5). In other words, since all nations will someday come, surely Israel, instead of acting like the old nature of Jacob, should take advantage of their present opportunity. God wanted them to live in fellowship with Him in the present. Isaiah was thus bringing in the future not to satisfy their curiosity but to challenge them to holiness and to spiritual growth and maturity.

Jesus' teachings about the future were also meant to challenge us. "They were not speculations about the end, nor visions to fascinate idle curiosity. But they were teachings on faithfulness to the end, steadfastness, courage, service and love."[45]

John gave the same kind of challenge to us when he declared that when Jesus returns we shall be like Him, that is, changed into His likeness with transformed, glorified bodies. Then John went on to say, "Everyone who has this hope in him purifies himself, just as he is pure" (1 John 3:2-3). The challenge to godly living is still the chief reason for preaching and teaching what the Bible says about the last things, or the end times.

This concern for holiness, purity, godliness, and righteousness is the chief reason for my writing this book. No part of the teachings of the Bible is more controversial than that of prophecy and the end times. Differences of opinion abound. Good people—people who are born again; love Jesus; believe the Bible as God's inspired, infallible Word; and are devoted to His worship and service—often have major differences in this area.[46]

But these truths are too important for any Christian to neglect. We all, in one way or another, are like the Thessalonians who "turned to God from idols to serve the living and true God, and to wait for his Son from heaven, whom he raised from the dead—Jesus, who rescues us from the coming wrath" (1 Thess. 1:9-10). What God did in and through the life, death, and res-

---

[45]Conyers, *The Eclipse of Heaven*, 49.

[46]At one time I avoided opportunities to teach and preach prophecy. I felt that no matter what I said, I would hurt someone's feelings or cause them to think I was trying to upset their ideas and hopes.

urrection of Jesus is the solid foundation for both faith and hope.[47]

Differences of interpretation should not keep us from fellowship with one another in Christ, however. Nor should difficulties of interpretation keep us from studying and preaching the truths of eschatology. As W. A. Whitehouse pointed out, "If through the Spirit, the humble believer is to be fed from the words and works of Jesus (and this, surely, is the substance for effective preaching), then the eschatological warp and weft of these words and works" must become part of our thinking in this modern day.[48] One thing we can agree on: The Bible holds out a sure hope for believers, a hope that will not disappoint us (Rom. 5:5). As the angels told those who saw Jesus ascend into heaven, "'This *same* Jesus, who has been taken from you into heaven, will come back in the same way you have seen him go into heaven'" (Acts 1:11).

A GREAT NEED

The world needs this hope and needs to know that our God is the God of hope. Modern society has made self the center of everything. Those who still have hope for automatic progress have forgotten that God is the God of the future as well as the past. In talking about a new order by which they hope to save the world from its problems, they have cut themselves off from the biblical foundation that first gave hope and direction, for it introduced the very idea of progress. The result has been exploitation of the environment along with increasing poverty, sin, and meaninglessness—along with the increasing danger of self-destruction.[49] Christians must take a stand against all these things. At the same time, these things draw attention to another side of the future.

---

[47]Kirkpatrick, "Christian Hope," 33.

[48]W. A. Whitehouse, "The Modern Discussion of Eschatology," 66.

[49]Schwarz, *On the Way to the Future,* 25.

A day will come, and must come, "when evil is finally abolished" and "righteousness finally holds full
sway."[50]

Our hope, like ancient Israel's, is in God alone. We
cannot depend on human progress or the mass of information now available from a human standpoint. In
the midst of the present corruption of society we
need the power of the Holy Spirit, not only to witness for Christ, but also to make us abound in hope,
knowing that God is faithful. The God who loved us
enough to send His Son to die for us loves us enough
to make every provision necessary to see us all the
way to the glory He is preparing for us (Rom. 5:5–
10). Thus, we need lack nothing we need now, and
the joy of our salvation is enough to contradict the
claims of communism, Freudian psychology, and everything else that attempts to contradict the good
news of the gospel.[51]

We can be sure also that God wants us to examine
the Scriptures every day as the Bereans did (Acts
17:11). The Holy Spirit inspired all Scripture (2 Tim.
3:16–17) and He wants to make our study of the
Scriptures a delight. With His help we can gain in-
sights into the truths of eschatology and use them to
encourage others and build them up in our holy faith.

As Stephen Travis points out, "This hope is not
wishful thinking . . . nor is it escapism." It is "a
powerful motive for positive Christian living and for
social change . . . for changing our lives and for influ-
encing society."[52] Though Satan is still "the god of
this age" who "has blinded the minds of unbelievers"
(2 Cor. 4:4), he is already a defeated foe. Jesus, the
Lord of glory, "gave himself for our sins to rescue us
from the present evil age" (Gal. 1:4). Though the final

---

[50]Thomas N. Finger, *Christian Theology: An Eschatological
Approach,* vol. 1 (Nashville: Thomas Nelson Publishers, 1985),
145.

[51]See Berkhof, *Well-Founded Hope,* 19.

[52]Travis, *The Jesus Hope,* 2.

victory is still future, His resurrection and the out-pouring of His Spirit enable us to live "on a new plane" (Acts 2:33; 5:32; Gal. 4:3-7), and "hope of Christ's return puts things in a new perspective."[53]

Waiting involves working (Matt. 24:45-51; Luke 19:12-26), and our hope gives new meaning to all our work, even the most mundane. Waiting also means fighting the fight of faith—the only good fight (2 Tim. 4:7). God has provided an armor that allows us to take a victorious stand against all the devil's schemes (Eph. 6:10-18). Our attitude, however, should differ from that of those who fight the world's battles: We need not be belligerent; we need not fear what the world fears. With Christ as Lord in our hearts, we can give the reason for our hope, and we can do it "with *gentleness* and *respect*" (1 Pet. 3:14-15). And without drawing attention to ourselves, we can do our good deeds (Matt. 6:1-4).

Thus we can move ahead, keeping our eyes on Jesus, rejoicing even in the midst of suffering, living by the Spirit, keeping in step with Him as He guides us (Gal. 5:25). We may not change the course of the world as a whole, in its headlong dash toward the days of the Antichrist, but we can do our part to help and save as many as possible. God told the Jewish exiles in Babylon, "'Increase in number there; do not decrease. Also seek the peace and prosperity of the city to which I have carried you into exile. Pray to the LORD for it, because if it prospers, you too will prosper'" (Jer. 29:6-7). We too need to pray for and seek the peace and prosperity of wherever we now live. Then by grace we will reach our God-appointed goal and we will take others with us. That truly is good news!

---

[53]Finger, *Christian Theology*, 37, 102.

STUDY QUESTIONS

1. Why is the study of eschatology essential to the understanding and proclamation of the gospel?

2. What are the reasons for saying all theology is ultimately eschatology?

3. Why does the Bible condemn occult practices, astrology, fortune-telling, and other such attempts to predict the future?

4. What effect does a linear view of history have on our daily lives, and how does this compare with the effect of a cyclical view?

5. What relation does Genesis 1 have to the study of eschatology?

6. In what ways does the Holy Spirit encourage our Christian hope?

7. What is the importance of the fourfold promise given to Abraham? How does it apply to us today?

8. How is God's covenant with David related to the promises of the first and second comings of Christ?

9. In what ways is the second coming of Christ tied to His first coming?

10. What is the chief purpose of teaching and preaching the second coming of our Lord Jesus Christ?

11. The Early Church expected Jesus to come soon, yet they were busy spreading the gospel. In what sense can we share the same expectation as we spread the gospel today?

12. What are some of the ways we can affect the needs of our community and nation and at the same time stir a living hope in the God of hope among people today?

Chapter One

Death and the Intermediate State

Part of eschatology deals with the last things with respect to our present life—the question of death and what happens in the intermediate state, the state between death and Christ's return.[1] Though the Bible has much to say about death, it has comparatively little to say about the afterlife. It is more concerned about how to live this present life in a way that pleases God. God wants us to be ready for Christ's return and the glories to follow. That is more important than the details of the temporary conditions that presently characterize the afterlife.[2]

LIFE AND DEATH

THE OLD TESTAMENT VIEW

The Old Testament recognizes the brevity and fragility of life. Job in his anguish said, "'My days are swifter than a weaver's shuttle. . . . My life is but a breath'" (Job 7:6-7). David spoke of death as "the way of all the earth" (1 Kings 2:2), observing, "As for man, his days are like grass, he flourishes like a flower of the field; the wind blows over it and it is gone" (Ps. 103:15-16).

---

[1]That is, for the believer. For the unbeliever the intermediate state is the state between death and the final judgment of the Great White Throne. See chap. 7.

[2]Loraine Boettner, *Immortality* (Philadelphia: Presbyterian & Reformed Publishing Co., 1956), 91.

On the other hand, the Old Testament encourages a healthy optimism, putting more emphasis on life as God's gift to be enjoyed along with His blessings (Ps. 128:5-6).[3] Long life was considered a special blessing from God (Ps. 91:16). Suicide was extremely rare. Death was to be avoided as long as possible. In the Law, God set before Israel a choice: Loving obedience would mean life and blessing; disobedience and the rebellion of idolatry would bring death and destruction (Deut. 30:15-20). This was true even when King Saul committed suicide, for the Bible says, "Saul died because he was unfaithful to the LORD. . . . So the LORD put him to death" (1 Chron. 10:13-14). God has the ultimate control over life and death; however, He allows intermediate causes, even our own carelessness, willfulness, or foolishness, to shorten or terminate life.

At the same time, death is in the world as a result of sin and is inevitable for all, for all have sinned (Gen. 2:17; 3:19,22-23; Rom. 3:23; 5:12; 6:23). This was recognized by the time of Enosh, whose name means "mortal one." The knowledge that everyone would have to die had a good effect initially, for "at that time men began to call on the name of the Lord" (Gen. 4:26). The godly in the Old Testament continued to follow that example as they looked again and again to the Lord to protect them from death and lengthen their lives. Death was considered an enemy, bringing sorrow usually expressed in loud wailing and deep mourning (Matt. 9:23; Luke 8:52). Even so, the mourning was for the loss of the bodily presence of the loved one, for, as Solomon wrote, "The spirit returns to God who gave it" (Eccles. 12:7).

---

[3]Cf. Robert Martyn-Achard, *From Death to Life: A Study of the Development of the Doctrine of the Resurrection in the Old Testament* (Edinburgh, Scotland: Oliver & Boyd, 1960), 3-5.

THE NEW TESTAMENT VIEW

The New Testament recognizes that death entered the world through sin, and because all have sinned, death comes to all (Rom. 5:12). It brings an end to our opportunity to make decisions that will affect our eternal future (Heb. 9:27; cf. Eph. 5:15-16; Col. 4:5).[4] The New Testament also looks at death as an enemy, "the last enemy," which will not be destroyed until the final judgment (1 Cor. 15:26; Rev. 20:14). However, for the believer, Jesus' victory over the devil has set free "those who all their lives were held in slavery by their fear of death" (Heb. 2:14-15). Death is no longer to be feared! "God has said, 'Never will I leave you; never will I forsake you.' So we say with confidence, 'The Lord is my helper; I will not be afraid. What can man do to me?'" (Heb. 13:5-6). Death has lost its sting (1 Cor. 15:56-57).

Even though the natural body inevitably wastes away, inwardly believers "are being renewed day by day" (2 Cor. 4:16). Consequently, we can face death and be "more than conquerors through him who loved us," for "neither death, nor life, . . . nor anything else in all creation, will be able to separate us from the love of God that is in Christ Jesus our Lord" (Rom. 8:36-39). Death does not break our communion with our Lord. We may sorrow at the death of loved ones because of our personal loss, but we do not "grieve like the rest of men [fallen, unbelieving humankind], who have no hope" (1 Thess. 4:13).

For unbelievers, death is a shattering experience and brings an end to all their hopes and dreams and to all they have lived and worked for. Because in this life they have remained "dead in . . . transgressions and sins" (Eph. 2:1), physical death also brings an end to their opportunities to find Christ and to obtain eternal life and reward in heaven. Nothing remains

---

[4]Thomas C. Oden, *Life in the Spirit*, vol. 3, *Systematic Theology* (San Francisco: Harper, HarperCollins Publications, 1992), 478-79.

for them but the continued effects of sin and evil that they will suffer in hell.

There will, however, be degrees of punishment in hell, just as there will be degrees of reward in heaven (Luke 12:47-48; 1 Cor. 15:41-42; cf. Matt. 23:15; Heb. 10:29). The degrees of punishment refer to the intensity of punishment, not the length of time, for those who die in their sins are eternally lost.[5]

Faith in Christ brings a new attitude. Death robs nothing from believers that they have lived and longed for. As the apostle Paul said, "To me to live is Christ and to die is gain" (Phil. 1:21); that is, to die would mean gain in Christ, more Christ—and that is better by far than anything in this life (Phil. 1:23). Paul was "already being poured out like a drink offering" (Phil. 2:17; 2 Tim. 4:6), an offering giving glory to God. His death, therefore, was not a defeat, but a "departure" (Gk. *exodos*), like the exodus from Egypt, a triumphant deliverance—a way out that leads into a better country than the promised land of Canaan (Heb. 11:16).[6] Paul expected to go directly into the presence of Christ and to experience joy and peace beyond anything we know in this life (Rom. 8:38-39; Phil. 1:23; cf. Luke 16:22; 23:43).

OLD TESTAMENT TEACHING

Though much of what we know about life after death was not revealed until New Testament times, the Old Testament does hold hope for life after death. Most Old Testament Israelites seem to have had at least a vague idea of the afterlife. But because the emphasis is on serving God in this life some scholars say that most Israelites did not believe in an afterlife at all. This would be very strange and quite contrary to all the culture around them. The Egyptians made great preparations for what they believed

---

[5]See chap. 8, pp. 227-233.
[6]Dale Moody, *The Hope of Glory* (Grand Rapids: William B. Eerdmans Publishing Co., 1964), 55.

Old Testament Teaching   43

Chapter 1
Death
and the
Intermediate
State

would occur in the afterlife. They also believed in judgment after death. In the tombs of the Valley of the Kings, across the Nile from Luxor, I saw paintings on the walls that depicted people coming before the gods, one line going away looking happy, another going away upside down—their heads cut off. Every Canaanite burial included a lamp, a jar of oil, and a jar of food.[7] Israelites, however, simply wrapped the body in linen, anointed it with spices, and laid it in a tomb or buried it in a grave. This did not mean any less of a belief in an afterlife, for they spoke of the spirit going to a place called $Sh^e{'}ol$[8] or into the presence of God (Ps. 23:6).

If the Israelites really did not believe in an afterlife, the Bible would certainly have drawn attention to this.[9] Instead, Solomon recognized that God has "set eternity in the hearts of men [humankind]" (Eccles. 3:11). This implies we are made for eternity and, therefore, though we can enjoy the good things He gives us, we cannot be satisfied with them. Unless deadened by sin, our very being cries out for eternal fellowship with God.

Another phrase indicates the Old Testament saints expected an afterlife. God told Moses, after Moses went up the mountain (Mount Nebo in the Abarim range) and looked across to the Promised Land, "'You too will be gathered to your people, as your brother Aaron was'" (Num. 27:13). Aaron, however, was buried at Mount Hor, and no one knows where

---

[7]I observed this while taking part in an archaeological expedition at Dothan where several Canaanite family tombs were explored, some of them including as many as five layers of burials over a period of two hundred years.

[8]Some derive $Sh^e{'}ol$ from $Sha{'}al$, "to ask," indicating a place of judgment. Others derive it from $Sha{'}al$, "to be hollow or deep," or from $Sha{'}ah$, "to lie desolate." See Martyn-Achard, *From Death to Life*, 37.

[9]The words of the Teacher (Solomon) during his backslidden state, when he looked on life as meaningless and said, "Who knows" (Eccles. 3:21), were not characteristic of Israelite thinking.

God buried Moses (Num. 20:27-28; Deut. 34:1,5-6). Therefore, being "gathered to one's people" can hardly refer to the grave. The phrase also implies that "his people" were still in existence, not annihilated, not nonentities, as Jesus himself pointed out (Luke 20:38).

THE PLACE OF THE AFTERLIFE

In the Old Testament the place of the afterlife for the wicked is most often called Sh^{e}'*ol* (usually translated "hell" or "the grave").[10] It is also identified with '*avaddon*, "Abaddon, the place of destruction" (Job 26:6; 31:12; Ps. 88:11; Prov. 27:20), and *bor*, "the pit," literally, a cistern, but used metaphorically as the entrance to Sh^{e}'*ol* or as a synonym for Sh^{e}'*ol* itself (Ps. 30:3; Isa. 14:15; Ezek. 31:14). When translated "hell" (KJV), however, it is not a place where Satan has his headquarters, nor is it controlled by Satan. God rules it (1 Sam. 2:6; Ps. 139:8; Amos 9:2).

Sh^{e}'*ol Not the Grave*. Because Sh^{e}'*ol*, "the pit," "the grave," "destruction," and "death" are sometimes parallel in grammatical construction (e.g., Pss. 30:3; 88:11-12), some say both Sh^{e}'*ol* and "the pit" always mean "the grave."[11] However, when the Bible speaks of *graves* in an unmistakable way, as when the Israelites asked Moses, "'Was it because there were no graves in Egypt that you brought us to the desert to die?'" (Exod. 14:11), another word, *qever*, is normally used. When Jacob thought Joseph was torn to pieces and obviously not in a grave, Jacob still thought he was in Sh^{e}'*ol* (Gen. 37:35). The Bible also pictures people as having some kind of existence in Sh^{e}'*ol*

---

[10]The KJV translates Sh^{e}'*ol* as "hell" thirty-one times, as "the grave" thirty-one times, and as "the pit" three times. The NIV usually translates it as "the grave," sometimes as "death," "the depths," or "the realm of death," but notes that the Hebrew is "Sheol."

[11]Martyn-Achard calls Sh^{e}'*ol* "a sort of vast grave of which the individual tombs are merely particular manifestations," *From Death to Life*, 38.

(Isa. 14:9-10; Ezek. 32:21). God acts powerfully and intervenes in $Sh^{e'}ol$ (Ps. 139:8; Amos 9:2), and it can do nothing against Him (Job 26:6). Consequently, others limit it to the place of the afterlife and say it never means the grave.[12]

Three passages (Pss. 6:5; 115:17-18; Isa. 38:17-19) are often cited to show that $Sh^{e'}ol$ is the grave.[13] Psalm 6:5 reads, "No one remembers you when he is dead. Who praises you from the grave [Heb. $Sh^{e'}ol$]?" The remembering is, however, parallel to the praising. The same word (Heb. *zakhar*) is used of a solemn naming of God among the people (Exod. 3:15). It speaks of an active reminding here on earth, which ends when a person dies. In other words, when the spirit goes to $Sh^{e'}ol$ that person's praise and testimony to the people here on earth ceases.

Psalm 115:17 speaks of the dead going down into silence. This is from the point of view of people on the earth. However, the Psalmist goes on to say, "It is we who extol the LORD both now and forevermore" (v. 18), which implies a better hope and certainly does not rule out praising the Lord in the afterlife.

King Hezekiah in his prayer stated, "In your love you kept me from the pit of destruction: you have put all my sins behind my back. For the grave [Heb. $Sh^{e'}ol$] cannot praise you, death cannot sing your praise; those who go down to the pit cannot hope for your faithfulness" (Isa. 38:17-18). Here Hezekiah was concerned about his testimony and its results among the people. God's forgiveness of his sins kept him from going to the place of punishment. Now that he was healed, he would see God's faithfulness—and he did—for fifteen additional years (Isa. 38:5).

---

[12]Ernest Swing Williams, *Systematic Theology,* vol. 3 (Springfield, Mo.: Gospel Publishing House, 1953), 178; George Eldon Ladd, *The Last Things: An Eschatology for Laymen* (Grand Rapids: William B. Eerdmans Publishing Co., 1978), 32.

[13]James Oliver Buswell, Jr., *A Systematic Theology of the Christian Religion,* vol. 2 (Grand Rapids: Zondervan Publishing House, 1963), 317.

Actually, *Sh^e'ol* is often described as a depth that contrasts with the height of heaven (Job 11:8; Ps. 139:8; Amos 9:2). Often the context refers to the anger or wrath of God (Job 14:13; Pss. 6:1,5; 88:3,7; 89:46,48), and sometimes to both wrath and fire (Deut. 32:22). In some cases the references are brief, and it seems it is treated simply as the place or the state of the dead. In it the dead are called *repha'im*, or what we might call "ghosts" (Isa. 14:9; 26:14).[14] Other passages refer to some of the dead as *'elohim*, in the sense of "powerful spirit beings" (1 Sam. 28:13).[15]

Sh^e'ol Translated as Hadēs. Where the New Testament quotes Old Testament passages referring to *Sh^e'ol*, it translates the word *Hadēs*, which it sees not as the vague place pagan Greeks talked about but as a place of punishment (Luke 10:15; 16:23-24; cf. Rev. 6:8; 20:13).[16] Peter also describes the wicked dead from Noah's day as "spirits in prison" (1 Pet. 3:19-20).[17]

---

[14]*Repha'im* possibly comes from the root *raphah*, "to become slack or feeble," "relax," or "fade," though others connect it with the idea of "awesome" or "wise." See Martyn-Achard, *From Death to Life*, 34.

[15]*'Elohim*, depending on its context, is used of the one true God, of pagan gods, of angels, and of departed heroes.

[16]In addition to *Hadēs* as a place of punishment, 2 Pet. 2:4 speaks of *Tartarus as* a place of punishment for fallen angels. This seems to be in the depth of *Hadēs*. See also Acts 2:27 where Peter quotes Ps. 16:10, clearly understanding *Sh^e'ol* as *Hadēs*.

[17]First Pet. 3:19-20 is a difficult passage. Some in the early centuries of the Church supposed that Jesus preached the gospel to people in *Hadēs* and gave them a second chance for salvation. Heb. 9:27 contradicts the idea of a second chance. Augustine and many reformers taught that Jesus preached through Noah to the people of Noah's day before the Flood, people who are now in *Hadēs*. A more modern view is that Jesus preached to fallen angels in *Hadēs*, not to offer them salvation, but simply to declare His victory. Some believe Jude 9 supports the latter view.

Sh^e'ol a Place for the Wicked. In view of this it is important to note that the Old Testament does not teach that everyone goes to *Sh^e'ol.* It is true that Job spoke of death as a *beth mo'ed,* a "meeting house" for all living (Job 30:23). But he was simply referring to the fact that all die, not that all go to the same place when they die.

Some Old Testament saints had a better hope. Enoch and Elijah were taken directly to heaven (Gen. 5:24; 2 Kings 2:11; Heb. 11:5). When David felt the wrath of God because of his sin, he cried out for mercy to escape going to *Sh^e'ol* (e.g., Ps. 6:1-5,9). But when his faith rose, his hope was to "dwell in the house of the LORD forever" (Ps. 23:6; cf. Ps. 17:15).

Though the New Testament identifies Psalm 16:10 with the death and resurrection of Jesus, the verse that follows it indicates that the path of life made known by God leads to joy in His presence and eternal pleasures at His right hand. Psalm 49:15 says, after considering the lot of the wicked, who are headed for *Sh^e'ol,* "God, however, will redeem my soul from the hand of *Sh^e'ol,* for He will take me [to himself]" (author's translation). That is, *Sh^e'ol* is personified as trying to grab him and take him down to the place of punishment, but God redeems and rescues him so that he escapes from having to go to *Sh^e'ol* at all and instead goes into the presence of God.[18]

Sh^e'ol a Place of Punishment. Several passages clearly indicate that *Sh^e'ol* is a place of punishment for the wicked (Ps. 9:17; cf. Num. 16:33; Job 26:6; Pss. 30:17-18; 49:13-15; 55:15; 88:11-12; Prov. 5:5; 7:27; 9:18; 15:10-11; 27:20; Isa. 38:18).[19] God said of idolaters, "'A fire has been kindled by my wrath, one

---

[18]See Martyn-Achard, *From Death to Life,* 155.

[19]R. H. Charles, *A Critical History of the Doctrine of a Future Life: In Israel, in Judaism, and in Christianity,* 2d ed., rev. and enl. (London: Adam & Charles Black, 1913), 33-35. He accounts for this by referring to "the biblical doctrine that death is the issue of sin."

that burns to the realm of *Sh^e'ol* below'" (Deut. 32:22). "The wicked return [change their total orientation] to *Sh^e'ol*, all the nations [Heb. *goyim*, "peoples," especially pagans] that *forget God*" (Ps. 9:17). "Let death take my enemies by surprise; let them go down alive to *Sh^e'ol, for evil finds lodging among them*" (Ps. 55:15; cf. 55:23). "My soul is full of trouble and my life draws near *Sh^e'ol.* I am counted among those who go down to the pit. . . . Your wrath lies heavily upon me" (Ps. 88:3-4,7). "Her house [the prostitute's house] is a highway to *Sh^e'ol*, leading down to the [dark] chambers of death" (Prov. 7:27). "The woman Folly is loud . . . calling out to those who pass by. . . . 'Let all who are simple come in here!' she says to those who lack judgment. . . . But little do they know that the dead are there, and her guests are in the *depths of Sh^e'ol*" (Prov. 9:13,15-16,18). When God pronounced judgment on the city of Tyre, He compared it to "those who go down to the pit," and said, "'I will bring you to a horrible end'" (Ezek. 26:19-21).

Then when judgment comes on the hordes of Egypt, "From *within Sh^e'ol* the mighty leaders will say of Egypt and her allies, 'They have come down and they lie with the uncircumcised, with those killed by the sword'" (Ezek. 32:18-21). In fact, all those Ezekiel mentions as being in *Sh^e'ol* are wicked.[20] When Korah gathered his followers in opposition to Moses and Aaron, God told Moses to warn the assembly, "'Move back from the tents of these wicked men! Do not touch anything belonging to them, or you will be swept away because of all their sins.' . . . And the earth opened its mouth and swallowed them. . . . They went down alive into *Sh^e'ol*" (Num. 16:23-33).

On the other hand, when the spiritist medium at Endor said she saw a spirit coming up out of *the*

---

[20]Daniel I. Block, "Ezekiel's Vision of Death and Afterlife," *Bulletin for Biblical Research* 2 (1992): 126.

Old Testament Teaching 49

Chapter 1
Death
and the
Intermediate
State

ground (Heb. *ha'arets*) looking like an old man wearing a robe (1 Sam. 28:13-14), it may be referring to his body rising from the grave and does not prove his soul was in an underworld any more than the fact Jesus called Lazarus from the tomb proves it (John 12:17).[21]

The psalmist Asaph wrote that, in contrast to the destruction of the wicked, "You guide me with your counsel," that is, while on earth, "and afterward you will take me into glory," that is, into heaven (Ps. 73:18-19,24-26; cf. Pss. 16:9,11; 17:15).[22] Solomon also declared that "the path of life leads upward [to the place above] for the wise [that is, for those who fear the Lord] in order to avoid *She'ol* beneath" (Prov. 15:24, author's translation).[23] God's message to Balaam made him recognize that the death of the righteous is better than the death of the wicked (Num. 23:10).

TWO COMPARTMENTS IN *SH^E'OL*

Possibly because of the influence of Greek ideas and possibly also because Jacob, mourning, spoke of going down to *She'ol* to his son Joseph, later Jews, considering Jacob and Joseph righteous, reasoned that both the righteous and the wicked went to *She'ol*. So they concluded there must be a special place in *She'ol* for the righteous. This would call for divisions in *She'ol*: a place for the righteous as well as

---

[21]William Grenough Thayer Shedd, *The Doctrine of Endless Punishment* (New York: Charles Scribner's Sons, 1886; repr. Minneapolis: Klock & Klock Christian Publishers, 1980), 67. For more about the woman at Endor and Samuel see pp. 61-62.

[22]The majority of Bible scholars hold that Ps. 73:24 means that at death "the righteous will be received to the presence of Yahweh and will dwell in His glory." Martyn-Achard, *From Death to Life,* 163.

[23]"Upward" (Heb. *le ma'elah*) is more literally "to the [place] above." "To keep him from" is a phrase that is used of avoiding something altogether (as when Job "shunned" evil [1:1]). Thus, *She'ol* in Prov. 15:24 cannot mean the grave, for even the wise who die cannot avoid the grave.

for the wicked (1 Enoch 22:1-14).[24] However, Jacob at that time refused to be comforted, no doubt thinking that both he and Joseph were somehow under God's judgment. There is no record of Jacob's seeking the Lord again until after he received the news that Joseph was alive (Gen. 45:28 through 46:1). Therefore, Jacob probably considered *Sh^e'ol* a place of punishment. Actually, no passage in the Old Testament clearly necessitates dividing *Sh^e'ol* into two compartments, one for punishment, one for blessing.[25]

Dr. William Shedd (1820-94) gave a classic argument against the idea of two compartments. He pointed out:

[Sh^e'ol] is a fearful, punitive evil, mentioned by the sacred writers to deter men from sin, . . . and any interpretation that essentially modifies this must therefore be erroneous. [For it to be an] alarm for the wicked, [it must pertain] to them alone. If it is shared with the good, its power to terrify is gone. . . . It is no answer to this to say that Sheol contains two divisions, Hades and Paradise, and that the wicked go to the former. This is not in the Biblical text, or in its connection. The wicked who are threatened with Sheol . . . are not threatened with a part . . . but with the whole. . . . Sheol is one, undivided, and homogeneous in the inspired representation. . . . The Biblical Sheol is always an evil, and nothing but an evil. . . . To say that "the wicked shall be turned into

---

[24]This is indicated in the pseudepigraphal book of 1 Enoch (22:1-14). Some rabbis said the compartments of the righteous were separated from the compartments of the wicked by only a handbreadth; others said by only a fingerbreadth. This contrasts with the "great chasm" Abraham mentioned in Jesus' account of the rich man and Lazarus (Luke 16:26).

[25]The pseudepigraphal book of Enoch does speak of four divisions in *Sh^e'ol*: one for martyrs, one for the righteous who die a natural death, one for sinners who suffered in this life, and one for sinners who did not. See H. A. Guy, *The New Testament Doctrine of the "Last Things": A Study of Eschatology* (London: Geoffrey Cumberlege, Oxford University Press, 1948), 19; Charles, *A Critical History*, 33-34.

Sheol" (Ps. 9:17), implies that the righteous shall not be; just as to say that "they who obey not the gospel of our Lord Jesus Christ shall be punished with everlasting destruction" (2 Thess. 1:8-9), implies that those who do obey it shall not be. To say that the "steps" of the prostitute "take hold on Sheol" (Prov. 5:5), is the same as to say that "whoremongers shall have their part in the lake which burneth with fire and brimstone" (Rev. 21:8). To "deliver the soul of a child from Sheol" by parental discipline (Prov. 23:14), is not to deliver him either from the grave or from the spirit-world, but from the future torment that awaits the morally undisciplined.[26]

NEW TESTAMENT TEACHING

The New Testament emphasis is on the resurrection of the body rather than on what happens immediately after death. Death was never God's original intention for humankind and ultimately "there will be no more death" (Rev. 21:4); death will be "swallowed up in victory" (1 Cor. 15:54). Although still an enemy,[27] death is no longer to be feared by the saved (1 Cor. 15:55-57; Heb. 2:15). For the believer, to live is Christ and to die is gain; that is, to die means a closer relationship with Christ, in effect, more of Him (Phil. 1:21). Thus, to die and go to be with Christ is far better than remaining in the present body, though we must remain as long as God sees that it is necessary (Phil. 1:23-24). Then death will bring a rest from (that is, a ceasing of) our earthly labors and sufferings and an entrance into glory (2 Cor. 4:17; cf. 2 Pet. 1:10-11; Rev. 14:13).

Jesus in Luke 16:19-31 describes an unnamed rich man[28] who dressed like a king and every day enjoyed a banquet complete with entertainment. At his gate

---

[26]Shedd, *The Doctrine of Endless Punishment*, 21-25.

[27]Erickson suggests that death is not natural to mankind. Millard J. Erickson, *Christian Theology* (Grand Rapids: Baker Book House, 1985), 1170-71.

[28]"Dives" is the transliteration of a Latin common noun, which means simply "a rich man"; it is not a proper name.

was laid a beggar named Lazarus, covered with sores, who wanted the scraps of food that would be swept out the door for the street dogs. These scavengers, unclean animals under the Law, licked his sores, making him unclean. Lazarus had only one thing in his favor—his name,[29] which means "God is my help" and indicates that in spite of everything he kept his faith in God.

At death the angels carried him away to Abraham's side,[30] which was certainly a place of blessing, for he received comfort there. The rich man after death found himself in agony in the fires of *Hadēs.* When he looked up, that is, to heaven (cf. Matt. 8:11–12; Luke 13:28–29), he saw Abraham and Lazarus "far away." But it was too late for him to receive help, for Abraham said, "'Between us and you a great chasm has been fixed, so that those who want to go from here to you cannot, nor can anyone cross over from there to us'" (Luke 16:26). In other words, we see that the destinies of both the wicked and the godly cannot be changed after death.[31] Some treat this account as a parable, since it follows a series of parables, but even in His parables Jesus never said anything that was misleading or contrary to the truth.[32]

The difference in the state of the rich man and that of Lazarus also seems to imply that at their death a judgment was made with respect to their destiny. Traditionally this has been called "particular judgment" in contrast to the judgment seat of Christ after

[29]Lazarus is a Greek form of "Eliezer."

[30]"Bosom" (KJV) was used of eating together while stretched out on the same couch (cf. John 13:23). It implies close communion and probably a place of honor.

[31]Origen, a few mystics, some Anabaptists, Friedrich Schleiermacher, and Jehovah's Witnesses are among those who hold to a second chance for salvation after death. But Boettner points out that this "depreciates the importance of the present life and . . . extinguishes missionary zeal." Boettner, *Immortality,* 104–8.

[32]Francis J. Hall, *Eschatology* (New York: Longmans, Green & Co., 1922), 9.

the Rapture and the Great White Throne Judgment after the Millennium.

WITH THE LORD

The apostle Paul's desire was to be not with Abraham, however, but with the Lord. He indicated that as soon as he was away from the body (at death), he would be present with the Lord (2 Cor. 5:6-9; Phil. 1:23). This was Jesus' promise to the dying thief on the cross, "'Today you will be with me in paradise'" (Luke 23:43), implying immediate fellowship.[33] In a vision Paul was caught up to the third heaven, which he also calls paradise (2 Cor. 12:1-5), thus identifying paradise with heaven.[34] There he "heard inexpressible things, things that man is not permitted to tell" (12:4).[35]

Stephen saw heaven open and Jesus standing at the right hand of God. Whereupon Stephen prayed, "'Lord Jesus, receive my spirit'" (Acts 7:56,59). Clearly, Stephen expected that upon his death, his spirit would be immediately in heaven with Jesus.[36]

Hebrews 8:1-2 also declares that Jesus "sat down at the right hand of the throne of the Majesty in heaven, and . . . serves in the sanctuary." This is in line with other passages which recognize that there is a

---

[33]This is very emphatic. The Greek word order is "Today, with me, you will be in paradise!"

[34]Paul seems to have thought of the first heaven as the atmosphere surrounding the earth, the second heaven as that of the stars, the third heaven as the heaven of heavens, the place where the throne of God and paradise are. The idea of seven heavens is not found in the Bible, though it became part of later Jewish theology. See Wilbur M. Smith, *The Biblical Doctrine of Heaven* (Chicago: Moody Press, 1968), 167; William O. E. Oesterley, *The Doctrine of the Last Things: Jewish and Christian* (London: John Murray, 1908), 172-73.

[35]"Not permitted" (Gk. *ouk exon*) can also mean "not possible."

[36]John Miley, *Systematic Theology,* vol. 2 (New York: Hunt & Eaton, 1893; repr. Peabody, Mass.: Hendrickson Publishers, 1989), 431.

special place in heaven where God manifests himself in a special way at His throne (Ps. 103:19; Isa. 57:15; 63:15; 66:1; Matt. 5:34).

Solomon recognized that "the heavens, even the highest heaven," cannot contain God (1 Kings 8:27), for God is everywhere present "in heaven above and on the earth below" (Deut. 4:39; cf. Josh. 2:11). But many passages show God is able to manifest himself and His glory in specific places, and He does so especially in heaven.[37]

A PREPARED PLACE

Jesus speaks of heaven as a prepared place where there is plenty of room (John 14:2), not temporary but "eternal dwellings" (Luke 16:9). It is a place of joy, of fellowship with Christ and other believers, and resounds with worship and singing (Rev. 4:10-11; 5:8-14; 14:2-3; 15:2-4). There they "rest from their labor" (Rev. 14:13). "Rest," however, does not mean sleep, nor being inert or idle. In the Bible, rest "carries with it the idea of *satisfaction in labor, or joy in accomplishment*," thus suggesting work, worship, and freedom from the effects of all that is evil.[38]

Paul longed to be with Christ (Phil. 1:23) and, because "our citizenship is in heaven," he was eager for Jesus to return and "transform our lowly bodies so that they will be like his glorious body" (Phil. 3:20-21). Because the resurrection body will be immortal, not subject to death or decay, and because Paul seems to withdraw from the idea of being a naked spirit (2 Cor. 5:3-4), some teach that in the intermediate state between death and resurrection believers will be disembodied spirits who, however, will be comforted by being with Christ.

Others teach that at death believers receive a temporary "heavenly" body, noting that Moses and Elijah appeared on the Mount of Transfiguration with

---

[37]Smith, *The Biblical Doctrine of Heaven*, 50, 61.
[38]Boettner, *Immortality*, 92-93.

some kind of a body and that white robes were given to the souls of the martyrs in heaven (Luke 9:30–32; Rev. 6:9-11). However, Paul was expecting to go to be with the Lord, and being absent from the body hardly means going into another body.[39] Further, the resurrection of the body is clearly at the time of Christ's coming for His church (Phil. 3:20–21; 1 Thess. 4:16-17).[40]

Whatever the case, it is clear that we shall know each other in heaven, just as the rich man knew who Abraham was.

OTHER VIEWS OF THE AFTERLIFE

SOUL SLEEP

Because Jesus spoke of Lazarus and the daughter of Jairus as "sleeping" (Matt. 9:24; John 11:11), and because Paul referred to death as "sleep" (1 Cor. 15:6,18,20,51; 1 Thess. 4:13-15; 5:10), some, especially the Christian Advent Church and the Seventh-Day Adventists, have developed a theory of psychopannychy, or soul sleep.[41] Jesus and Paul used "sleep" simply as a figure, however, to indicate that death was not to be feared but was an entrance into

---

[39]Moody, *The Hope of Glory*, 65; William W. Stevens, *Doctrines of the Christian Religion* (Nashville: Broadman Press, 1967), 378-79; Herman Ridderbos, *Paul: An Outline of His Theology*, trans. John R. De Witt (Grand Rapids: William B. Eerdmans Publishing Co., 1975), 505.

[40]Ladd, *Last Things*, 35–36.

[41]See Boettner, *Immortality*, 109–113; Smith, *The Biblical Doctrine of Heaven*, 156. Seventh-Day Adventists modify this by saying that "death is not complete annihilation; it is only a state of temporary unconsciousness while the person awaits the resurrection." Ministerial Association General Conference of Seventh-Day Adventists, *Seventh-Day Adventists Believe* (Hagerstown, Md.: Review & Herald Publishing Association, 1989), 352.

quietness and rest, which Jesus also identified with paradise.[42]

Oscar Cullmann, reacting to Greek ideas of the immortality of the soul, taught that the dead were indeed asleep, but "in proximity to Christ."[43] They would awake refreshed, as a person does who has had a pleasant dream. Most of those who teach soul sleep, however, go to an extreme. They say that the soul, or spirit, is not simply in a state of stupor after death, but that the total person is dead and the soul or spirit goes out of existence until recreated at the resurrection.[44] Some compare this to switching off a light bulb. The light is out until its circuit is reconnected by putting the switch in the on position. But the light that comes on again is not the same light. If the "soul ceased to exist at death, and a new soul were created at the resurrection[,] it could not possibly be the same soul, and could not justly be rewarded or punished for what the former soul had done."[45]

That God is "not the God of the dead but of the living" also means that Abraham, Isaac, and Jacob were (and are) alive, not out of existence (Matt. 22:32). Then, Moses and Elijah at the Mount of Transfiguration knew what was going on and talked to Jesus "about his departure [Gk. *exodos,* including His death, resurrection, and ascension], which he was

---

[42]Ray Summers, *The Life Beyond* (Nashville: Broadman Press, 1959), 9.

[43]Oscar Cullmann, *The Immortality of the Soul, or Resurrection of the Dead?* (London: Epworth Press, 1958), 11, 48-57.

[44]Victor Paul Wierwille, founder of the cult The Way, taught that "when you are dead, you are dead," and that there is no one in heaven now but Jesus Christ. Passages used as proof texts for soul sleep (Pss. 6:5; 13:3; 115:17; 146:3-4; Eccles. 9:5-6; Matt. 9:24; John 11:11-14; Acts 7:60; 1 Cor. 15:51; 1 Thess. 4:13-14) all deal with the dead body as it appears from the standpoint of the ordinary person who is still living. These texts do not deal with what happens to the person who goes to hell or who goes to be with the Lord after death.

[45]Boettner, *Immortality,* 110.

about to bring to fulfillment at Jerusalem" (Luke 9:31). They understood this would mean something to them as well. Peter used the same word, *exodos,* referring to his death (2 Pet. 1:15), as does Paul (2 Tim. 4:6).

As with the Old Testament saints, and as the Church throughout its history has generally held, death for the believer can only mean entering into the presence of the Lord, not into sleep.[46] When one of the criminals crucified with Jesus said, "'Remember me when you come into your kingdom,'" Jesus answered him, "'I tell you the truth, today you will be with me in paradise'" (Luke 23:42-43)—not in sleep, not out of existence.[47]

Paul understood that after death he would be able to feel whether he was a naked spirit or not.[48] "Sleep," therefore, is a term used from our present point of view and can apply only to the body.[49] It is the body that is raised to life in the resurrection (cf. Matt. 27:52).[50] The spirit remains consciously alive. Not only so, the dead are "in Christ" (1 Thess. 4:16; Rev. 14:13), not "enveloped by Him after a quietistic, unproductive fashion," but sharing "after their own degree in his glorified state," with the "certitude of being themselves changed in due time."[51]

Others suppose that after death the person is not out of existence but in a state of stupor. Certainly

---

[46]Smith, *The Biblical Doctrine of Heaven,* 161, 165.

[47]Some who teach soul sleep make Jesus' statement a question. However, the Greek is very emphatic, "This day, with me, you will be in paradise."

[48]Stevens, *Doctrines,* 381.

[49]For a discussion of three Greek verbs translated "sleep," see Thomas R. Edgar, "The Meaning of 'Sleep' in 1 Thessalonians 5:10," *Journal of the Evangelical Theological Society* 22:4 (December 1979): 345-47.

[50]See Boettner, *Immortality,* 109-16, for a good discussion of the doctrine of soul sleep; Edgar, "The Meaning of 'Sleep,'" 345-49; Moody, *Hope of Glory,* 67-69.

[51]Geerhardus Vos, *The Pauline Eschatology* (Grand Rapids: William B. Eerdmans Publishing Co., 1972), 158.

neither Lazarus, Abraham, nor the rich man were unconscious or in a state of stupor. They knew what was going on, and Lazarus was being "comforted" (Luke 16:25).[52] The Book of Revelation also draws attention to the conscious life and blessing enjoyed by those who are in heaven (5:9; 6:10-11; 7:9-10).

PURGATORY

Roman Catholics declare by the authority of their church that all the future elect except special saints and martyrs[53] must go through purgatory (a condition rather than a place) to purify them, rejuvenate them, render them immortal, and prepare them for entrance to heaven.[54] This doctrine has no basis in Scripture. Augustine introduced the idea in the fourth century,[55] but the word "purgatory" was not used until the twelfth century, and the doctrine was not fully worked out until the Council of Trent in the sixteenth century.[56]

Some Catholics speculate that purgatory is nearer to heaven than to hell. Some take the fires as literal, with frightening, ever-intensifying flames, but this is "not part of the dogmatic pronouncements of the

---

[52]Gk. *parakaleitai* implies an atmosphere of encouragement.

[53]Alois Winklhofer, *The Coming of His Kingdom: A Theology of the Last Things,* trans. A. V. Littledale (Freiburg, West Germany: Herder; Montreal: Palm Publishers, 1965), 114.

[54]Some Roman Catholics will admit there is no scriptural support for purgatory, but they say there is nothing in the Bible contrary to the doctrine. Zachary Hayes, "The Purgatorial View," in *Four Views on Hell,* ed. William Crockett (Grand Rapids: Zondervan Publishing House, 1992), 107. Catholic "tradition commonly appeals to 2 Maccabees 12:38-46." Zachary Hayes, *Visions of the Future: A Study of Christian Eschatology* (Wilmington, Del.: Michael Glazier, 1985), 112.

[55]Some Catholics claim the idea goes back to Tertullian (A.D. 160-230). Winklhofer, *The Coming of His Kingdom,* 100.

[56]Jacques Le Goff, *Birth of Purgatory,* trans. Arthur Goldhammer (Chicago: University of Chicago Press, 1984), 3, 41, 61. The Council of Trent said nothing about the nature of the fire, the location of purgatory, or even that it is a place. Hayes, "The Purgatorial View," 113.

Church," though the Church of Rome has allowed and still allows such teachings to circulate. Others spiritualize the fires or combine them with water as a sort of spiritual sauna. Thus, they say that purgatory is "not a state of horror and misery," but has "a note of confidence and joy" and "an element of sweetness and hope," even though the suffering is real. However, the suffering may be intense for some, but "it may be that many souls pass through this purification as through a spring-breeze."[57]

Augustine also introduced the idea that prayer, good works, and the saying of the Mass would help the dead through their sufferings. Gregory the Great went further and said that the saying of the Mass, as a repetition of Christ's sacrifice, would release souls from purgatory. By the eleventh century indulgences were made a convenient way to lessen or shorten the sufferings of purgatory.[58] Luther reacted against their misuse, and the misuse of Luther's day is no longer allowed in Catholic churches.

LIMBO

Some Roman Catholics also conjectured that there is a condition called Limbo for unbaptized babies and another Limbo for Old Testament saints, where they suffered temporary punishment until Jesus died.[59] Then the soul of Jesus descended into the Limbo of the Old Testament saints "to introduce them to the

---

[57]Winklhofer, *The Coming of His Kingdom,* 102, 104, 107–10.

[58]Hans Schwarz, *On the Way to the Future: A Christian View of Eschatology in the Light of Current Trends in Religion, Philosophy, and Science,* rev. ed. (Minneapolis: Augsburg Publishing House, 1979), 181.

[59]Limbo (Lat. *limbus,* "fringe," "outskirts") was connected by some with the "spirits in prison" (1 Pet. 3:19). See Boettner, *Immortality,* 102. Boettner, however, takes the preaching to be that done long ago by the Spirit of Christ through Noah to the people of his day who are now "in prison."

beatific vision of God," and since His ascension they have been in heaven.[60]

Limbo (for infants) is "now generally rejected" in favor of the idea that infants and the severely retarded will, after death, be presented with God's offer of eternal life and allowed to accept or reject it.[61] One Roman Catholic professor points out that "the hierarchical magisterium has offered no clear, definitive position on the matter of limbo" and suggests the doctrine should be "removed from the map of eschatology."[62]

SPIRITISM

Spiritism (often called spiritualism) teaches that mediums can communicate with the dead, usually through a "control" spirit, and that the spirits of the dead remain in the vicinity of the earth. [63] "There is almost universal insistence that the supraterrestrial world is composed of seven or eight spheres, each a little higher than its predecessor."[64] This is contrary to the assurance that at death the believer is "present with the Lord."

The Bible emphatically warns against any attempt to communicate with the dead. "'Do not turn to me-

---

[60]Joseph Pohle, *Eschatology, or the Catholic Doctrine of the Last Things: A Dogmatic Treatise,* English version by Arthur Preuss (Westport, Conn.: Greenwood Press, Publishers, 1971; repr. from 1917), 26–27.

[61]Francis X. Cleary, "Roman Catholicism," in *How Different Religions View Death and Afterlife,* ed. Christopher J. Johnson and Marsha G. McGee (Philadelphia: Charles Press, Publishers, 1991), 271.

[62]Hayes, *Visions,* 120.

[63]"There is no satisfactory proof that the mediums actually do contact those spirits. . . . Even the most famous mediums have been detected in fraud." Also, the witch at Endor was very surprised at Samuel's appearance. God took over and used this occasion to pronounce judgment upon King Saul (1 Sam. 28:12). Boettner, *Immortality,* 138, 149.

[64]G. W. Butterworth, *Spiritualism and Religion* (London: Society for Promoting Christian Knowledge, 1944), 129.

diums or seek out spiritists, for you will be defiled by them. I am the LORD your God'" (Lev. 19:31). "'I will set my face against the person who turns to mediums and spiritists to prostitute himself by following them, and I will cut him off from his people'" (Lev. 20:6). Any reliance on spiritist mediums is a rejection of God's guidance as well as any relationship to Him. Thus the Law called for mediums to be put to death (Lev. 20:27).

The practices of spiritists and mediums were among the detestable ways of the nations that called for God's judgment (Deut. 18:9-12). Isaiah referred to these teachings of the Law when he said,

When men tell you to consult mediums and spiritists, who whisper and mutter, should not a people inquire of their God? *Why consult the dead on behalf of the living?* To the law and to the testimony! If they do not speak according to this word, they have no light of dawn. Distressed and hungry, they will roam through the land; when they are famished, they will become enraged and, looking upward, will curse their king and their God. Then they will look toward the earth and see only distress and darkness and fearful gloom, and they will be thrust into utter darkness (Isa. 8:19-22).

Thus, spiritists and those who consult them are identified as rebels who will come under the judgment of God.[65]

This was true of King Saul when he consulted the spiritist medium at Endor (1 Sam. 28:4-25). Because Saul was estranged from the Lord, the sight of the Philistine army filled him with terror. He tried to get a word from the Lord, but the Lord did not answer him personally, not through dreams, nor by the Urim of the priests, nor through prophets. Even though Saul had previously outlawed spiritism and sentenced

---

[65]René Pache, *The Future Life,* trans. Helen I. Needham (Chicago: Moody Press, 1962), 77.

spiritists to death, he now turned to a pagan spiritist medium for aid.

The Bible says, "The woman saw Samuel" (v. 12). Samuel's appearance before her has been understood in various ways: Some suppose the woman simply saw Samuel in her mind and then by some sort of mental telepathy discerned Saul's thoughts. Others suppose a demon appeared impersonating Samuel.[66] However, she was startled by Samuel's appearance; it was obviously something different from what she was used to. In view of her amazed and terrified reaction it seems more likely that the woman was expecting a demonic spirit, whereas God actually permitted the spirit of Samuel to appear in order to confirm to Saul God's sentence of defeat and death. What Samuel said accords with his previous prophecies (1 Sam. 15:26,28). In fulfillment, Israel's armies were defeated. Then Saul committed suicide (1 Sam. 31:4). Thus, there is nothing in this account to indicate that spiritist mediums can really communicate with the dead.

Jesus also made it clear that the rich man in *Hadēs* was unable to communicate with his five brothers who were still living, and his request that someone from the dead be sent was denied (Luke 16:27-30).

REINCARNATION

A number of Eastern religions, because of their cyclic view of history that denies a beginning and an end, teach reincarnation: At death a person is given a new identity and is born into another life as an animal, a human being, or even a god. They hold that a person's actions generate a force, *karma,* that demands transmigration and determines the destiny of

---

[66]Ralph W. Klein, *1 Samuel,* Word Biblical Commentary, vol. 10 (Waco, Tex.: Word Books, 1983), 271-73.

that person in the next existence.[67] Thus, by going from one existence to another, a person is supposed to gradually purify and save himself or herself. In India they suppose this may take as many as six hundred thousand reincarnations.[68]

The Bible, however, makes it clear that "now is the day of salvation" (2 Cor. 6:2). We cannot save ourselves by our good works. God has provided a full salvation through Jesus Christ that atones for our sin and cancels our guilt. We do not need another life to try to take care of sins and mistakes of this life or any supposed former existences. Furthermore, "Man is destined to die once, and after that to face judgment, so Christ was sacrificed once to take away the sins of many people; and he will appear a second time, not to bear sin, but to bring salvation [including the full blessings of our inheritance] to those who are waiting for him" (Heb. 9:27–28).

It is evident also that the judgment of believers deals only with "the things done while in the body" during this present life (2 Cor. 5:10). Nor do unbelievers have a second chance after death (Rom. 2:5–6,8; cf. Rom. 1:18). At death a person's destiny is fixed (Matt. 13:42; 24:51; 25:30; Luke 16:19–31; John 8:24; 2 Cor. 5:10; 6:2; Heb. 9:27).

It is clear also that when Moses and Elijah appeared on the Mount of Transfiguration they were still Moses and Elijah. Jesus Christ also retained His identity after His death and resurrection. He said, "'Look at my hands and my feet. *It is I myself!* Touch me and see; a ghost does not have flesh and bones, as you see I have'" (Luke 24:39). "This same Jesus"—not some reincarnation—will come back from heaven to earth again (Acts 1:11). We shall know Him, and we shall know each other.

---

[67]See Anne C. Klein, "Buddhism," and Swami Adiswarananda, "Hinduism," in *How Different Religions View Death,* ed. Johnson and McGee, 85–108, 157–84.

[68]Pache, *Future Life,* 92.

Paul expected to know the Thessalonians, for they would be his hope, joy, and the crown in which he and his fellow workers would glory "in the presence of our Lord Jesus when he comes" (1 Thess. 2:19; cf. 2 Cor. 1:14). At our Lord's coming, believers will receive rewards, an eternal "inheritance that can never perish, spoil or fade," and all the blessing that is included in "the salvation that is ready to be revealed in the last time" (1 Pet. 1:4-5).

STUDY QUESTIONS

1. What are some of the ways the Old Testament saints looked at life?

2. What are some of the ways the Old Testament saints looked at death?

3. What are the reasons the New Testament believer no longer needs to fear death?

4. How does the Old Testament view of life after death compare with that of Israel's pagan neighbors?

5. What does the Old Testament reveal about the place of the afterlife for the wicked?

6. What does the Old Testament reveal about the place of the afterlife for the godly (the "wise")?

7. What lessons can we learn from the account of the rich man and Lazarus?

8. What assurance do we have that New Testament believers will be with Christ in paradise immediately after death?

9. What are the chief reasons for not accepting the theories of soul sleep, spiritism, reincarnation, and purgatory?

Chapter Two

Resurrection and Rapture

NOT FULLY DEVELOPED

The idea of resurrection in the Old Testament is not fully developed. Sometimes it is connected with the restoration of the nation of Israel, as in Ezekiel 37:12-14, "'This is what the Sovereign LORD says: O my people, I am going to open your graves and bring you up from them; I will bring you back to the land of Israel. Then you, my people, will know that I am the LORD, when I open your graves and bring you up from them. I will put my Spirit in you and you will live, and I will settle you in your own land. Then you will know that I the LORD have spoken, and I have done it, declares the LORD.'"

The idea of resurrection is stronger in Hosea 6:2: "'After two days he will revive us [Heb. $y^echayyenu$, "bring us back to life"]; on the third day he will restore us [Heb. $y^eqimenu$, "raise us up" (that is, from the earth)], that we may live in his presence.'"[1]

Resurrection seems to be implied also in Job 19:25-27. In Job 14:14 Job asks, "'If a man dies, will

---

[1]Robert Martyn-Achard, *From Death to Life: A Study of the Development of the Doctrine of the Resurrection in the Old Testament* (Edinburgh, Scotland: Oliver & Boyd, 1960), 74.

he live again?'" But in 19:25[2] he reaches a place of renewed faith and confidence as he says, "'I know that
my Redeemer lives, and that in the end he will stand
upon the earth.'" Then he goes on to say, "'After my
skin has been destroyed, yet in my flesh I will see
God; I myself will see him with my own eyes—I, and
not another. How my heart yearns within me!'"

Isaiah 26:19 is more specific for individuals, though
it does not seem to teach a universal resurrection: "Your dead will live; their bodies will rise. You
who dwell in the dust, wake up and shout for joy.
Your dew is like the dew of the morning; the earth
will give birth to her dead." Psalm 17:14 indicates
that unbelievers have no reward except in this life, "a
statement which implies that there is more than this
present life."[3]

Daniel 12:2 then reveals that there will be a bodily
resurrection for the wicked as well as the righteous: "'Multitudes who sleep in the dust of the earth
will awake: some to everlasting life, others to shame
and everlasting contempt.'" Then (v. 3), "'those who
are wise will shine like the brightness of the heavens,
and those who lead many to righteousness, like the
stars for ever and ever.'"[4] There was also future hope
in the prophecy: "He will swallow up death forever.
The Sovereign LORD will wipe away the tears from all
faces" (Isa. 25:8).

---

[2]Some of the older commentators supposed that Job would
see his Redeemer only in his soul or spirit. R. H. Charles, *A Critical History of the Doctrine of a Future Life: In Israel, in Judaism, and in Christianity,* 2d ed., rev. and enl. (London:
Adam & Charles Black, 1913), 49. The Hebrew, however, is best
translated as the NIV does.

[3]Leon Morris, *New Testament Theology* (Grand Rapids: Academie Books, 1986), 266.

[4]See French L. Arrington, *Paul's Aeon Theology in 1 Corinthians* (Washington, D.C.: University Press of America, 1978), 101.

THE SADDUCEES

The Sadducees, because of the influence of Greek philosophy, rejected the idea of resurrection as well as the authority of the prophets who taught it. For the Sadducees, the Law (the Torah, the Pentateuch) was their only sacred and authoritative book. Consequently, Jesus, in dealing with them, said, "'Are you not in error because you do not know the Scriptures or the power of God?'" Then He took a passage they did accept and added, "'Now about the dead rising—have you not read in the book of Moses, in the account of the bush, how God said to him, "I am the God of Abraham, the God of Isaac, and the God of Jacob"? He is not the God of the dead, but of the living. You are badly mistaken!'" (Mark 12:24,26-27; cf. Exod. 3:6).

CHRIST'S RESURRECTION FORESEEN

The New Testament also recognizes that the Old Testament foresaw the resurrection of Jesus. On the Day of Pentecost, Peter quoted Psalm 16:8-11 and said David "spoke of the resurrection of the Christ" (Acts 2:25-32). Paul also referred to the same passage in speaking of the resurrection of Jesus (Acts 13:35-37). It may be that he had Isaiah 53 in mind also when he wrote, "Christ died for our sins according to the Scriptures [the Old Testament], . . . he was buried, . . . he was raised on the third day according to the Scriptures" (1 Cor. 15:3-4).

Isaiah 53 clearly refers to the Servant of the LORD who, without any sin on His part, suffers completely for others, dying as a guilt offering, and then, seeing His offspring [His spiritual descendants] and prolonging His days, "after the suffering of his soul, he [as the Dead Sea Scrolls read] will see the light of life and be satisfied"—an obvious reference to Christ's resurrection.

RESURRECTION IN THE NEW TESTAMENT

CHRIST'S RESURRECTION AS A GUARANTEE

Jesus declared that it will be "His voice" that will bring about resurrection: "'Those who have done good will rise to live, and those who have done evil will rise to be condemned'" (John 5:28-29). Most Bible scholars also recognize that "in the New Testament the future is seen as the unfolding of what is given in the resurrection of Christ."[5] It inaugurates the "end times," the last age before the Millennium. Because of it, those who find life in Christ experience a foretaste of the powers of the age to come. In Him we are "enriched in every way—in all [our] speaking and in all [our] knowledge" (1 Cor. 1:5).

Eternal life is not simply unending life; it is Christ's life in us, a life that will be fully manifest in us in the age to come, but which is also our present possession if we are "in Christ" by faith (John 5:24; cf. John 1:4; 3:14-16; 5:40; 6:40; 11:25; 14:6).

Christ's resurrection was a key theme in the preaching of the Early Church, for its truth is vital to the gospel (1 Cor. 15:2,12-21). By opening up the Scriptures in the light of His resurrection, Jesus changed the whole outlook and attitude of His followers (Luke 24:25-27,44-48). On the Day of Pentecost, Peter centered attention on the risen Jesus.[6] All the apostles preached that in and through the resurrection of Jesus the resurrection of the dead is now a reality and is assured to us (Acts 4:2). Paul proclaimed that "Christ has indeed been raised from the dead, the firstfruits of those who have fallen asleep" (1 Cor. 15:20).[7] That is to say, the resurrection of the

---

[5]Louis Berkhof, *Systematic Theology*, 4th ed., rev. (Grand Rapids: William B. Eerdmans Publishing Co., 1941), 18.

[6]Francis J. Hall, *Eschatology* (New York: Longmans, Green & Co., 1922), 10.

[7]The firstfruits were usually a sheaf. That may be why many holy people were raised to life, came out of the tombs, and after Jesus' resurrection appeared to many people (Matt. 27:52-53). They drew attention to the fact that Jesus' resurrection means the resurrection of others.

dead is not simply something future. It has begun already in Jesus' resurrection.

Jesus is also "the firstborn from among the dead, so that in everything he might have the supremacy" (Col. 1:18; cf. Rev. 1:5). "Firstborn" has nothing to do with origin. God said, "'Israel is my firstborn son'" (Exod. 4:22; cf. Jer. 31:9). Of David, the youngest son of Jesse, God said, "'I will appoint him my firstborn'" (Ps. 89:20,27). The term "firstborn" was used to designate the heir, the one to have the supremacy. So Jesus is the heir, the one who will be in control, "the firstborn over all creation. . . . And he is the head of the body, the church" (Col. 1:15,18).

THE HOLY SPIRIT'S WORK

The Holy Spirit is the Spirit of sonship who "testifies with our spirit that we are God's children. Now if we are children, then we are heirs—heirs of God and co-heirs with Christ, if indeed we share in his sufferings in order that we may also share in his glory" (Rom. 8:15-17). That future glory will include the redemption of the bodies of those who have "the firstfruits of the Spirit" (Rom. 8:23). Our having only the firstfruits of the Spirit is a further guarantee that we will receive the fullness at the resurrection.

"If the Spirit of him who raised Jesus from the dead is living in you, he who raised Christ from the dead will also give life to your mortal bodies through the Spirit, who lives in you" (Rom. 8:11; cf. Rom. 6:4-5; 1 Cor. 6:14). This hope, however, puts a responsibility on us, for Paul goes on to say in Romans 8:11-17 that since Christ will resurrect us through the Spirit who now lives in us, "we have an obligation—but it is not to the sinful nature, to live according to it. For if you live according to the sinful nature, you will die; but if by the Spirit you put to death the misdeeds of the body, you will live [that is, be resurrected in the resurrection to life, rather than the resurrection to condemnation or judgment; John 5:29], because those who are led by the Spirit of God are sons of God."

Peter also spoke of "a living hope through the resurrection of Jesus from the dead, . . . into an inheritance that can never perish, spoil or fade—kept in heaven for you" (1 Pet. 1:3-4).

Christ's resurrection by the Spirit is, therefore, the guarantee that we will be raised and changed, so that our resurrection bodies will be immortal and imperishable (1 Cor. 15:42-44,47-54). For us believers the resurrection will be our personal sharing in Christ's victory over the last enemy, death (1 Cor. 15:54).

THE GIFT OF THE SPIRIT AS A GUARANTEE

The gift of the Spirit is also a guarantee of what is to come (2 Cor. 5:5). As Ralph Riggs put it, "This resurrection and translation of the saints has an extent of glory which we cannot comprehend. . . . The time is coming when the Spirit will envelop us with His power, transform our bodies by His might, and transport us to glory. . . . This will be the manifestation of the sons of God, the glorious liberty of the children of God . . . the triumphant climax to the work of the Holy Spirit."[8]

As always, there is perfect cooperation within the Trinity—so that our resurrection is not only by the Holy Spirit, but also by the power of God (Rom. 4:17; 1 Cor. 6:14; 2 Cor. 1:9; 13:4; 1 Thess. 4:14) and by Jesus himself (John 5:25-29; 6:39-40,44,54; 1 Cor. 15:21-23; Phil. 3:20-21).

THE RESURRECTION BODY

The Christian hope for the future always centers on God and Christ. Greek philosophers, except for the Epicureans, taught the immortality of the soul, but all

---

[8]Ralph Riggs, *The Spirit Himself* (Springfield, Mo.: Gospel Publishing House, 1949), 188-89. Riggs was general superintendent of the Assemblies of God, 1953-59.

of them rejected the idea of resurrection of the dead. They based their idea of immortality on their view of the nature of the soul, and they centered their hope on a supposed quality of life that would necessarily continue after death.[9] They considered the body a prison or at least "a burden, a hindrance to the soul."[10] This caused some of them at Athens to sneer at Paul's idea of the resurrection (Acts 17:32), and Greek influence undoubtedly was the cause of some Christians at Corinth saying "there is no resurrection of the dead" (1 Cor. 15:12).[11] But Paul in the same chapter gives a marvelous defense of the truth of our future resurrection.

The Bible is also clear in its teaching that as finite beings we need a body for the full expression of what God created us to be. As born-again believers, our bodies "are members of Christ himself," temples of the Holy Spirit meant to become means of honoring God (1 Cor. 6:15,19-20).

Changed Bodies. Our resurrection bodies will be the bodies we now possess, changed to be like the glorified nature of Christ's body (Phil. 3:21; 1 John 3:2).[12] God created humanity in His own likeness, and the image was still there after the Fall (Gen. 9:6). We are also told that Adam "had a son in his own likeness, in his own image" (Gen. 5:3). Therefore Paul can say, "Just as we have borne the likeness of

---

[9]A. J. Conyers, *The Eclipse of Heaven: Rediscovering the Hope of a World Beyond* (Downers Grove, Ill.: InterVarsity Press, 1992), 43-45.

[10]George Eldon Ladd, *The Last Things: An Eschatology for Laymen* (Grand Rapids: William B. Eerdmans Publishing Co., 1978), 29-30.

[11]Dale Moody, *The Hope of Glory* (Grand Rapids: William B. Eerdmans Publishing Co., 1964), 78.

[12]It should be noted that the human body is constantly changing in form and with respect to the molecules that make it up, yet it keeps its identity. God is able to bring together whatever is necessary for the resurrection of the body, even if that body was decayed, burned, or eaten by crocodiles (as was the body of missionary J. W. Tucker).

the earthly man, so shall we bear the likeness of the man from heaven" (1 Cor. 15:49). Our transformed bodies will be as much different from our present bodies as a wheat plant is from a bare grain (1 Cor. 15:37). The contrast can also be seen by comparing the raising of Lazarus, still wrapped in graveclothes (John 11:44), and the resurrection of Jesus, who rose up through the wrappings, leaving them behind (John 20:5-8). The torn, beaten, bloody body of Jesus was laid in the tomb. He arose healthy, able to walk to Emmaus, though He still bore the scars in His hands and side. This would imply also that babies and the elderly will not be resurrected in exactly the same form as when they died. Each will indeed be the same individual, the same person, but in a form that will be mature and healthy.[13]

In a passage that has stirred controversy, Paul speaks of "a building from God, an eternal house in heaven," "our heavenly dwelling," which will clothe us "so that what is mortal may be swallowed up by life" (2 Cor. 5:1-4). Some take this to mean we receive a temporary body while in heaven waiting for the resurrection, though Ray Summers says, "This view is foreign to the New Testament."[14] Others take it to refer to the environment dead believers enjoy in heaven. Some take it that in the resurrection a new body will become a "topcoat" for the present body. The majority of Bible scholars over the centuries have rejected that idea.[15]

In view of the passages that place the transformation of the body at the time of the resurrection and the Rapture (e.g., Phil. 3:20-21), George Ladd suggests that Paul is simply anticipating the resurrection

---

[13]A person at seventy years of age is still the same person he or she was at five, ten, or twenty even though the physical form changes, as does the chemical composition of the body's molecules.

[14]Ray Summers, *The Life Beyond* (Nashville: Broadman Press, 1959), 17.

[15]See Moody, *Hope of Glory,* 81-91, 94.

body, which is as good as his already, and that he longs to be further clothed at the resurrection.[16]

Spiritual Bodies. The believers' resurrection bodies are also described as "spiritual" in contrast to our present "natural" bodies.[17] It is generally agreed that "spiritual" (Gk. *pneumatikon*) does not mean "consisting of spirit"; nor is the body immaterial, ethereal, or lacking in physical density.[18] The disciples knew from experience that Christ's resurrection body was real, touchable, not ghostly, yet at the same time of a different order suited for both earth and heaven. It was not limited to the conditions of our present "space-time dimensions."[19] Consequently, our resurrection bodies are described as "of heaven" (Gk. *epouranios*). Jesus also said we would be like the angels in heaven, not spirit beings as they are, but rather no longer involved in marriage or having children (Mark 12:25).

Our present bodies are earthly, natural (Gk. *psuchikon*), with capacities, abilities, passions, and emotions adapted to the present earthly order, and with the same limits Adam had after the Fall. In contrast, our resurrection bodies will take on supernatu-

---

[16]Ladd, *Last Things,* 35–37.

[17]"Spiritual" (Gk. *pneumatikos* [nominative]) is used of the manna as "spiritual bread," bread from heaven (1 Cor. 10:3); of "spiritual songs" (Eph. 5:19; Col. 3:16); of "spiritual wisdom and understanding," wisdom and understanding given by the Spirit (Col. 1:9); of "spiritual gifts" given and empowered by the Spirit (1 Cor. 12:1); and of people who are filled with and used by the Holy Spirit (1 Cor. 14:37; Gal. 6:1).

[18]Geerhardus Vos, *The Pauline Eschatology* (Grand Rapids: William B. Eerdmans Publishing Co., 1972), 166–67; see also Geerhardus Vos, *Redemptive History and Biblical Interpretation: The Shorter Writings of Geerhardus Vos,* ed. Richard B. Gaffin, Jr. (Phillipsburg, N.J.: Presbyterian & Reformed Publishing Co., 1980), 49–50.

[19]Henry Blamires, "The Eternal Weight of Glory," *Christianity Today* 35:6 (27 May 1991): 30–34.

ral qualities involving power and glory.[20] Though we will still be finite beings, dependent wholly on God, our bodies will be the perfect instruments to enable us to respond to the Holy Spirit in new and marvelous ways.[21]

Changed Babies. We can be sure that babies and children who die will also be changed, brought to the complete physical and spiritual stature of Christ that we all will miraculously share. "Our citizenship is in heaven. And we eagerly await a Savior from there, the Lord Jesus Christ, who, by the power that enables him to bring everything under his control, will transform our lowly bodies so that they will be like his glorious body" (Phil. 3:20–21).

Nothing in the Bible says babies will be excluded from this. Life, including the life in aborted babies, is something that God put there and He knows how to bring it to perfection. Further, as René Pache points out, "The Bible gives no description of children playing in the courts of heaven."[22]

PREPARATION BY THE HOLY SPIRIT FOR
RESURRECTION AND RAPTURE

When Jewish believers cry, *"Abba!"* or Gentile believers cry, "Father!" the Holy Spirit "testifies with our spirit" that what we are saying is not mere

---

[20]Marriage relationships and sexual passions will no longer be a part of life after the resurrection (Mark 12:25). They will be superseded by a greater experience of spiritual relation with Jesus. But this does not necessarily mean that our resurrection bodies will be sexless, for identification as male and female seems to be an essential part of being human. See H. Wayne House, "Creation and Redemption: A Study of Kingdom Interplay," *Journal of the Evangelical Theological Society* 35:1 (March 1992): 9–10.

[21]Henry Barclay Swete, *The Holy Spirit in the New Testament* (Grand Rapids: Baker Book House, 1976; repr. from 1910), 190–91.

[22]René Pache, *The Future Life,* trans. Helen I. Needham (Chicago: Moody Press, 1962), 353.

words, confirming to us that God really is our Father. Our relation to God as His children, however, is not limited to this life. It makes us heirs of God and co-heirs with Christ (Rom. 8:17). Now we have "the firstfruits of the Spirit" (v. 23). The fullness will come with the fullness of the adoption ("the placing of sons") and with the redemption of our bodies (v. 23), that is, at the time of the resurrection.

In the meantime the Spirit prepares us for the fulfillment of our hope of glory in many ways. He helps us pray (Rom. 8:26-27)[23] as "by faith we eagerly await through the Spirit the righteousness for which we hope" (Gal.5:5). The gift of the Holy Spirit is a seal and a "first installment" of what we will receive in greater fullness in our future inheritance as the children of God (Eph. 1:13-14). It is also a "pledge" that we will indeed receive our promised inheritance if we keep our faith in Jesus[24] and continue to sow "to please the Spirit" rather than our sinful nature (Gal. 6:7-10; Rom. 2:7-10).[25]

In Paul's writings the work of the Spirit in preparing for the coming age is very much in view. The point of Romans 14:17 is that righteousness, peace, and joy in the Holy Spirit are what show that we are under the rule of God—that God is really King in our lives. Yet Paul is not limiting the Kingdom to these present blessings. They are, in fact, blessings of the future Kingdom. But through the Spirit, they are ours now as well. Paul goes on to show that they prepare us for the future and increase our anticipation of our future hope (Rom. 15:13). This hope was behind the

---

[23]The "groans" of 8:26 seem to be related to the "groanings" of verses 22-23 that look forward to future fulfillment when Jesus returns to earth. See Neill Quinn Hamilton, *The Holy Spirit and Eschatology in Paul*, Scottish Journal of Theology Occasional Papers, no. 6 (Edinburgh, Scotland: Oliver & Boyd, 1957), 36.

[24]Charles Webb Carter, *The Person and Ministry of the Holy Spirit: A Wesleyan Perspective* (Grand Rapids: Baker Book House, 1974), 300-302.

[25]Cf. Moody, *Hope of Glory*, 46.

cry *"Marana tha"* ("Our Lord come!" 1 Cor. 16:22), which recognized that Jesus is Lord now and that His lordship will be fully manifested on earth when He returns.[26]

A Needed Warning

Along with these first installments of the blessings of the age to come believers can have special times of refreshing from the Lord whenever they repent or change their attitude toward the Lord (Acts 3:19). We must keep in mind also His warnings. Over and over Jesus emphasized the importance of being ready and living in the light of His return (Matt. 24:42,44,50; 25:13; Luke 12:35,40; 21:34-36).[27]

Jesus compared the world at the time of His coming to the world of Noah's day. In spite of the warnings, the preaching, the building of the ark, the gathering of the animals, the people were unheeding and unprepared. They did not really believe God's judgment would come. To them, the day of the Flood dawned like any other: They had their meals planned, their good times planned, their parties and weddings planned. But that day brought an end to the world as they knew it. In the same way the present world will go blindly on, making its own plans. But one day Jesus will suddenly come (Matt. 24:37-39). The suddenness of His coming is further emphasized in Matthew 24:43-50.[28]

---

[26]Thomas N. Finger, *Christian Theology: An Eschatological Approach,* vol. 1 (Nashville: Thomas Nelson Publishers, 1985), 37.

[27]Schwarz observes, "Immediate readiness does not necessarily express belief in the chronologically near return of the Lord, but shows that our present attitude is expressive of our ultimate future. . . . Christians are asked to live their lives in active anticipation, as if each moment were their last." See Hans Schwarz, "Eschatology," in *Christian Dogmatics,* ed. Carl E. Braaten and Robert W. Jenson, vol. 2 (Philadelphia: Fortress Press, 1984), 583.

[28]R. Earl Allen, *The Hereafter* (Old Tappan, N.J.: Fleming H. Revell Co., 1977), 85-92.

To emphasize that it will be like any other day, Jesus said, "'Two men will be in the field; one will be taken and the other left. Two women will be grinding with a hand mill; one will be taken and the other left'" (Matt. 24:40-41). That is, people will be going about their normal, everyday tasks, and suddenly there will come a separation. "Taken" (Gk. *paralambanetai*) means "taken along or received." Jesus "*took* Peter and the two sons of Zebedee *along* with him" (Matt. 26:37). He promised, "'I will come back and *take* you to be with me'" (John 14:3). In this way, the one who is taken is graciously received into Jesus' presence to be with Him forever (1 Thess. 4:17). "Left" (Gk. *aphietai*) means "left behind" (as in Mark 1:18,20)— left behind and abandoned to face the wrath and judgments of God.

In other words, there will be no prior warning and no opportunity to get ready at the last minute. The same truth is brought out in the Parable of the Ten Virgins (Matt. 25:1-13). All this reminds us that in spite of Christ's delay, we must always consider His return imminent.

OTHER THEORIES OF JESUS' RETURN

The fact that Jesus is coming back to earth again is clear in the Scriptures. Evangelicals in general accept Acts 1:11 as assuring His personal, visible return. Various theories have arisen, however, to try to explain it away.

RETURN AT PENTECOST

Some say Christ returned in the person of the Holy Spirit on the Day of Pentecost. However, the exalted Christ was at the right hand of God the Father, and from heaven He poured out the Spirit at that time (Acts 2:32-33).

RETURN AT CONVERSION

Others say that Christ's second coming occurs when He enters the believer's heart at conversion (Rev. 3:20 is usually cited), but the Scriptures teach that those who receive Him then wait for His coming (Phil. 3:20; 1 Thess. 1:10).[29]

RETURN AT DEATH

Still others say His coming is fulfilled when He comes for the believer at death. In fact, this became almost the only expectation in the Roman Catholic Church.[30] However, both the dead and the living will be "caught up together" at His appearing (1 Thess. 4:17).

RETURN IN A.D. 70

On the basis of passages such as Matthew 10:23; 16:28; 24:34; Mark 9:1; 13:30; and 14:62, some tie the return of Jesus to the Romans' destroying Jerusalem and its temple in A.D. 70, thus bringing an end to the Old Testament sacrificial system. They say He was invisibly present bringing that judgment, perhaps as a step in a series of judgments where Christ's presence (Gk. *parousia*) brings ongoing victories.[31] Those who hold this view base part of their argument on the assumption that the Book of Revelation, with its view of a future return, was written before A.D. 70. Howev-

---

[29]"Hebrews 9:28 is decisively against" the idea that the *parousia* can "be spiritualized away into the mere continued presence of Jesus with His beloved at all times." Bernard Ramm, "A Philosophy of Christian Eschatology," in *Last Things,* ed. H. Leo Eddleman (Grand Rapids: Zondervan Publishing House, 1969), 33.

[30]Alois Winklhofer, *The Coming of His Kingdom: A Theology of the Last Things,* trans. A. V. Littledale (Freiburg, West Germany: Herder; Montreal: Palm Publishers, 1965), 11.

[31]Willibald Beyschlag, *New Testament Theology,* trans. Neil Buchanan, vol. 1 (Edinburgh, Scotland: T. & T. Clark, 1895), 196–200.

er, the vast majority of ancient and modern Bible
scholars date Revelation during the reign of Domitian,
about A.D. 95.[32] (It is also obvious that the glories of
the future Kingdom and the personal reign of Christ
on earth did not follow the events of A.D. 70.)

Luke 21:20-24 does specifically refer to the fall of
Jerusalem. The following verses indicate that after the
times of the Gentiles are fulfilled, signs in the sun,
moon, and stars will cause anguish and perplexity in
the nations on earth. Then "they will see the Son of
Man coming in a cloud with power and great glory"
(Luke 21:27). Mark 13:14-26 supplements this "from
the same fundamental viewpoint."[33] George Beasley-
Murray points out that the destruction of Jerusalem
and the temple is related to Christ's return, not because both events occur at the same time, but because the events of A.D. 70 were part of a long series
of God's judgments that prepare for the coming end
of the age. Jesus did not reveal the time span between the destruction of the city and His return, just
as the Old Testament prophets did not reveal the
time gap between the first and second comings of
Christ. He was more concerned with declaring the
power and glory of His return.[34]

SWEDENBORG THEORY

Emanuel Swedenborg (1688-1772) dated the last
judgment in 1757 in the spiritual world and said June
19, 1770, was the day the Lord sent His angels to
gather the elect. He also claimed that the "New
Church" he founded fulfilled the prophecies of the
new heaven, the new earth, and the New Jerusalem.[35]

---

[32]George Raymond Beasley-Murray, *Jesus and the Future: An
Examination of the Criticism of the Eschatological Discourse,
Mark 13 with Special Reference to the Little Apocalypse Theo-
ry* (London: Macmillan & Co., 1954), 167-71.

[33]Ibid., 204.

[34]Ibid.

[35]See T. Francis Glasson, *His Appearing and His Kingdom:
The Christian Hope in the Light of Its History* (London: Epworth Press, 1953), 53-54.

JEHOVAH'S WITNESSES

Jehovah's Witnesses say Christ returned invisibly in 1874. Others follow C. T. Russell and say He returned invisibly in judgment when Jerusalem was destroyed in A.D. 70.[36]

OTHER GROUPS

Still others take "the manifestation of the sons of God" (Rom. 8:19, KJV) out of context and claim they are the manifested sons. They say that Christ's second coming is fulfilled in them as His matured sons, who are maturing the Church to take over the kingdoms of this world. They reject the Rapture[37] and claim they are fulfilling it by being "caught up" into spiritual maturity. They also claim they are already the New Jerusalem and they are as well the "clouds" of power and glory in whom Christ is now appearing and through whom Christ will reign on the earth.[38]

A similar group call themselves theonomists and want to bring in the Kingdom by bringing the whole world under God's law, specifically, some or all of the law of Moses, even if it takes twenty thousand years.

All these groups take great liberties in spiritualizing plain biblical statements and forget that we do not have our hope yet, but "we wait for it patiently" (Rom. 8:25). The personal return of Jesus Christ to earth is the only way we will receive the fullness of the hope we are waiting for. Our hope is not in the fulfillment of a long process of what the individual believer or the Church can accomplish. We should be looking for a sudden, unexpected, visible return of Christ (Matt. 24:27,30,44; Mark 13:26; Luke 21:27; Acts 1:11; Phil. 2:10–11) that will suddenly change us

---

[36]Beasley-Murray, *Jesus and the Future*, 167, 170.
[37]See note 39.
[38]Hobart E. Freeman, *Exploring Biblical Theology* (Warsaw, Ind.: Faith Ministries and Publications, n.d.), 298–99.

and cause us to share His glory (Rom. 8:18-23; 1 Cor. 15:51-52), making it possible for us to return with Him in glory (Col. 3:4).

TWO ASPECTS OF CHRIST'S SECOND COMING

THE RAPTURE OF THE CHURCH

The Bible indicates two aspects of Christ's coming. On one hand, He will come as the Preserver, Deliverer, or Rescuer "from the coming wrath" (1 Thess. 1:10). "Since we have now been justified by his blood, how much more shall we be saved from God's wrath through him!" (Rom. 5:9). We are to keep awake spiritually, living sober, well-balanced, self-controlled lives, and wear the gospel armor of faith, love, and the hope of salvation—"God did not appoint us to suffer wrath but to receive salvation through our Lord Jesus Christ. He died for us so that, whether we are awake or asleep, we may live together with him. Therefore encourage one another" (1 Thess. 5:9-11).

These verses of encouragement refer to the promise that "the Lord himself will come down from heaven, with a loud command, with the voice of the archangel and with the trumpet call of God, and the dead in Christ will rise first. After that, we who are still alive and are left will be caught up together with them in the clouds to meet the Lord in the air. And so we will be with the Lord forever. Therefore encourage each other" (1 Thess. 4:16-18).

Only the resurrection of believers who died "in Christ" is in view here. They are changed, clothed with immortality, "in a flash, in the twinkling of an eye" (1 Cor. 15:52-54), their bodies transformed "so that they will be like his glorious body" (Phil. 3:21). Then those believers who are still alive will be changed and caught up together with them, in one Body. The one requirement for both the dead and, obviously, the living believers is to be "in Christ," that is, in a relationship of faith in Him and faithfulness to Him.

"Caught up" (Gk. *harpagēsometha*)[39] refers to what is often called "the Rapture."[40] "To meet the Lord" (Gk. *eis apantēsin tou kuriou*) can be translated "for a meeting with the Lord." "Meeting" was often used as a technical term for people meeting a king or general some distance outside their city and escorting him in.[41] This is parallel to the use of parousia, "presence," "coming," of the Lord (1 Thess. 4:15), which has a technical status when it refers to Christ's return,[42] and is most often used of the Rapture.[43]

---

[39]The same verb is used of the male child who was "snatched up" to God and His throne (Rev. 12:5). It is also used of Paul being "caught up" to the third heaven, to paradise (2 Cor. 12:2,4), and of the Spirit when He "suddenly took Philip away" (Acts 8:39). In addition to being used of supernatural transfer, the verb is used of a wolf seizing the sheep (John 10:12), the evil one snatching away the Word (Matt. 13:19), and the instruction by the Roman officer that his soldiers "snatch away" Paul from the Jews (Acts 23:10). Thus, the word involves the idea of a powerful "snatching away."

[40]"Rapture" is from the Latin *raptus,* the past participle of *rapere,* "to seize," and has the original meaning of being snatched up and carried away. Therefore, "the Rapture" is a proper designation of our "being caught up together . . . to meet the Lord in the air." In today's English it has come to mean "being carried away or exalted in joyful emotion or ecstasy." We can be sure the Rapture will also be a joyful experience as we meet the Lord in the air.

[41]See the usage of the word in the Parable of the Ten Virgins (Matt. 25:1–10) and in the case of Paul being met by Christians from Rome who escorted him into the city (Acts 28:15). See also Polybius, 18,48,4 (2d century B.C.), ed. Th. Buttner-Wobst, 1882–1904.

[42]Thoralf Gilbrant, ed. *The Complete Biblical Library,* vol. 15 (Springfield, Mo.: Complete Biblical Library, 1991), 101–2.

[43]*Epiphaneia* ("appearing") and *apokalupsis* ("revelation," "disclosure") are also used of Christ's return. These three words (i.e., including *parousia*) can be used interchangeably for Christ's coming for His waiting saints (cf. 1 Cor. 1:7; 1 Thess. 2:19; 1 Tim. 6:14) as well as for His coming in flaming fire at the end of the Tribulation (cf. 1 Thess. 3:13; 2 Thess. 1:7; 2:8; 1 Pet. 1:7). *Parousia* emphasizes His arrival and personal presence; *apokalupsis,* His descent from the heaven to which He ascended; and *epiphaneia,* the awesome manifestation of His glory and power.

THE REVELATION OF CHRIST

On the other hand, God's justice will be vindicated "when the Lord Jesus is revealed from heaven in blazing fire with his powerful angels. He will punish those who do not know God and do not obey the gospel of our Lord Jesus . . . on the day he comes to be glorified in his holy people and to be marveled at among all those who have believed" (2 Thess. 1:7–10). This fits with other passages which show that the Kingdom must be brought in through judgment (Dan. 2:34–35,44–45; Rev. 19:11–16).

Revelation 19:14 also says that when Jesus returns to judge the world, not only will angels be with Him but also the armies of heaven, "dressed in fine linen, white and clean." Such a description identifies them as the raptured believers who are already in heaven, who have been before the judgment seat of Christ, and who have enjoyed the Marriage Supper of the Lamb (Rev. 17:14; 19:7–8; see below).

THE JUDGMENT SEAT OF CHRIST

JESUS THE JUDGE

Throughout the Bible God is seen as a righteous Judge. He brought judgment on both Israel and the surrounding nations in ancient times. At the end of the age He will still be the Righteous Judge, but He will mediate that judgment through the Son, for "the Father judges no one, but has entrusted all judgment to the Son, that all may honor the Son just as they honor the Father" (John 5:22–23; cf. Acts 3:21; 10:42; Rom. 2:16; 1 Thess. 1:10; 2 Tim. 4:8). Jesus has the right and the authority to judge "because he is the Son of Man" (John 5:27). In other words, just as He is a High Priest who is able "to sympathize with our weaknesses," for He "has been tempted in every way, just as we are—yet was without sin" (Heb. 4:15), so He is a Judge who truly understands us and will do what is right.

This means all peoples are responsible both to God the Father and to Jesus. We must "give account" of ourselves (Matt. 12:36). When the Lord comes, He "will bring to light what is hidden in darkness and will expose the motives of men's hearts. At that time each will receive his praise from God" (1 Cor. 4:5). In other words, God looks on everything we do and say as important.

We have different backgrounds and different natural gifts that we have inherited. We cannot change that. But we can make right choices that will develop Christian character and bring glory to God. We are responsible to "fight the good fight [the only fight worth fighting]" and "finish the race," as we keep the faith (2 Tim. 4:7)—letting our faith express itself through love (Gal. 5:6-7). That is, we must make every effort to develop the fruit of the Spirit and be true followers of Jesus (2 Pet. 1:3-11).

With the prospect of judgment in mind, we can see that the Rapture is no mere "escape." Believers will forever be with the Lord. But all without exception will be subject to judgment when brought into His presence (Rom. 14:10-12; 1 Cor. 3:12-15; 2 Cor. 5:10).

God's judgment seat, or throne (Gk. *bēma,* Rom. 14:10), is also called "the judgment seat of Christ" (2 Cor. 5:10). There each one will "receive what is due him for the things done while in the body, whether good [Gk. *agathon,* "spiritually and morally good or useful in God's sight"] or bad [Gk. *phaulos,* "worthless, evil; including selfishness, envy, and laziness"]" (2 Cor. 5:10).[44]

EVERYTHING JUDGED

No secret thing can be hidden (Rom. 2:16). Everything will be judged: our words, our acts, our mo-

[44]Some ancient Greek manuscripts have *kakos,* a more general word for "bad," "evil," "lack," "harm," "wrong," instead of *phaulos.*

tives, our attitudes, our character, our sufferings, the use of spiritual gifts, and the use of material goods and money (Matt. 5:22; 12:36-37; Mark 4:22; Rom. 2:5-11,16; 1 Cor. 3:13; 4:5; 13:3; Eph. 6:8).[45] Of these, our motives (especially love) and our faithfulness seem to be the most important (Matt. 25:21,23; Luke 12:43; 1 Cor. 13:3; Col. 3:23-24; Heb. 6:10). They can make the difference between whether our deeds are judged as "gold, silver, costly stones" or "wood, hay or straw" (1 Cor. 3:12).[46] If our works are not built on Christ or if there is pride, selfishness, self-will, or envy involved, they will disappear in the fire (1 Cor. 3:12-15; cf. Matt. 6:1-2,5; 7:22-23; Gal. 6:8-10; Phil. 1:17).

In other words, the judgment includes the possibility of either "loss" (1 Cor. 3:15) or "reward" (Rom. 2:10; 1 Cor. 3:12-14; Phil. 3:14; 2 Tim. 4:8; 2 John 8). We must continue "in him [Christ] so that when he appears we may be confident and unashamed before him at his coming" (1 John 2:28). Otherwise, there is the danger of having all our works burned up (1 Cor. 3:13-15).

Only those who respond in love and faith to the grace, abilities, and responsibilities God gives them will hear Jesus say, "'Well done, good and faithful servant. You have been faithful with a few things; I will put you in charge of many things. Come and share your master's happiness!'" (Matt. 25:21,23). Though we are not saved by our works, we are "created in Christ Jesus to do good works [not our own ideas of what is good, but those works], which God prepared in advance for us to do" (Eph. 2:10).

PRINCIPLES OF JUDGMENT

Paul emphasizes that all judgment will be according to the principles laid down in the gospel (Rom. 2:16).

---

[45]See p. 87 on sins covered by the blood of Christ.

[46]Note that all this has to do with deeds done in the body, that is, in this present life. There is no second chance after death.

He summarizes these principles of God's righteous judgment in Romans 2:6-11:

God will give to each person according to what he has done. To those who by persistence in doing good seek glory, honor and immortality, he will give eternal life. But for those who are self-seeking and who reject the truth and follow evil, there will be wrath and anger. There will be trouble and distress for every human being who does evil, first for the Jew, then for the Gentile; but glory, honor and peace for everyone who does good; first for the Jew, then for the Gentile. For God does not show favoritism.

REWARDS

The matter of rewards should not be dismissed; the Bible shows it is very important. As Jesus said, "'Do not be afraid, little flock, for your Father has been pleased to give you the kingdom. Sell your possessions and give to the poor. Provide purses for yourselves that will not wear out, a treasure in heaven that will not be exhausted, where no thief comes near and no moth destroys. For where your treasure is, there your heart will be also'" (Luke 12:32-34).

From what Jesus and Paul state it is clear also that there will be differences in reward. Some, including Martin Luther, have objected to this and have supposed that since salvation is by grace, that all believers must share equally in the glory and grace that God offers, and that there cannot be any differences in what is received. Augustine, however, had already pointed out that any differences in reward will not cause envy or jealousy because of the love all will have for Christ and for each other.[47]

---

[47]Joseph Pohle, *Eschatology, or the Catholic Doctrine of the Last Things: A Dogmatic Treatise,* English version by Arthur Preuss (Westport, Conn.: Greenwood Press, Publishers, 1971; repr. from 1917), 40, 42.

When Paul does address the subject, however, in Romans 2:6-16, he does not mean that everyone will be judged at the same time. His purpose is to point out that God's righteous judgment means justice for all and that Jews and Gentiles will be judged by the same principles, the same standards. In 1 Thessalonians 4, only the resurrection of those "in Christ" is in view. This is true also of the passages that deal with the judgment seat of Christ.

Paul's mention of judging "men's secrets" also draws attention to the fact that faults, errors, and sins that have been repented of and confessed with contrition before the Lord have already been forgiven and will not be brought up before the Judgment Seat. When the wicked forsake their way (including their plots and plans) and turn to the Lord, He has mercy and He freely pardons them (Isaiah 55:7).

Sins that have been forgiven are behind God's back (Isa. 38:17). Since God is everywhere present, this must mean they are out of existence. God removes them from us "as far as the east is from the west" (Ps. 103:12), an infinite distance. Then when God forgives sins, He no longer remembers them (Jer. 31:34). When the Bible speaks of God remembering, it always means He is about to enter into the situation and do something about it. But when sins are forgiven they are really gone, and the guilt is gone as well.

Jesus became our guilt offering (Isa. 53:10), so that both our sins and all our guilt are under His blood. In this way, we are justified ("declared righteous") in God's sight. We come before Him as redeemed, the blood of Christ having paid the price for our redemption. We are acquitted—God's verdict is "not guilty." Therefore, we can even now approach God's throne, in the holiest place in heaven's temple, with confidence (Heb. 10:19).

THE WEDDING SUPPER OF THE LAMB

The Parable of the King's Wedding Banquet for His Son, though it encourages our present activity for the Lord, has a future consummation, as seen by the judgment on the man who was not wearing wedding clothes (Matt. 22:1-14). Jesus is the heavenly Bridegroom that Paul had in mind when he wrote to the Corinthian believers, "I am jealous for you with a godly jealousy. I promised you to one husband, to Christ, so that I might present you as a pure virgin to him" (2 Cor. 11:2).

Paul says further, "Husbands, love your wives, just as Christ loved the church and gave himself up for her to make her holy, cleansing her by the washing with water through the word, and to present her to himself as a radiant church, without stain or wrinkle or any other blemish, but holy and blameless" (Eph. 5:25-27). The Book of Revelation also draws attention to the Bride who "has made herself ready" and who was given "fine linen, bright and clean," to wear (19:7-8).

The armies of heaven who follow Jesus, riding on white horses (symbolizing triumph), are "dressed in fine linen, white and clean" (Rev. 19:14). This identifies them with the Lamb's bride (the Church),[48] who take part in the Wedding Supper of the Lamb (Rev. 19:6-9). That is, they have already been in heaven, they are already fully clothed with "the righteous acts of the saints" (v. 8). This implies also that those acts are complete and the believers have been resurrected, changed, and taken to heaven. This would imply also that they have already appeared before the judgment seat of Christ (2 Cor. 5:10). What a time of joy and delight that wedding supper will be!

---

[48]Stanley M. Horton, *The Ultimate Victory* (Springfield, Mo.: Gospel Publishing House, 1991), 277-79.

STUDY QUESTIONS

1. In what ways did the Old Testament prepare for the New Testament teaching of bodily resurrection?

2. How is the resurrection of Jesus related to the resurrection of believers?

3. What is the work of the Holy Spirit in relation to our resurrection and how does He prepare us for it?

4. In what ways will our resurrection bodies be like our present bodies and in what ways will they be different?

5. What warnings did Jesus give concerning His return and how should they affect us today?

6. What are some of the Scripture passages and other evidences that indicate Jesus could come at any time, even today?

7. Why did Jesus show concern about the fall of Jerusalem, which took place in A.D. 70, in connection with prophecies of the distant future?

8. What is the biblical evidence that points to two distinct aspects of Christ's return?

9. On what basis will believers be judged at the judgment seat of Christ?

10. What attitude should believers have toward the matter of the gaining or losing of rewards?

11. What is the purpose of the Wedding Supper of the Lamb?

12. What does the fact that heaven's armies following Jesus are clothed in white linen tell us about them?

Chapter Three

The Tribulation

Jesus declared that the gospel of the Kingdom, the gospel of God's power and rule, must be preached to all nations before the consummation of this age (Matt. 24:14). This gospel, or good news, revealed several aspects of the Kingdom. It centered in the King, our Lord Jesus Christ. While He was here on earth He manifested divine power and rule, even over nature and demons. That is to say, the Kingdom was present in and through Jesus. He commissioned His disciples and sent the Holy Spirit at Pentecost so that they would manifest God's power throughout the world in this age. Therefore, the Kingdom is present in and through the Church. But He also looked ahead to a future Kingdom on earth where He would again drink of the fruit of the vine and where His twelve apostles would sit on twelve thrones judging the twelve tribes of Israel (Matt. 19:28; 26:29).

This Kingdom will fulfill the Old Testament prophecies of restoration and blessing on earth in the age to come. In spite of the spread of the gospel and the outpouring of the Holy Spirit, this present age is an evil age, from which our Lord Jesus Christ will "rescue" us (Gal. 1:4). It will be replaced by the Kingdom Age. But the transition will not be gradual, over an extended time, as the postmillennialists teach.[1] There will be a crisis time at the end of this age, when God's wrath and judgment will be outpoured as never before.

---

[1]See chap. 5, p. 163.

THE KINGDOM BROUGHT IN THROUGH JUDGMENT

Many passages in the Old Testament picture God's judgment that must come on a sinful world before the promised restoration and blessings. Because the earth is defiled with immorality and wickedness, the fires of God's judgment will consume the earth's inhabitants and few will be left (Isa. 24:5-6). Joel compares this judgment to a harvest in which the nations are gathered into the Valley of Jehoshaphat, literally, the "valley where Yahweh (Jehovah) judges"—also called the "valley of decision"—where the Lord renders His decision and pronounces judgment because wickedness is so great (Joel 3:2,12-14). Zechariah also prophesied judgment on the nations gathered against Jerusalem in what John called the Battle of Armageddon (Zech. 14:2-4; Rev. 16:16; 19:19).[2]

A KEY PICTURE

Daniel 2 gives us a key picture. Nebuchadnezzar in a dream saw "a large statue—an enormous, dazzling statue, awesome in appearance. The head of the statue was made of pure gold, its chest and arms of silver, its belly and thighs of bronze, its legs of iron, its feet partly of iron and partly of baked clay." While Nebuchadnezzar was watching, "a rock was cut out, but not by human hands. It struck the statue on its feet of iron and clay and smashed them. Then the iron, the clay, the bronze, the silver and the gold were broken to pieces at the same time and became like chaff on a threshing floor in the summer. The wind swept them away without leaving a trace. But

---

[2]Some writers consider these passages in Isaiah, Joel, and Zechariah as apocalyptic. However, they do not show many of the marks of being apocalyptic. They are eschatological prophecies. See H. H. Rowley, *The Relevance of Apocalyptic: A Study of Jewish and Christian Apocalypses from Daniel to the Revelation,* new and rev. ed. (New York: Association Press, 1964), 25-26.

the rock that struck the statue became a huge mountain and filled the whole earth" (Dan. 2:31-35).

THE BABYLON IMAGE STILL WITH US

Daniel's God-given interpretation of the dream showed that the statue represented a sequence of empires, beginning with Nebuchadnezzar and Babylon. This was followed by Medo-Persia, Alexander the Great's Greek Empire, the Roman Empire, and finally by nationalistic states that, like iron and baked, or fired, clay, were partly strong and partly brittle— some nations lasting a long time, others always breaking up—none remaining united.[3]

This iron and clay condition has been characteristic of the states descending from the former Roman Empire since its fall. Attempts at further empire building have failed again and again. Charlemagne tried to set one up. So did Napoleon. The kaiser dreamed of one in 1914. Mussolini dreamed of one and proclaimed that he would make the Mediterranean a Roman lake. Hitler attempted to take over all of Europe. They all failed. Other attempts to unite Europe have failed. The World Court and the League of Nations did not

---

[3]Modern critical scholars who do not believe in the supernatural deny the reality of prophecy. Thus, they interpret the sequence to be Babylon, Media, Persia, Greece, and the divided Greek Empire that came under Alexander the Great's generals after his death. They do this to fit their view that the Book of Daniel was history written during the persecution of the Jews by Antiochus Epiphanes (175-164 B.C.), written as if it were prophecy. However, the Book of Daniel itself (8:20) pictures Medo-Persia as a single animal (the ram), in this way confirming the interpretation that Medo-Persia is the second empire of Dan. 2. A number of conservative scholars uphold the early date of the Book of Daniel, including Edward Young, H. C. Leupold, Kenneth Kitchen, R. D. Wilson, John H. Raven, and Carl F. Keil. See Michael Kalafian, *The Prophecy of the Seventy Weeks of the Book of Daniel: A Critical Review of the Prophecy as Viewed by Three Major Theological Interpretations and the Impact of the Book of Daniel on Christology* (Lanham, Md.: University Press of America, 1991), 201-6.

last. The United Nations has never been very united. The European Common Market and the European Community may bring a temporary or apparent unity that could possibly prepare for the Antichrist. But his rule will also be temporary.

Notice, too, that even though one empire gives way to another, they are all part of the same statue, the same world system. There is never a really new world order until the statue is destroyed and every remnant of it blown away. The present world system still bears the marks of the empires that preceded it. We still have Babylonian idolatry and love of luxury. Medo-Persian religion supposed the world would end with everyone having to go through a river of fire. If a person's good deeds outbalanced the bad deeds, the fire would seem like warm milk; otherwise, it would really burn. This encouraged an ethic that caused people to go around trying to do their good deed for the day. That ethic of good works is still all too common. Greek philosophy is the basis of most modern philosophy, and Greek art and its exaltation of the human is still everywhere present. Roman law and Roman ideas of might makes right and keeping the peace by force still influence world politics. In effect, the present world system with its breakup of many European states is still iron and clay—part of the same statue. None of the present human or political attempts at bringing a new order or a new age will change that.

THE IMAGE HIT IN THE FEET

Daniel 2 does not discuss the Antichrist because his kingdom is part of the iron and fired clay of the statue's feet. The important point is that the rock cut out of a mountain hits the statue in the feet, not in the head or any other part of the statue, so that the dream does not call for Babylon to be rebuilt or for the Medo-Persian, Greek, or Roman Empire to be reestablished.

Some have taken Isaiah 13:19, which prophesies the overthrow of Babylon, to mean that Babylon must be rebuilt in order to have the kind of overthrow described. Verse 20, "She will never be inhabited or lived in through all generations," in the NIV (and most English versions) implies that after a sudden destruction Babylon would never be rebuilt. King Sennacherib did destroy Babylon suddenly in 689 B.C., shocking the known world by leveling it to the ground and digging trenches from the river to make a swamp out of it, as Isaiah 14:23 prophesied. The city, however, was too important in those days and was rebuilt by his son Esarhaddon, and its present condition is the result, not of sudden destruction, but of gradual deterioration and desertion in favor of Baghdad. However, the Hebrew verbs in verse 20 are actives, not passives. A more literal translation is "She will not sit endlessly and she will not live on unto generation and generation." Why? Verse 22 gives the answer: "Her time is at hand, and her days will not be prolonged." In other words, this prophecy was simply saying that Babylon would soon be destroyed, not that it would never be rebuilt.[4] So God will move in judgment on the world in its present iron and clay condition (made worse by the Antichrist and his false prophet). Then the Kingdom will be supernaturally established "without human hands," and for the first time we will see a brand-new world order.

Neither does Daniel 2 see a gradual taking over of the kingdoms of this world by the gospel, as postmillennialism and its modern variations, such as "kingdom now" and dominion theology, teach.[5] The rock does not penetrate the statue and transform it. Rather, it shatters not only the feet, but the entire statue. And "the God of heaven will set up a kingdom that

---

[4]Archaeologists have discovered Sennacherib's records and they verify the above. This is discussed in an unpublished doctoral dissertation, "A Defense on Archaeological Grounds of the Isaian Authorship of the Passages in Isaiah Dealing with Babylon," by Stanley M. Horton, Kansas City, Kans.: Central Baptist Theological Seminary, 1959.

[5]See chap. 5, p. 164.

will never be destroyed, nor will it be left to another people. It will crush all those kingdoms and bring them to an end, but it will itself endure forever" (Dan. 2:44). Three things stand out. The Kingdom must be brought in through judgment. The Kingdom will be established by God's direct, sudden, drastic intervention. And when established, the Kingdom will continue forever. Even the end of the Millennium will not bring an end to the Rock, for that Rock is Christ, and the rule He establishes will continue on into the new heavens and the new earth.

AN OVERVIEW OF HISTORY

In his early life Daniel interpreted the dreams of others, but toward the end of his life God gave him a series of four visions, which provide further details of the sequence of empires, revealing their inner character. Daniel 7 gives an overview of history beginning in Daniel's own time and climaxing with the second coming of Christ in the clouds and great glory. The three visions that follow give more information about certain aspects of the history covered in chapter 7 down to Armageddon and the Final Judgment (Dan. 11:46 through 12:3).[6]

Some writers identify the "four great beasts" of chapter 7 with end-time nations.[7] However, Daniel 8 deals further with Medo-Persia and Alexander's Greek Empire. The parallel with chapter 2 in both chapters 7 and 8 seems clear. The fourth beast of chapter 7 seems to represent the Roman Empire and all that follows, down to the end of the age. The ten horns on

---

[6]J. Barton Payne, "The Goal of Daniel's Seventy Weeks," *Journal of the Evangelical Theological Society* 21:2 (June 1978): 114.

[7]Some take the lion to be Great Britain; the eagle's wings, the U.S.; the bear, Russia; the leopard, Japan and China; the fourth beast, the European Community. See Michael B. Wieteska, *Intimations of Empire: The Great Powers in Prophecy* (Geneva: N.A.T.I.O.N., 1993), 10–15, 45.

the fourth beast are rulers or kingdoms at the end of the age that may be identified with the ten kings who are contemporary with the Antichrist (Dan. 7:24; Rev. 17:12). That they are still future is seen by the fact that the little horn uproots three of those horns (Dan. 7:8).

The fourth beast and the little horn (the Antichrist) are to be destroyed, and then Daniel sees after that "one like a son of man, coming with the clouds of heaven," who "was given authority, glory and sovereign power; all peoples, nations and men of every language worshiped him. His dominion is an everlasting dominion that will not pass away, and his kingdom is one that will never be destroyed" (Dan. 7:13-14). This clearly identifies the One "like a son of man" with the Rock of chapter 2. The New Testament also identifies the Rock with Jesus, and Jesus himself declared His identification with the One coming in the clouds of heaven (Matt. 26:64).

SEVEN YEARS OF TRIBULATION

The Book of Revelation shows that this age ends with an outburst of evil and a series of judgments which will culminate in the final end of the present world system. In other words, a period of time is involved: From Daniel 9:24-27, this is often taken to be a period of seven years. In that chapter Daniel was concerned about what the Lord said to the Judean exiles in Babylon: "'When seventy years are completed for Babylon, I will come to you and fulfill my gracious promise to bring you back to this place [Jerusalem]'" (Jer. 29:10). The seventy years were about up, and there was still no evidence that a return from exile was about to take place. Daniel then identified himself with Israel, confessed their sin, recognized that no righteousness on their part or on his deserved the return, and prayed for forgiveness and for the return for the Lord's sake.

The angel Gabriel brought the Lord's answer. Obviously, Jeremiah's prophecy of the seventy years would be fulfilled. However, God was not through dealing with Israel. Gabriel said, "'Seventy "sevens" are decreed for your people and your holy city to finish transgression, to put an end to sin, to atone for wickedness, to bring in everlasting righteousness, to seal up the vision and prophecy and to anoint the most holy'" (Dan. 9:24). Since the seventy "sevens" are something beyond the seventy years of Jeremiah's prophecy, the "sevens" ("weeks," KJV) are periods of seven years each.[8] A total of sixty-nine "sevens" (483 years) leads up to the time of the "Anointed One" who will be "cut off" (Dan. 9:26).

Different times for the beginning of the 483 years have been proposed. Some take it to be 538 B.C. when Cyrus decreed the return of the Jews to Jerusalem. But that was to rebuild the temple, not the city. Others take it to be the decree of 445 B.C. that sent Nehemiah back to rebuild the walls of Jerusalem, but that involves using 360-day years to bring the end of the 483 years at A.D. 32.[9] The letter quoted in Ezra 4:11–16 indicates Ezra went back to rebuild the city in 458 or 457 B.C., which would bring the end at A.D. 26 or 27, when Jesus most likely began His ministry.[10]

---

[8]The fact that Daniel was dealing with a prophecy of seventy years that was fulfilled literally shows that the seventy weeks should be taken as an actual number and the entire prophecy should be interpreted literally.

[9]See Robert Anderson, *The Coming Prince* (Grand Rapids: Kregel Publications, 1957; repr. of the 10th edition), xiii. Anderson claimed April 6, A.D. 32, was the date of the Triumphal Entry when Jesus "was acclaimed as 'Messiah the Prince, the King, the son of David.'" The problem with this is that the Jews always added an extra month from time to time in order to make their years average 365 days. Most Bible scholars today take the Triumphal Entry to be in A.D. 30, which makes the date beginning in 457 B.C. seem more reasonable.

[10]The repetition in Ezra 4:5 and 4:24 indicates that the verses in between are a parenthesis: bringing the opposition of the Samaritans up to Ezra's own time and making the "force" of Ezra 4:23 the cause of the situation recorded in Neh. 1:3. As a result, the correspondence of the sixty-nine weeks is exact. See Payne, "Goal of Daniel's Seventy Weeks," 101.

After the 483 years the Anointed One would be "cut off" (cf. Isa. 53:8). "'The people of the ruler who will come will destroy the city and the sanctuary. The end will come like a flood: War will continue unto the end, and desolations have been decreed. He will confirm a covenant with many for one "seven." In the middle of the "seven" he will put an end to sacrifice and offering. And on a wing of the temple he will set up an abomination that causes desolation, until the end that is decreed is poured out on him'" (Dan. 9:26–27).

"The people" who destroy the city and the sanctuary are the Romans who did this in A.D. 70 (cf. Luke 21:20); they are the people "of the ruler who will come" only in the sense that they belong to the same anti-God world system. "The ruler who will come" is connected with the end and therefore refers to the end-time Antichrist.[11] Notice that the destruction of Jerusalem and the temple by the Romans did not occur immediately after Christ's crucifixion, making it clear that there is an interval of time between the sixty-ninth and the seventieth "seven."[12] And since the prophecy speaks of the end, many Bible scholars believe the Church Age is the interval. It is also clear that the seventy weeks are decreed for Israel and Jerusalem "to finish transgression, to put an end to sin, to atone for wickedness, to bring in everlasting righteousness, to seal up vision and prophecy and to anoint the most holy" (Dan. 9:24). Some of these goals for Israel are still in the future (Rom. 11:25–29). Israel has not yet experienced "everlasting righteous-

Chapter 3
The
Tribulation

---

[11]See Robert D. Culver, "Daniel," in *The Wycliffe Bible Commentary,* ed. Charles F. Pfeiffer and Everett F. Harrison (Chicago: Moody Press, 1962), 151.

[12]Amillennialists and others who take the seventieth "seven" to follow the sixty-ninth without a gap do not interpret Dan. 9:27 literally and are not able to find anything that "resembles a clear fulfillment in history." Kalafian, *Prophecy of the Seventy Weeks,* 96; cf. Jay E. Adams, *The Time Is at Hand* (Philadelphia: Presbyterian & Reformed Publishing Co., 1974), 3.

ness," nor is the vision sealed up by being totally ful-filled. The "anointing of the most holy" may also refer to the restoring of the millennial temple.[13] Conse-quently, the seventy weeks have not been totally ful-filled.[14]

The ruler who will come will then "confirm a cov-enant with many for one 'seven.'"[15] The making of this covenant will thus indicate the beginning of the seven years of tribulation. The covenant or treaty may be made with Israel, possibly with respect to a land dispute (cf. Dan. 11:39). Then after three and one-half years, the ruler will break the covenant, put an end to sacrifices and offerings in a rebuilt temple, and set up an abomination that causes desolation (9:27).[16]

THE ABOMINATION THAT CAUSES DESOLATION

After declaring that the gospel of the Kingdom must be preached, Jesus went on to talk about the "abomination that causes desolation, spoken of through the prophet Daniel" (Matt. 24:15). The initial fulfillment of Daniel's prophecy took place in Decem-ber 167 B.C., when Antiochus Epiphanes set a hea-then altar on the altar of burnt offering and dedicated the Jerusalem temple to the Greek god Zeus.[17]

Both Daniel and Jesus saw a greater fulfillment. Daniel 11:36 through 12:1 jumps ahead to the Anti-christ and to the time of the Tribulation, which it identifies as "a time of distress such as has not hap-pened from the beginning of nations until then."

---

[13]Payne, "Goal of Daniel's Seventy Weeks," 102.

[14]Robert H. Gundry, *The Church and the Tribulation* (Grand Rapids: Zondervan Publishing House, 1973), 189–90.

[15]This covenant cannot be the one made by Christ. His cov-enant, put into effect by His death and the shedding of His blood, will never be broken.

[16]Many refer to this time as "a time of trouble for Jacob" (Jer. 30:7), a "time of distress" (Dan. 12:1). There is no reference to the Church's being present on earth during this time.

[17]First Macc. 1:47,54,59; 2 Macc. 6:2.

Jesus also identified the time as "great distress" (Matt. 24:21).

In the present world many believers are already suffering distress, but the Great Tribulation will receive the wrath of God in a way beyond anything that has ever been known in the past (Rev. 14:10; 16:17-21). Satan and the nations will also be full of anger and wrath at this time (Rev. 11:18; 12:12). This time will also see the climax of world rebellion against God, with the rise of the Antichrist as a world dictator, and it will bring terrible judgments on the nations of the world.

THE WRATH OF GOD AND THE LAMB

These judgments, however, are not just for the nations' outward sins. The wrath of the Book of Revelation is not only the wrath of God, but also the wrath of the Lamb (Rev. 6:16). The Antichrist is pictured as a wild, destructive beast, but Jesus, even in judgment, is still the Lamb, the One who gave himself as a sinless sacrifice in our place on the cross, the One still bearing the marks of having been slain (Rev. 5:6). Therefore, the wrath is visited upon those who have rejected His sacrifice and His love. They have, by their deep-seated sin of unbelief, cut themselves off from the salvation and blessing Jesus died to give them.[18]

As the Lamb He is also the Lion of the tribe of Judah who has triumphed—the victory is already His (Rev. 5:5). But His victory was really won at the Cross, so John sees not a lion but a Lamb. He does His work and wins His victories, not by human might or power, not by worldly methods, but through the seven horns and the seven eyes which represent the power and wisdom of the sevenfold Holy Spirit

---

[18]Stephen Travis, *The Jesus Hope* (Downers Grove, Ill.: Inter-Varsity Press, 1974), 61, 62.

prophesied in Isaiah 11:2.[19] Satan and the forces gathered by the Antichrist will be no match for Him. Because of His sacrifice as God's Lamb, He will work powerfully in all the earth. Then, "he will reign for ever and ever" (Rev. 11:15).[20]

INTERPRETATIONS OF THE BOOK OF REVELATION

THE IDEALIST VIEW

From the time of Origen (ca. 185–ca. 254) and other Alexandrians until the present, some have taken a "spiritualist" or "idealist" view of the Book of Revelation. They understand it as a general picture of the conflict between good and evil that is always going on and, therefore, do not see any specific identifications in history. Rather, they look for general principles of God's activity in history and for the assurance of final victory.

THE HISTORICIST VIEW

During the Middle Ages a historicist view became popular. That is, its proponents took the events of the Book of Revelation to be scattered throughout church history, connecting them with such events as the rise of the papacy and the Moslem invasions of Europe. With the fall of Constantinople to the Turks in 1453, Turkey was considered an antichrist. Then the Turkish advance into Europe continued. In 1520 they captured Belgrade and in 1529 advanced against Vienna, causing many to describe Turkey as the sixth trumpet of the Book of Revelation.

---

[19]See Rev. 1:4–5, which refers to the Trinity, thus identifying the sevenfold Spirit as the Holy Spirit himself. Note also the omniscience of Jesus seen in seven mentions of the word "know" (Gk. *oida*) in Rev. 2:2,9,13,19; 3:1,8,15.

[20]J. Daryl Charles, "An Apocalyptic Tribute to the Lamb (Rev. 5:1–14)," *Journal of the Evangelical Theological Society* 34:4 (December 1991): 462, 468.

The Turks were driven back. The events of the seventh trumpet did not follow. Consequently, a new generation of historicists had to reevaluate their interpretations. Historicists are concerned always to make the sequence end in their own day. In effect, each generation feels it necessary to go over history and redefine what they think the visions in the Book of Revelation signify. Some historicists believe that the seals, the trumpets, and the bowls ("vials," KJV)[21] of judgment are parallel to each other and each covers the time from the first to the second comings of Christ.

During the seventeenth century, Protestants, such as Joseph Mede and William Hicks, took a historicist view. Some, like Nathaniel Stephens (1656), recognized rightly that the Old Testament prophets saw the first and second comings of Christ as joined together. The prophets, in their perspective, were like people traveling toward two distant mountains whose tops seem near together. But when they arrive at the first one, they find there is a great valley between the two peaks and the second one is still many miles away. However, as historicists, they "viewed the prophecies of Daniel and Revelation as a panorama of successively unfolding events spanning twenty centuries or more of the church's history."[22]

THE PRETERIST VIEW

In contrast to them, Hugo Grotius and the Jesuit theologian Alcazar took a preterist[23] view of the Book

---

[21]Gk. *phialē* is the root of our words "vial" and "phial" through the Lat. *phiala*. In modern English "vial" has come to mean a small closable vessel for liquids. The Greek definitely means a large bowl.

[22]Bryan W. Ball, *A Great Expectation: Eschatological Thought in English Protestantism to 1660*, vol. 12 in *Studies in the History of Christian Thought*, ed. Heiko A. Oberman (Leiden, Netherlands: E. J. Brill, 1975), 63, 72.

[23]From Lat. *praeteritus,* "gone by," "passed by," indicating the action was all in the past.

of Revelation. That is, they supposed that most of the visions refer to events in the first century, and they tied them to Roman persecutions under Nero (A.D. 64) and Domitian. This view contends that the prophecies in the book have already been fulfilled and really do not concern us. Some, such as William Gild and Thomas Hall, argued that the Millennium was already past and that nothing awaited the Church but the coming of Christ, immediately followed by a general judgment of both the righteous and the wicked.[24] The preterist view is still popular in many denominations today.

THE FUTURIST VIEW

Since Revelation calls itself a prophecy (1:3),[25] many in the Early Church were futurists: They believed the judgments of Revelation 5 through 19 will take place during a short period of time at the end of the Church Age, that is, during the Tribulation. This view had little appeal to Bible believers in the time when the King James Version was being translated.[26] In fact, Thomas Brightman (1615) claimed that a Jesuit priest, Ribera, invented futurism, and a little later James Durham said the idea that the Antichrist would reign just three and one-half years was promoted by Roman Catholics to avoid the Reformation idea that the pope of Rome was the true Antichrist.[27] In more

---

[24]Ball, *Great Expectation,* 162–63.

[25]John calls the book "The revelation (Gk. *apokalupsis*) of Jesus Christ" (1:1). As a result, some classify the book with the very speculative and imaginative apocalyptic Jewish literature (most patterned after the visions of the Book of Daniel) that flourished from about 200 B.C. until after the time of Christ. Though the Book of Revelation does use language and imagery that is similar to Daniel and Ezekiel, it is not a mere imitation or repetition. It uses Old Testament language to bring new prophetic revelations and to give a new picture of Jesus as the Lamb of God and as the triumphant Lord.

[26]Ball, *Great Expectation,* 72–73.

[27]Ibid., 74–75.

recent times, however, the futurist view has become dominant among premillennialists.

JOHN'S VISIONS

John's visions of the seals, trumpets, and bowls (Rev. 6 through 9; 11; 15; 16) are the chief events described in the central part of the Book of Revelation. Some take them to be parallel descriptions of the same events from different viewpoints. However, the seventh seal introduces and initiates the seven trumpets. The trumpets introduce partial judgments. Then the bowls pour out more complete judgments. Therefore, it is more likely that the bowl judgments follow the trumpet judgments and take place in a short period of time near the end of the Tribulation.

THE SEALS

Revelation 6 reveals Jesus as the Lamb at the throne in heaven breaking the seals on the scroll of God's judgments one by one. The breaking of the first four seals introduces the four horsemen, personifying conquest, war, famine, and death. The fifth seal is clearly anticipatory, looking forward to further judgment on a world that has so often martyred Christ's witnesses. Since it is not likely that the four horsemen represent a sequence (conquest for a while, then war, then famine, then death), it seems probable that all the judgments pictured in connection with the seals are also anticipatory. That is, when each seal is broken, John in heaven sees a vision of what will happen in the future, but nothing actually happens at the time. The sixth seal, then, is a vision presenting an overview of the whole period of divine judgment that will bring an end to this age and bring in the millennial kingdom.

The interlude between the sixth and seventh seals is also anticipatory in the sense that it pictures events that precede the judgments of the Tribulation. No harm is allowed to come to the land or the sea until the 144,000 of God's servants (Gk. *doulous,* "slaves") "from all the tribes of Israel" receive the seal of the living God (Rev. 7:1-8). By this seal they are identified as His, under His care and protection. As His "slaves" they are ready to carry out His will. It seems probable that the sealing on their foreheads will also be accompanied by the New Testament sealing: the baptism in the Holy Spirit with the initial outward evidence of speaking in other tongues. Even in the Old Testament, when God gave an outward sign He also gave the inward reality.[28]

The tribe of Dan, however, is left out of this number, possibly because it never claimed the inheritance given it under Joshua and it was the first to turn to idolatry (Judg. 18:1,27-30).[29] Ephraim is also recognized as the true heir of Joseph and is called the tribe of Joseph. Levi is included in the list, for it is no longer the priestly tribe since the Messiah has come and, by His death and the shedding of His blood, put the new covenant into effect.

The 144,000 seem to remain on earth for a time, since the direct judgments of God fall only on "those people who [do] not have the seal of God on their foreheads" (Rev. 9:4). Some Bible scholars speculate that the 144,000 will be commissioned and anointed by the Holy Spirit to preach the gospel during the early part of the Tribulation. They do not seem to be present, however, when the sixth trumpet sounds (Rev. 9:20) or when the two witnesses are active on earth (Rev. 11:10). It may be that they are martyred, or perhaps taken into heaven.

Then in another vision, John sees a great multitude in long white robes standing before the throne in heaven. In contrast to the 144,000, their number is too great to count. Instead of being from the tribes of

---

[28]Stanley M. Horton, *The Ultimate Victory* (Springfield, Mo.: Gospel Publishing House, 1991), 111.

[29]The tribe of Dan, however, does have a place in the land during the millennial kingdom (see Ezek. 48:1).

Israel, they are from every nation, tribe, people, and language.[30] This hardly means that Israel is excluded in their number, however, for Israel is a people and John's designation of the multitude is certainly inclusive.

With regard to the vision, one of the elders tells John that these clothed in white are the ones coming out of the Great Tribulation. Some take the present participle "coming" (Gk. *erchomenoi,* see Rev. 7:14, Williams) to mean that part of the great multitude were already coming out of great tribulation in John's own day. Others take the participle as continuous, referring to all those saved during the entire Church Age. Similarly, they understand the phrase "great tribulation" to be a Hebraistic way of saying the "long tribulation," since the Hebrew word for "great" can also mean "long," "tall," or "numerous." Further, they appeal to Jesus' statement that in the world (i.e., in this age) we shall have "tribulation" (Gk. *thlipsis*), a word that includes "pressure," "trouble," "affliction," "hardship," "suffering," and "persecution" (see John 16:33; cf. Acts 14:22; Rom. 12:12; 2 Cor. 1:4; 7:4; 2 Thess. 1:4; Rev. 1:9; 2:9). Therefore, the "great multitude" would be the whole number of the redeemed who have finished their time of testing on earth and stand before God. Others take the participle to mean that the great multitude is coming out just at this time before the breaking of the seventh seal. Thus, they are coming out of the final Great Tribulation and are martyrs added to the number revealed in the vision of the fifth seal. Whoever they are, they "have washed their robes and made them white in the blood of the Lamb" (7:14) and therefore are born-again believers who will serve God forever.

---

[30]Some have tried to identify the 144,000 with the "great multitude," but, as Dale Moody points out, "the descriptions of each defies the identity." See Dale Moody, *The Hope of Glory* (Grand Rapids: William B. Eerdmans Publishing Co., 1964), 168.

THE TRUMPETS

With the breaking of the seventh seal the scroll can be unrolled and its contents put into action. There is silence in heaven as attention is turned from the throne to what is about to happen on earth. Seven angels with seven trumpets then announce and pour out plagues as partial judgments on the earth: hail and fire are mingled with blood; a mountain is thrown into the sea; a star, blazing like a torch, falls on the rivers and springs; a third part of the sun, moon, and stars is darkened; the abyss is opened; locusts torment like a scorpion; four angels are loosed and a third of humankind are killed. But in spite of all this judgment, no one left alive repents.

THE BOWLS

Before the more complete judgments of the bowls, seven thunders have a message, which John was not allowed to record. Then there is an interlude describing two witnesses. The seventh trumpet brings praise in heaven. Further interludes give visions of the woman (Israel) clothed with the sun who gives birth to a male child (Rev. 12), the beast rising out of the sea (the Antichrist), and another beast out of the earth (the false prophet), with his deceptive miracles and the demand that all take the mark of the beast (Rev. 13). In contrast, three visions (Rev. 14) give a positive note: the Lamb appears on Mount Zion, the eternal gospel is proclaimed by an angel, and the fall of Babylon is announced.

Finally, the seven last plagues bring the judgments of the Tribulation to a climax as victors in heaven sing the song of Moses and the Lamb. These bowl judgments are more severe and more complete: foul, angry sores come on those who have taken the mark of the beast; the sea becomes like coagulating and decaying blood; fresh water becomes blood; the sun's heat increases; the kingdom of the Antichrist is plunged into total darkness; the River Euphrates dries up; an earthquake changes the topography of the earth; and great hailstones devastate the people. Again, no one repents; instead, they blaspheme God. They know the judgments are coming from God, but their hearts remain hard as they obstinately refuse to repent.[31] They are ready for the Antichrist and his false prophet to recruit them to defy Christ at the Battle of Armageddon.

THE ANTICHRIST

The apostle Paul had to deal with false teachers who were saying that the Day of the Lord had "already come" (2 Thess. 2:2). The Thessalonians were unsettled and alarmed because these teachers apparently denied the literal return of the Lord and "our being gathered to him" in the Rapture (v. 1). Obviously, they were no longer encouraging one another as Paul had commanded them (1 Thess. 4:18; 5:11). So Paul declared, "That day will not come, until the rebellion occurs and the man of lawlessness[32] is revealed, the man doomed to destruction" (2 Thess. 2:3). That is, the rebellion and the revelation of the Antichrist would be the first things to take place on the Day of the Lord. This would not happen until "the secret power of lawlessness" is no longer held back (2 Thess. 2:6-7). Since these things had not taken place, the Thessalonians were not in the Day of the Lord, and they could still encourage each other with the sure hope of being caught up to meet the Lord in the air.

---

[31]J. Dwight Pentecost, *Will Man Survive?* (Chicago: Moody Press, 1971), 75.

[32]Many early manuscripts, as well as church fathers such as Tertullian, have "the man [Gk. *anthrōpos,* "a human being"] of sin," but this does not essentially change the meaning. The Antichrist will put himself above the law and make his will supreme as an absolute dictator. He fits the description of the one who "will do as he pleases" (Dan. 11:36-45).

THE REBELLION

Paul had already explained this while at Thessalonica, but we do not have his explanation. The "rebellion" (Gk. *apostasia*) may mean a spiritual rebellion but more commonly refers to a military rebellion, possibly a world war or a fulfillment of Ezekiel 38 and 39. Some suppose it could mean "departure" and interpret it to be the Rapture.[33] However, *apostasia* never means simple departure elsewhere in the New Testament, in the Septuagint, or in the secular Greek of New Testament times.[34] Those who take it to be a fulfillment of Ezekiel 38 and 39 see a battle that will bring such devastation that the world will look for someone to take control and the Antichrist will take advantage of the situation to establish his power.

Ezekiel prophesies an invasion of Israel by enemy hordes that will not only be defeated, but whose corpses will be scattered over the land. The invasion will come from the far north (Ezek. 38:6,15; 39:2), led by "Gog, chief prince of Meshech and Tubal" (38:3). "Chief prince" could also mean "prince of Rosh," though this is not the normal meaning of the Hebrew. Some identify Rosh with Russia, though this cannot be proved.[35] The identification of Meshech and Tubal with Moscow and Tobolsk is clearly without foundation. Ancient cuneiform texts discovered by archaeologists locate Meshech and Tubal in central and eastern Anatolia, now the part of Turkey in northern Asia Minor that was "far north" to the Jews

---

[33]See note 39.

[34]See Gundry, *Church and Tribulation,* 115.

[35]Gvil Gesenivs, *Lexicon Manvale Hebraicvm et Chaldaicvm* (Lipsiae, Germany: Vogeli, 1833), 916–17, suggested that "Rosh" meant *Russorum* (Russia), but there is no connection between the Hebrew and Russian words. See also Dwight J. Wilson, *Armageddon Now! The Premillennarian Response to Russia and Israel Since 1917* (Grand Rapids: Baker Book House, 1977), 152; Arthur E. Bloomfield, *A Survey of Bible Prophecy* (Minneapolis: Bethany Fellowship, 1971), 85.

of Ezekiel's day.[36] The important thing is that the armies led by Gog come from all directions—from the east (Persia, modern Iran), from the south (Cush, modern Sudan and Ethiopia), from the west (Put, modern Libya), and from the north (Gomer and Togarmah)—but they are totally defeated.

Another possible interpretation is that after the Antichrist is defeated at Armageddon, Gog gathers others who were not included in the Antichrist's armies and makes a final attack on Israel during a transition period before the establishing of the millennial kingdom. Or it may be that Ezekiel 38 and 39 have more than one fulfillment in the end times.[37]

THE SECRET POWER OF LAWLESSNESS

The "secret power of lawlessness" (2 Thess. 2:7) certainly refers to "behind-the-scenes activity of evil powers throughout the course of human history."[38] The Antichrist is held back by something ("what" in 2 Thess. 2:6 is neuter), while the secret power of lawlessness is held back by someone ("the one" in verse 7 is masculine).

An interpretation promoted by Tertullian (ca. 160–230), and common in both ancient and modern times, is that verse 6 refers to the Roman Empire and verse 7 to the emperor. Though Paul did take advantage of his Roman citizenship and took a positive attitude toward government (Rom. 13:1-7; 1 Tim. 2:1-2), he would hardly have thought of the Roman Empire, with all its idolatry and immorality, as a force for the

---

[36]Edwin Yamauchi, "Meshech, Tubal, and Company: A Review Article," *Journal of the Evangelical Theological Society* 19:3 (Summer 1976): 243-44.

[37]Ralph H. Alexander, "A Fresh Look at Ezekiel 38 and 39," *Journal of the Evangelical Theological Society* 17:3 (Summer 1974): 160-69. Alexander also proposes that on the basis of multiple fulfillment Gog is the Antichrist in Rev. 19 and Satan in Rev. 20.

[38]Donald C. Stamps, ed., *The Full Life Study Bible* (Grand Rapids: Zondervan Publishing House, 1992), 1895-98.

true God, a force restraining evil. Nor would the Roman emperor, who claimed to be a god, be holding back the appearance of the Antichrist.[39]

Oscar Cullmann favors the idea of Theodore of Mopsuestia (ca. 350–428) that verse 6 refers to the preaching of the apostles, which must be done before Christ returns, and verse 7 to the apostle Paul himself.[40] Nothing in the context of 2 Thessalonians 2 favors this, however. Nor is it likely that Paul would think of himself as holding back the secret power of lawlessness until he would be taken out of the way by his death. How would his death leave the way open for the Antichrist to take over? The same difficulty applies to those, like Luther, who consider the pope or the papal system as the restraining one or the restraining power.

The phrase "that he [the Antichrist] may be revealed in his own time" refers to the beginning of the Day of the Lord (2:3), in effect, after the rapture of the true believers. Dale Moody, following a suggestion of Ferdinand Prat, points out that the chief angel Michael is "the commander of the heavenly hosts and protector of the people of God" (Dan. 10:13,21; 12:1; Rev. 12:7–9). Thus, he and the angels under him could be the ones holding back the secret power of lawlessness and the revelation of the Antichrist.[41]

Herman Ridderbos suggests that we should not try to be specific and that perhaps a supernatural power or person or even God himself might be meant.[42]

---

[39]For the absurdity of identifying the Roman Empire as the restrainer of evil, see Oscar Cullmann, *Christ and Time*, rev. ed., trans. Floyd V. Filson (Philadelphia: Westminster Press, 1964), 164–66.

[40]Ibid.

[41]Moody, *Hope of Glory*, 180.

[42]Herman Ridderbos, *Paul: An Outline of His Theology*, trans. John R. De Witt (Grand Rapids: William B. Eerdmans Publishing Co., 1975), 525; William Neil, *The Epistle of Paul to the Thessalonians*, The Moffatt New Testament Commentary (London: Hodder & Stoughton, 1950), 170.

However, it is hard to understand how they could be "taken out of the way," since both God and angels are active all during the Tribulation period.

Among premillennialists, another interpretation of this difficult passage is common. Some, even in the Early Church, taught that the One holding back the revelation of the Antichrist is the Holy Spirit.[43] He is a Person with all power and is most certainly able to hold back the forces of Satan. The word "spirit" (Gk. *pneuma*) is neuter, and the Greek normally uses neuter pronouns to refer to neuter nouns, even when referring to the Holy Spirit. John's Gospel is an exception, using the masculine to emphasize that the Holy Spirit is a Person (John 16:7-8,13-14). Paul, however, usually uses the grammatically correct neuter (as in Rom. 8:16). Consequently, many understand that the One who holds back the revelation of the Antichrist is the Holy Spirit.

But it is not the Holy Spirit who is taken out of the way (leaves the scene, or is swept out of the midst). During the Church Age the Holy Spirit is working through believers. Paul calls our bodies temples of the Holy Spirit (1 Cor. 6:19). When believers come together as an assembly, they also are the temple of the Spirit (1 Cor. 3:16). Thus, there is no reason why the masculine word of John 16:7 could not refer to the true believers who will be taken out of the way, caught up in the Rapture. This fits the facts which indicate that the Rapture will take place before the Antichrist is revealed. As believers we look for Jesus Christ, not the Antichrist: Revelation 1:1 makes it clear; the visions John saw were primarily a revelation of Jesus, rather than of the Antichrist.[44]

---

[43]Henry Alford, *The Greek Testament*, 5th ed., vol. 3 (Cambridge, London: Deighton, Bell, & Co., 1871), 57-58.

[44]Stanley M. Horton, *It's Getting Late* (Springfield, Mo.: Gospel Publishing House, 1975), 105-6.

THE NATURE OF THE ANTICHRIST

The name "Antichrist" comes from John's letters, in which he implies that the Antichrist will indeed come. His readers, however, needed to be concerned about the "many antichrists" (who falsely claimed to be "anointed ones"), as well as "the spirit of antichrist" that was already at work (1 John 2:18–19,22; 4:2; 2 John 7). On the other hand, the final Antichrist is doomed to destruction, and his time will be comparatively short.[45] He will also be a distinct person, a real person, a man in whom will be concentrated the climax of lawlessness (that is, the disregard of God's instructions and God's will).

Many antichrists will foreshadow him, but he will concentrate all their rebellions in his person as he becomes the final agent of Satan in this age. He will be "the man of lawlessness." But from the moment he is revealed he is already doomed to destruction. Since the same phrase (Gk. *ho huios tēs apōleias,* "the son of destruction") is used of Judas Iscariot, some have suggested that Judas will be raised and come back as the Antichrist. However, Judas "left to go where he belongs" (Acts 1:25), the place of his own choice. There he awaits the final judgment (Heb. 9:27). Furthermore, only God can raise the dead, and the phrase simply means that the Antichrist is headed for destruction just as Judas was.[46]

Since he "will oppose and will exalt himself over everything that is called God or is worshiped," that is, be against the true God and Christ, we can take the "anti" to mean "against." However, the Greek *anti*

---

[45]Cf. Matt. 24:22 where in God's plan those days have been cut short (but not shorter than the three and one-half years of the second half of the Tribulation).

[46]Walter Bauer, *A Greek-English Lexicon of the New Testament,* trans. William F. Arndt and F. Wilbur Gingrich (Chicago: University of Chicago Press, 1957), 103.

most often means "instead of" or "in place of,"[47] and the Antichrist will set himself up "in God's temple, proclaiming himself to be God" (2 Thess. 2:4).[48] In other words, he will most likely not call himself Antichrist. He will be the ultimate of all the counterfeit christs but may or may not claim to be Christ, though he will eventually claim to be God.[49] Possibly he may claim that Moses, Confucius, Buddha, Jesus, Mohammed, and others were all forerunners and that he is the true "one to come."

His coming will appear to be supernatural, for it "will be in accordance with the work of Satan displayed in all kinds of counterfeit miracles, signs and wonders, and in every sort of evil that deceives those who are perishing" (2 Thess. 2:9–10).[50] This description fits the little horn with "a mouth that spoke boastfully" (Dan. 7:8,20) and the world ruler who makes the covenant with Israel and later breaks it (Dan. 9:27), as well as the beast, the blasphemous world ruler who is energized and indwelt by Satan

---

[47]Cf. Matt. 20:28 where Jesus came "to give his life as a ransom for [*anti*] many," which indicates substitutionary Atonement.

[48]This indicates a rebuilt temple in Jerusalem (cf. Dan. 9:26; Matt. 24:15; 2 Thess. 2:4) that will be destroyed when religious Babylon is destroyed (Rev. 17:16–18). See Horton, *Ultimate Victory*, 194; Payne, "Goal of Daniel's Seventy Weeks," 106.

[49]Cf. Matt. 24:4,23–24. Some suggest that the Antichrist claims to be God in such an absolute sense that he could not also claim to be the Messiah. Geerhardus Vos, *The Pauline Eschatology* (Grand Rapids: William B. Eerdmans Publishing Co., 1972), 113; Ridderbos, *Paul*, 519. However, a man inspired by Satan surely could do both.

[50]Posttribulationists usually say that those who have been taught a pre-Tribulation Rapture will be so disillusioned when they have to face the Antichrist that they will fall away and be deceived by him. See J. Rodman Williams, *Renewal Theology*, vol. 3 (Grand Rapids: Zondervan Publishing House, 1992), 381. However, it is only those who refuse "to love the truth and *so be saved*" that the Antichrist will deceive (2 Thess. 2:10). No saved person will be deceived by the Antichrist.

and whose false prophet does counterfeit miracles (Rev. 13:1–17).[51]

THE MARK OF THE BEAST

By the middle of the Tribulation the Antichrist requires everyone to receive a mark on the right hand or forehead, a mark "which is the name of the beast or the number of his name." This number is identified as 666, a number that has caused all kinds of speculation.[52] Most interpret this number to mean that by using letters of the alphabet as numerals (Arabic numbers were not invented until later), and then adding them up, the total would be 666. For example, by spelling "Nero Caesar" in Hebrew letters (as Neron Kaisar, a transliteration) the total is 666, and many ancients believed Nero would come back to life. Because the Greek *Benedictos* adds up to 666, Pope Benedict XI was once singled out as the Antichrist.[53] A former student of mine from Italy told me that the letters that represent Roman numerals in the inscription around the inside of St. Peter's Cathedral in Rome total 666, which he applied to the pope. In 1962 a Jewish believer in Jerusalem told me to watch out for Richard Nixon, for his name in Hebrew letters (Rikard Nigson) added up to 666.[54] The list goes on. However, the idea of adding up Hebrew letters is not reasonable, for the Book of Revelation was written in Greek and makes reference to letters in the Greek al-

---

[51]Horton, *Ultimate Victory,* 183–94. This does not mean that the Antichrist is Satan incarnate or Satan taking the form of a man. He is a real man who opens himself up to being possessed by Satan.

[52]For example, Pope Innocent III (1198–1216) said that the Saracens were the Antichrist and Mohammed his false prophet and that Muslim power was to last 666 years. Because this time was about up, he called for a new Crusade against Islam.

[53]T. Francis Glasson, *His Appearing and His Kingdom: The Christian Hope in the Light of Its History* (London: Epworth Press, 1953), 41.

[54]Nixon died in 1994.

phabet. Jesus is called by the first and last letters of the Greek alphabet. He is the Alpha and the Omega, not the Aleph and the Tau of the Hebrew. Since 666 "is a man's [a human being's] number" (Rev. 13:18), it is somehow identified with the fact that the Antichrist claims to be God but is really just a man.[55] But by the demand that all take the mark on the right hand or forehead he will gain economic control and become the dictator of the whole world. Even so, he will not be able to prevent the fall of the Babylonian world system and total economic collapse (Rev. 18:1–24).[56]

ARMAGEDDON

At the end of the Tribulation he will lead the armies of many nations, armies gathered by Satan, at Armageddon. It is then that Jesus will "overthrow [him] with the breath of his mouth and destroy [him] by the splendor of his coming" (2 Thess. 2:8). This is pictured powerfully in Daniel 2:34–35,44–45; Zechariah 14; and Revelation 19:11–21. Daniel sees the stone both destroying the great image and becoming a mountain that fills the whole earth.

Zechariah sees the Lord in control, bringing the nations together, while they are thinking that they are dealing with "the Jewish question" (Zech. 14:1–2).[57] "On that day his feet will stand on the Mount of Olives, east of Jerusalem, and the Mount of Olives will be split in two from east to west, forming a great valley. . . . Then the Lord my God will come, and all

---

[55]Horton, *Ultimate Victory*, 196–97.

[56]Because the sixth plague announces preparation for the Battle of Armageddon, some identify the fall of the "modern world-Babylon" with the Battle of Armageddon. See Hans K. LaRondelle, "The Biblical Concept of Armageddon," *Journal of the Evangelical Theological Society* 28:1 (March 1985): 23–24.

[57]Walter C. Kaiser, Jr., *Toward an Old Testament Theology* (Grand Rapids: Academie Books, 1978), 256.

the holy ones [saints] with him" (Zech. 14:4–5).[58] In Zechariah 12 through 14 "on that day" is found fifteen times; "Jerusalem," twenty-two times; and "nations," thirteen times. It will be a glorious appearing when Jesus returns "to complete what He had promised to do."[59]

Though the world does not recognize Him, Jesus is now reigning in heaven. His return in glory will reveal His lordship. The world will then know that He is the true Christ, the King of kings and Lord of lords. The Antichrist will then be seen as the impostor that he is. His final destiny is "the fiery lake of burning sulfur" (Rev. 19:20).

STUDY QUESTIONS

1. What are the reasons severe judgments will be necessary before the future Kingdom can be established?

2. What are the evidences that the present godless world system will not improve before Christ returns?

3. How do the later visions of Daniel 7 through 12 confirm the message of Nebuchadnezzar's dream in chapter 2?

4. On what grounds may we take the Tribulation at the end of this age to be a period of seven years?

5. What is the significance of "the abomination that causes desolation"?

---

[58]Some have stated that there is a major geological fault line running through the Mount of Olives. Cf. H. A. Ironside, *The Lamp of Prophecy* (Grand Rapids: Zondervan Publishing House, 1940), 99. However, when I searched the geologic maps of the region at the Institute of Oriental Studies, I found no such fault.

[59]Kaiser, *Old Testament Theology,* 256.

6. What is meant by picturing Jesus as a Lion and as a Lamb?

7. What are the chief arguments for and against each of the views of the Book of Revelation (idealist, historicist, preterist, and futurist)?

8. What are the advantages of taking the futurist view?

9. On the basis of the futurist view of the Book of Revelation, how should we interpret the seals, trumpets, and bowls described in the book?

10. What does the Bible teach about the Antichrist?

11. What is the significance of the mark of the beast, and does modern technology give us any ideas about how it might be applied?

12. What will happen at the Battle of Armageddon?

Chapter 3
The
Tribulation

Chapter Four

The Time of the Rapture

Those with an allegorical, idealist, preterist, or historicist view of the Book of Revelation do not put its events into a special time of great tribulation at the end of the age. They interpret "tribulation" to mean the believers' struggles down through church history. If they look for a Rapture at all, they see it coming in connection with Christ's return in flaming fire to judge the world. Some do recognize that there will be an unusual resurgence of evil at the end of this age. Futurists, however, recognize something more: the "Tribulation," a definite, limited time period when the judgments of Revelation 6 through 19 take place.

Such a time of trouble is prophesied for Israel in Daniel 12:1: "At that time Michael, the great prince who protects your people [Israel], will arise. There will be a time of distress such as has not happened from the beginning of nations until then." Jeremiah said, "How awful that day will be! None will be like it. It will be a time of trouble for Jacob, but he will be saved out of it" (30:7). Isaiah saw that it would also involve "the [satanic, demonic] powers in the heavens above and the kings on the earth below" (24:21). Zechariah 14:1-3 also indicates that it will involve "all the [Gentile] nations."

Those who recognize that the Bible reveals the Tribulation are divided into pre-, mid-, and posttribulationists. There are also some who propose multiple Raptures taking place at various times during the Tribulation.

121

Pretribulationists emphasize the New Testament concept of the imminence of Christ's return, that it could be soon, though the actual time is in the Father's hands (Acts 1:7). They teach that the Rapture will take place before the Tribulation begins, that the departure of believers to be forever with the Lord will signal the beginning of the Tribulation. They recognize that Jesus comes "for" His saints at the Rapture, then returns in judgment "with" His saints at the end of the Tribulation (Rev. 19:14). This truth was largely neglected during the course of church history because of the rise of amillennialism and postmillennialism.[1] It was first given expression in modern times by Edward Irving in 1828,[2] though it was not as clearly identified as it was later by J. N. Darby and the Plymouth Brethren.[3] Even so, this did not involve a totally new concept, but rather a return to the imminence that was taught in the Early Church and to a literal interpretation of Bible prophecy.

Midtribulationists have a variety of opinions concerning the exact time of the Rapture, but agree that the believing Church will be on earth through at least the first part of the Tribulation.

POSTTRIBULATIONISTS

Posttribulationists believe that the Church will be present on earth during the entire period.[4] They take

[1]See chap. 5, pp. 168-74.

[2]This was before the first outbreak of tongues and prophecies in late 1831 in his church. See Robert H. Gundry, *The Church and the Tribulation* (Grand Rapids: Zondervan Publishing House, 1973), 185-87. Thus, Irving's teaching came from Scripture, not from a message in tongues and interpretation or from a prophecy by Margaret MacDonald, as some have claimed. Later, however, tongues and interpretation may well have confirmed Scripture.

[3]John F. Walvoord, *The Blessed Hope and the Tribulation: A Historical and Biblical Study of Posttribulationism* (Grand Rapids: Zondervan Publishing House, 1976), 42-48.

[4]George Eldon Ladd, *The Blessed Hope* (Grand Rapids: William B. Eerdmans Publishing Co., 1956).

the Greek words *parousia* ("presence," "coming"), *epiphaneia* ("appearing"), and *apokalupsis* ("revelation") to be technical words that apply only to the second coming of Christ after the Tribulation. However, an examination of the context of the various passages that use these words does not uphold their view. Posttribulationists deny that the return of the Lord will be in two stages and argue that their view has been the dominant one through most of church history. But they are including the preterists, who say the events of the Tribulation took place in the first century, so that the Tribulation is already over; the historicists, who say we have been in the Tribulation all through church history; and the idealists, or allegorists, who spiritualize the Tribulation, identifying it with the struggles of this age. None of them teach a special tribulation period at the end of the age.

Some refer to Matthew 24:25, "'See, I have told you ahead of time,'" and Mark 13:23, "'I have told you everything ahead of time,'" and claim that since Jesus did not mention the Rapture as a distinct event in these chapters, pretribulationists must be wrong. But arguments from silence are always very weak. These passages must mean either that Jesus told the disciples everything they needed to know in answer to their question (Matt. 24:3; Mark 13:4) or that He told them everything but not everything is recorded (see John 21:25). Certainly Paul in 1 and 2 Thessalonians gives details that he received from Jesus (Gal. 1:11,12; 1 Thess. 4:2) but that Matthew and Mark did not record.

Some draw attention to Hebrews 9:28: "He will appear a second time, not to bear sin, but to bring salvation to those who are waiting for him." They say this does not allow one to split the Second Coming into two stages.[5] Actually, it definitely calls for two stages when compared with 2 Thessalonians 1:7–10.

---

[5]William R. Kimball, *The Rapture: A Question of Timing* (Joplin, Mo.: College Press Publishing Company, 1985), 113.

Hebrews 9:28 is talking to those who are waiting for Christ to come and bring them the promised salvation. Second Thessalonians 1:7-10 pictures His coming in flaming fire to bring judgment on unbelievers and His glorification in His holy people—who must therefore have already been before the judgment seat of Christ.

Posttribulationists also claim that the writings of the early church fathers do not indicate two stages of Christ's return.[6] However, those fathers were primarily concerned with refining the doctrines of Christology and the Trinity. Many said nothing about the rapture of the Church, and those who did usually wrote about their expectation of the imminent coming of the Lord in a general way, without refining their views.[7] Then, because of the influence of the Alexandrian school and later that of Augustine, the tendency was to spiritualize prophecy and give little attention to the details of the Bible's prophetic program.

Most posttribulationists interpret the wrath we are to escape (1 Thess. 5:9) to be the final state of the wicked, the lake of fire. The context, however, is that of the Rapture. They expect that all living believers will go through the Great Tribulation. Some suppose that many of these believers will become martyrs; others suppose that God will protect them in some special way, perhaps as He protected the Israelites from the plagues of Egypt.[8] They argue that the New Testament does not promise that believers will escape tribulation and suffering.[9] The point they miss is that the Bible uses the word "tribulation" (Gk.

---

[6]Ladd, *Blessed Hope,* 31.

[7]Walvoord, *Blessed Hope,* 16-17, 24.

[8]J. Rodman Williams, *Renewal Theology,* vol. 3 (Grand Rapids: Zondervan Publishing House, 1992), 378.

[9]Some take a historicist view that identifies the Tribulation with the problems of this age. J. Barton Payne, *The Imminent Appearing of Christ* (Grand Rapids: William B. Eerdmans Publishing Co., 1962).

thlipsis) to talk about two different things. Sometimes the Greek word refers to the distress, persecution, trouble, pressure, and anguish of heart that outward circumstances may bring upon a Christian as he or she serves the Lord in a Christ-rejecting world. For example, the same word is translated "troubles" when Paul talks about "our light and momentary *troubles . . .* achieving for us an eternal glory that far outweighs them all" (2 Cor. 4:17). But the judgments of the Great Tribulation are not in the same class— they are God's wrath (Rev. 6:16-17; 15:1,7; 16:1).

MIDTRIBULATIONISTS

Midtribulationists usually conceive of the first part of the Tribulation as being peaceful, while the Antichrist is establishing his rule. Most of them believe the Rapture will take place at the sounding of the seventh trumpet of the Book of Revelation (Rev. 11:15), which they identify with the last trumpet of 1 Corinthians 15:52, which seems to be the same as the trumpet of 1 Thessalonians 4:16.[10] However, in 1 Thessalonians 4:16 only one trumpet is mentioned, not a sequence. The same is true of the last trumpet of 1 Corinthians 15:52. Paul uses the word "last" here to indicate the close of the Church Age. He goes on to say, "*The* trumpet will sound." He does not indicate that it is the last in a series. It sounds before the wrath of God falls on the earth. It summons the believers and is called the trumpet of God. At the same time, calling it "last," meaning the final one for this age, does not rule out the sequence of seven angelic trumpets coming later during the Tribulation.

Others take the two witnesses as representative of the Church and suppose that when these witnesses

---

[10]James Oliver Buswell, Jr., *A Systematic Theology of the Christian Religion,* vol. 2 (Grand Rapids: Zondervan Publishing House, 1963), 398, 431, 444, 450, 456, 458-59.

go "up to heaven in a cloud" (Rev. 11:12), this will be the time of the rapture of the Church.[11]

Midtribulationists sometimes speak of a "prewrath Rapture" and take the last three and one-half years of the Antichrist's rule as the period of wrath.[12] Some place the wrath only at the very end of the Tribulation.[13] However, the vision of the sixth seal would indicate the wrath extends throughout the entire Tribulation (Rev. 6:12–17).[14]

THE PARTIAL-RAPTURE THEORY

Some midtribulationists teach a partial Rapture, that part of the Church goes through the Tribulation. They take the exhortations to watch and be alert to mean that mature believers will watch, while immature believers will fail to watch and thus miss the Rapture and have to go through the Tribulation. The Parable of the Ten Virgins shows, however, that those who are not ready to go in when the Bridegroom comes lose out altogether (Matt. 25:12). That is, the contrast is not between mature and immature believers, but between those who have the oil—the Holy Spirit's preparation of the believer for the Lord's coming and the inward reality of God's grace—and those who have only the appearance of waiting for Christ's coming but have no genuine relationship with Him.

Many who teach a partial Rapture are also very legalistic and look at the Rapture as something they

---

[11]Ibid., 456. Posttribulationists consider this "fanciful" and argue that the two witnesses will minister during the second three and one-half years of the Tribulation, because only after the Antichrist breaks his covenant with Israel will the Gentiles "trample on the holy city for 42 months" (Rev. 11:2). See Gundry, *Church and Tribulation,* 200–201.

[12]Martin J. Rosenthal, *The Prewrath Rapture of the Church* (Orlando, Fla.: Zions Hope, 1989).

[13]Gundry, *Church and Tribulation,* 89.

[14]Stanley M. Horton, *The Ultimate Victory* (Springfield, Mo.: Gospel Publishing House, 1991), 104–7.

must deserve, rather than seeing it as part of the blessing of being heirs of God and joint heirs with Christ, something that is ours by grace through faith.[15] Robert Gundry rightly points out that "viewing the tribulation period as a time of purgation for living believers who failed to qualify for the Rapture" calls for some sort of purgatory for believers "who died in a state of Christian immaturity."[16]

THE TEACHING OF MULTIPLE RAPTURES

Other midtribulationists teach multiple Raptures.[17] Many of these teachings divide the Church into various groups, such as the Bride, the Friends of the Bridegroom, the Servants, the Guests. They argue that for the Marriage Supper of the Lamb to be complete, all these categories must be present; usually they treat the Bride as a special company that only those holy enough will attain. However, just as Jesus is the Lamb and is also the Shepherd, His parables treat the Church as the Bride, the Guests, the Servants, and the Friends. Jesus does not treat these categories as separate divisions. Each is actually an aspect of the true Church. When the New Testament talks about the bride of Christ, the entirety of the true Church is in view. All who do God's will are His servants (Gk. *douloi,* "slaves"). The apostles and others humbly referred to themselves as servants or slaves of the Lord (Rom. 1:1; Col. 4:12; Titus 1:1; James 1:1; 2 Pet. 1:1; Jude 1; Rev. 1:1). Jesus refers to His own disciples as the friends or "guests of the bridegroom" (Matt. 9:15;

---

[15]A gentleman from Illinois wrote me that he was sure he was not good enough to go up in the Rapture, but he was sure he would be able to stand against the Antichrist during the Tribulation. This sounds like salvation by works. See Stanley A. Ellisen, *Biography of a Great Planet* (Wheaton, Ill.: Tyndale House Publishers, 1975), 117.

[16]Gundry, *Church and Tribulation,* 201.

[17]Glen Menzies and Gordon L. Anderson, "D. W. Kerr and Eschatological Diversity in the Assemblies of God," *Paraclete* 27:1 (Winter 1993): 8–16.

Mark 2:19; Luke 5:34). In the Parable of the Wedding Banquet, the guests previously invited are the Jews. The people from the streets and alleys are those despised by the Jewish leaders. Those brought in from the roads and country lanes are the Gentiles (Luke 14:15-24; cf. Matt. 22:2-10).

Paul makes it clear that all the dead in Christ and all the believers who remain are caught up "together" in one Body in the Rapture (1 Thess. 4:16-17).[18] "We will not all sleep, but we will *all* be changed—in a flash, in the twinkling of an eye, at the last trumpet. For the trumpet will sound, the dead will be raised imperishable, and we will be changed" (1 Cor. 15:51-52). The only requirement for the dead to go up in the Rapture is to be "in Christ." The same applies to those who are still alive when He comes. Then, since Jesus descends not to the earth but to the air, and the meeting is in the air, it is probable that with Jesus they will return to heaven for the judgment seat of Christ and the Marriage Supper of the Lamb.[19]

PRETRIBULATIONISTS

Pretribulationists recognize that the apostle Paul still had the Rapture in mind when he said, "God did not appoint us to suffer wrath but to receive salvation through our Lord Jesus Christ" (1 Thess. 5:9).[20] Christ's sacrificial death guarantees that whether we die before the Rapture or are still alive at that time, we will "live together with him" (1 Thess. 5:10), for

---

[18]See John F. Walvoord, *The Rapture Question* (Findlay, Ohio: Dunham Publishing Co., 1957), 105-25, for a discussion of this.

[19]James Everett Frame, *A Critical and Exegetical Commentary on the Epistles of St. Paul to the Thessalonians,* International Critical Commentary (Edinburgh, Scotland: T. & T. Clark, 1912), 176.

[20]Paul D. Feinberg, "The Case for the Pretribulation Rapture Position," in *The Rapture: Pre-, Mid-, or Post-Tribulational?* Richard Reiter, Paul D. Feinberg, Gleason L. Archer, and Douglas J. Moo (Grand Rapids: Academie Books, 1984), 50-72.

He will "rescue us from the coming wrath" (1 Thess. 1:10). The same verb *(rhuomai)* is used of the rescue of Lot *before* God's judgment fell on Sodom (2 Peter 2:7). Some see this contradicted in Matthew 24:30–31 ("At that time the sign of the Son of Man will appear in the sky"); however, "at that time" (Gk. *tote*) is very general. Jesus, in speaking of His coming, covers a period of time that includes both His coming for His elect, or chosen (that is, for true believers from all nations as well as from Israel),[21] and a coming that the whole world will see. But Jesus does not deal with this period in chronological fashion. Like the Old Testament prophets, He moves back and forth, teaching about one aspect of His coming and then another, not always in order, and without indicating the time interval between. But the time interval is there.[22]

Though 2 Thessalonians 1 speaks of the revelation of Jesus in flaming fire, Paul's purpose is not chronological, and that revelation should not be confused with the appearance of Christ to catch away the believers in the Rapture (1 Thess. 4:17). In the case of the Rapture, the attention is on the believers and on what will happen to them as they rise for a meeting with the Lord in the air and then go on to be with Him. In Christ's return in glorious triumph, the attention is on what will happen to the unbelievers as Christ pours out the fire of His judgment on them. At that time the believers are already with the Lord.

In 2 Thessalonians 2:1–2 Paul returns to the subject of Christ's coming to gather the believers. These verses might be paraphrased:

---

[21]"Many nations will be joined with the LORD in that day and will become my people" (Zech. 2:11). See George Raymond Beasley-Murray, *Jesus and the Last Days: The Interpretation of the Olivet Discourse* (Peabody, Mass.: Hendrickson Publishers, 1993), 434.

[22]Stanley M. Horton, *Welcome Back, Jesus* (Springfield, Mo.: Gospel Publishing House, 1967), 33.

**Chapter 4
The Time of
the Rapture**

Now in contrast to what we have been talking about [in chapter 1], we request of you brothers (and sisters), for the sake of advocating the true view of the coming [Gk. *parousia*] of our Lord Jesus Christ, even our being gathered with Him, that you be not so easily (so quickly, so hastily) unsettled, shaken from your mental balance, and confused so that you are alarmed and in a continual state of agitation because of some prophecy, report, or letter supposed to have come from us, saying that the day of the Lord has already come.

In 1 Thessalonians Paul gave positive assurance that all believers will be caught up in the Rapture to meet the Lord in the air. In spite of his warning against giving attention to times and dates (1 Thess. 5:1), some began to make excited speculations. They passed over the exhortations to keep awake and maintain sober balance and self-control (1 Thess. 5:6). In this state they were only too willing to follow every wind of teaching that came along (see Eph. 4:14).

Instead of acting like intelligent people with sound judgment, they were departing from their senses like ships blown from their moorings. The result was they were disturbed, frightened, continually agitated, and filled with feverish anxieties. Jesus used the same expression when He told His disciples not to be alarmed when they heard of wars and rumors of wars (Mark 13:7).

The cause of all this confusion was false teaching promoted by people who claimed the authority of both the Holy Spirit and the apostle Paul. They even produced letters that they claimed came from Paul. (Letters were dictated to scribes or secretaries rather than personally written, so it was easy to circulate a forgery.) But at the end of 2 Thessalonians (3:17) Paul called attention to the closing salutation in his own handwriting. He wanted the believers to pay close attention to it so they would not be taken in by any more frauds.

THE DAY OF THE LORD

The false teaching that so upset the Thessalonians' thinking was that the Day of the Lord (the period of time in which judgment would fall) had already come. In other words, these false teachers were saying that since the Day of the Lord had already begun, there was no prospect of a literal Rapture to encourage them. Paul denied their claim as emphatically as possible (2 Thess. 2:3). Their teaching was a deception, no matter what means they used to promote it. (These may have included false tongues and interpretation or false prophecy.) The Greek of verse 3 clearly indicates that the first thing on the Day of the Lord will be "the rebellion,"[23] followed by "the man of lawlessness" (the Antichrist) being revealed. These events do not precede the Day of the Lord, but are part of the judgment that God allows to come on the earth on the Day of the Lord.[24] In effect, Paul emphasized that we can expect the Rapture before the Day of the Lord and before the appearance of the Antichrist, and we can still encourage one another (1 Thess. 4:18; 5:11; 2 Thess. 2:17).

[23]Some interpret the Greek *apostasia* as "departure" rather than "apostasy" or "rebellion." They use this interpretation as a further indication that the Rapture precedes the revelation of the Antichrist. See Ellisen, *Biography of a Great Planet,* 121–23. However, "rebellion" or "abandonment" is the common meaning. Though Tyndale, Coverdale, Cranmer, and the Geneva Bible did translate the word as "a departynge," departure from God was probably what they meant. Most take the rebellion to be religious apostasy, though it may possibly refer to the events of Ezek. 38 and 39. See Stanley M. Horton, *It's Getting Late* (Springfield, Mo.: Gospel Publishing House, 1975), 100; William Neil, *The Epistle of Paul to the Thessalonians,* The Moffatt New Testament Commentary (London: Hodder & Stoughton, 1950), 160. Neil sees it as "a definite event," conceivably "an earthly parallel to the revolt in heaven (Rev. 12:7ff.)," and also mentions the assault of Ezek. 38 and 39.

[24]Robert L. Thomas, "A Hermeneutical Ambiguity of Eschatology: The Analogy of Faith," *Journal of the Evangelical Theological Society* 23:1 (March 1980): 52.

The fact that "the man of lawlessness" will set "himself up in God's temple, proclaiming himself to be God" (2 Thess. 2:4), also indicates that the temple will be rebuilt at least by the first part of the Tribulation. Consequently, for post- and midtribulationists, there can be no thought of the imminence of Christ's coming as long as the temple is not rebuilt.[25]

OUR FUTURE HOPE

The pretribulational view fits in best with the future hope the Bible presents.[26] Believers, who are told repeatedly to be watchful and to wait for God's Son from heaven (1 Thess. 1:10), are never told "to watch for the Great Tribulation or the appearance of the Antichrist. To expect that such things must happen before the Rapture destroys the teaching of imminence with which the New Testament is replete."[27] In that some passages dealing with the Rapture speak of Christ's coming to snatch up believers to be with Him (1 Thess. 4:17), and other such passages speak of believers being with Him at His coming (Col. 3:4; Jude 14), it is scriptural to recognize two phases of Christ's coming. The fact that we are not appointed to wrath indicates that the Great Tribulation occurs between these two phases of His coming.[28]

Luke 21:34-36 is also important: "'Be careful, or your hearts will be weighed down with dissipation, drunkenness and the anxieties of life, and that day

---

[25]J. Dwight Pentecost, *Will Man Survive?* (Chicago: Moody Press, 1971), 41.

[26]See pp. 121-22, 128-30.

[27]Assemblies of God, *Where We Stand* (Springfield, Mo.: Gospel Publishing House, 1990), 129.

[28]Some accuse pretribulationists of being "escapists." However, pretribulationism is a practical doctrine and its emphasis on imminence keeps the thought of the Lord's return before us, encouraging witnessing and missions as well as godly living. Cf. James Montgomery Boice, *Foundations of the Christian Faith* (Downers Grove, Ill.: InterVarsity Press, 1986), 707-8.

will close on you unexpectedly like a trap. For it will come upon all those who live on the face of the whole earth. Be always on the watch, and pray that you may be able to escape all that is about to happen, and that you may be able to stand before the Son of Man.'"

That Jesus spoke of these things coming on "the whole earth" shows that He is looking beyond the time of Jerusalem's destruction in A.D. 70 to the end of the age. That He speaks of escaping "all" that is about to happen (on the whole earth) shows that those on the earth will suffer all these things and also shows that the believers who are ready will not go through any part of the Tribulation. Since He speaks of standing before the Son of Man, He must be referring to the Rapture.[29] It is noteworthy also that the Church is not mentioned in Revelation 4 through 18, nor is anything mentioned that could specifically refer to the Church or its relationships.

Nevertheless, let us not allow differences of opinion with respect to the time of the Rapture separate believers. All around us we can see increasing deception, terrible apostasy, false prophets, satanic cults, New Age teachings. To avoid the spiritual shipwreck of those who depart from the faith, our attention must always be on Jesus, the Christ who "was sacrificed once to take away the sins of many people" and who "will appear a second time, not to bear sin, but to bring salvation to those who are waiting for him" (Heb. 9:28). A "crown of righteousness" is not limited to those who have right ideas about the Rapture, but is promised "to all who have longed for his appearing" (2 Tim. 4:8). The commendation that we all want to hear is "Well done, good and faithful servant!" So let us all be about the Lord's business and, at the same time, keep that longing for, that expecta-

---

[29]Guy Duty, *Escape from the Coming Tribulation: How to Be Prepared for the Last Great Crisis of History* (Minneapolis: Bethany Fellowship, 1975), 13–19.

tion of, Christ's coming, which might take place at any moment.

THE LAST DAYS

The Bible is full of hope for the future. The fulfillment of prophecies with Christ's first coming indeed gives assurance of His second coming. The fact that the Holy Spirit is present now gives us further assurance that we are in "the last days" (Acts 2:17). It also guarantees that "the last days" will not go on indefinitely, for in this age we have only "the firstfruits of the Spirit" (Rom. 8:23), and the baptism in the Holy Spirit gives us only a deposit (Gk. *arrabōn,* "first installment") of our future inheritance, which will surely be ours when Jesus comes.[30] This was prominent in the thinking of first-century believers and should always be a part of the believer's vision today.

It should be noted also that on the Day of Pentecost Peter did not use the word "fulfilled" when speaking of Joel's prophecy. Rather, he indicated that Pentecost was only the beginning of an outpouring that would continue to be available to all who would ask (Luke 11:13). "'The promise is for you and your children and for all who are far off—for all whom the Lord our God will call'" (Acts 2:39; cf. Acts 8:14-17; 9:17; 10:44-47; 11:15-17; 19:1-7; Gal. 3:14).[31]

LOOKING FOR CHRIST'S COMING

THE EARLY CHRISTIANS

Though the Lord did not return immediately, there was "no loss of faith in the second coming."[32] Many believe part of the purpose of Luke's Gospel was to

---

[30]David Ewert, *And Then Comes the End* (Scottdale, Pa.: Herald Press, 1980), 17.

[31]Hobart E. Freeman, *An Introduction to the Old Testament Prophets* (Chicago: Moody Press, 1969), 155-56.

[32]Francis J. Hall, *Eschatology* (New York: Longmans, Green & Co., 1922), 12.

address the delay of Christ's return. On the other hand, a sense of the imminence of our Lord's return can be seen in all Christian literature "up to the middle of the second century." Then arguments over the nature and person of Christ began to dominate the attention of the Church.[33] After that, the truth that the world in all its history is headed for consummation, which will again reveal God's judgment and mercy, receded into the background of most Christian thinking, especially in the Western church.[34] For many the only "coming" of Christ they thought of was His coming at their death.[35]

The New Testament, however, inspires a sense of joy as it encourages us to live in the light of our blessed hope of Christ's return, though it does not give all the details curiosity seekers would like. Rather than keeping their attention on Jesus, too many today want to treat God's Word as if it were a fortune-telling book. They scan its pages trying to determine what will happen next. Every new political or religious leader who comes along becomes a subject of speculation.[36] Worst among these speculations are those who set dates for our Lord's return. Satan at-

---

[33]R. P. C. Hanson, *The Attractiveness of God: Essays in Christian Doctrine* (Richmond, Va.: John Knox Press, 1973), 191. Hanson also points out here that the words "Second Coming" are not in the New Testament because Jesus' second coming is really the consummation of His first coming.

[34]J. E. Fison, *The Christian Hope: The Presence and the Parousia* (London: Longmans, Green & Co., 1954), 22.

[35]Alois Winklhofer, *The Coming of His Kingdom: A Theology of the Last Things*, trans. A. V. Littledale (Freiburg, West Germany: Herder; Montreal: Palm Publishers, 1963), 11.

[36]I learned a lesson about this when I walked into the Biola College book room the day after Italy's premier, Benito Mussolini, died in 1945. There I saw a big stack of books marked down to "5 cents each." The title was *Is Mussolini the Antichrist?* The author implied he could be. In 1990 another book proclaimed Saddam Hussein of Iraq as the Antichrist who would soon take over the world.

tempts to use the failures of these date setters to turn people away from the sure hope the Bible gives.

DATE SETTING

Date setters for the return of Christ have arisen from time to time throughout the history of the Church. Lactantius set the date at A.D. 200. Hippolytus said it would be about 500. The Epistle of Barnabas (15.4) suggested that a thousand years equals a day, and drawing a parallel with the six days of creation, the writer supposed that after six thousand years the millennial Sabbath rest would begin. This theory was repeated again and again in later writings.[37] Such date setters misinterpreted Psalm 90:4, "A thousand years in your sight are like a day that has just gone by," and 2 Peter 3:8, "With the Lord a day is like a thousand years, and a thousand years are like a day." These passages simply let us know that God is not limited by time the way we are.[38] They were never intended to give us grounds for dating the Second Coming.

As the year 1000 approached, there was a bit of excitement because some of the early church fathers

---

[37]G. W. H. Lampe, "Early Patristic Eschatology," in *Eschatology,* William Manson, G. W. H. Lampe, T. F. Torrance, W. A. Whitehouse (Edinburgh, Scotland: Oliver & Boyd, 1953), 31.

[38]Our view of time is conditioned by the movement of the earth and its relation to other parts of the universe. As Fison points out, "Our clock or calendar time . . . is the abstraction needing correction from God's point of view." Fison, *Christian Hope,* 104.

suggested that the date of creation was about 5000 B.C.[39] But the excitement affected only a very few. The Roman Catholic Church paid little attention, for, following Augustine, it rejected the idea of a millennial kingdom, spiritualized it, identified the church with the eternal Kingdom, and put the return of Christ in the far distant future. It looked on its apparent success in dominating Europe as proof it was "building the city of God here on earth, and took upon itself presumptuously the authority of that city."[40]

The Reformation, by its "rediscovery of the living God of the Bible, who actively intervenes" in human affairs, powerfully brought new attention to the hope of Christ's second coming.[41] Martin Luther did not set a date, but thought that he was living in the last days and that "Christ stood poised to return, to deliver His own, and to deal the final blow to a corrupt world."[42] Some of his followers, however, did project dates for the end of the world, between 1588 and 1673.[43] John Calvin was more balanced, recognizing that the hope of the Lord's coming helps us to stand firm for Christ and to follow Him, knowing that He

---

[39]Augustine and Eusebius actually put it about 5202 B.C. It should be noted, however, that the year 1000 did not become "a major focus of expectancy." There was no panic. Major plans for the time beyond that year were common in the years preceding it. See T. Francis Glasson, *His Appearing and His Kingdom: The Christian Hope in the Light of Its History* (London: Epworth Press, 1953), 45–47; Robin Bruce Barnes, *Prophecy and Gnosis: Apocalypticism in the Wake of the Lutheran Reformation* (Stanford, Calif.: Stanford University Press, 1988), 21.

[40]Hanson, *Attractiveness of God,* 194.

[41]F. F. Torrance, "The Eschatology of the Reformation," in *Eschatology,* Manson et al., 38.

[42]Robin Bruce Barnes, *Prophecy and Gnosis,* 3.

[43]Ibid., 60, 93, 110, 116, 131–132, 134, 165, 168, 189.

will come and restore everything according to God's design.[44]

King James I in 1588 published an exposition of the Book of Revelation in which he said that of all the Scripture, "the buik of the reuelatioun is maist meit for this our last age."[45] Puritans in England made computations that put Christ's return between 1640 and 1660.[46] John Napier used his new invention of logarithms to arrive at a date between 1688 and 1700.[47] The successor of Sir Isaac Newton, William Whiston, said the Millennium would begin in 1715. After 1715 he fixed on 1734, and then on 1866. William Miller (1742–1849) predicted Christ would return in 1843; then in 1844 he changed the date to October 22 of that year.[48] Jehovah's Witnesses have announced various dates, including 1874, 1914, 1915, and 1975.[49] In 1988 a book containing eighty-eight reasons why Christ could return during the Jewish feast of *Rosh Hashshanah*[50] of that year received unusual attention. It contained a number of mistakes and misinterpretations that were probably not apparent to the casual reader. Of course, it proved to be no different from other such books that preceded it and have followed it.

None of the date setters pay enough attention to Mark 13:33, "Be on guard! Be alert! You *do not*

---

[44]Bryan W. Ball, *A Great Expectation: Eschatological Thought in English Protestantism to 1660,* vol. 12 in *Studies in the History of Christian Thought,* ed. Heiko A. Oberman (Leiden, Netherlands: E. J. Brill, 1975), 16.

[45]Quoted in Ball, *Great Expectation,* 23.

[46]Ibid., 1–4, 19–23.

[47]Stephen Travis, *The Jesus Hope* (Downers Grove, Ill.: InterVarsity Press, 1974), 86.

[48]Glasson, *His Appearing,* 49–50.

[49]Travis, *The Jesus Hope,* 86.

[50]That is, the Feast of Trumpets (Lev. 23:23–25; Num. 29:1–6; the beginning of the secular or fiscal year, later celebrated as New Year's Day). Misspelled as "Rosh-Hash-Ana" in Edgar C. Whisenant, *88 Reasons Why the Rapture Could Be in 1988* (Nashville: World Bible Society, 1988).

know when that *time* will come." Nor do they deal adequately with the answer Jesus gave His disciples just before His ascension when they asked, "'Lord, are you at this time going to restore the kingdom to Israel?'" His reply was "'It is not for you to know the times or dates the Father has set by his own authority.'" This was a nice way of telling them that the times and dates were none of their business.[51] Then He went on to tell them what He wanted them to make their business: "'You will receive power when the Holy Spirit comes on you; and you will be my witnesses in Jerusalem, and in all Judea and Samaria, and to the ends of the earth'" (Acts 1:6-8). This rules out all date setting, including suggestions about the time and even the season of the year when Christ might return.[52] The attention of believers is to be on Jesus (Heb. 12:2-3) and on faithfully fulfilling the Great Commission (Matt. 24:14,45-46; 25:21,23).

On the other hand, we must not let date setters dull our sensitivity to the possible nearness of our

---

[51]We can expect more speculation about dates, some from people who may be sincere but who misinterpret Scripture, some from deceivers who use people's fears and curiosity to get them to send money. It should be noted also that "generation" (Gk. *genea;* Matt. 24:34) can also mean "race" and may refer to the Jewish people not passing away or being destroyed utterly. Even if it is taken to mean "generation," it could refer to a length of thirty, forty, or one hundred years, or even an indefinite time, since "all these things" are probably meant to include the destruction of Jerusalem as well as the consummation and the *parousia.* See Henry Barclay Swete, *Commentary on Mark* (London: Macmillan & Co., 1913; repr. Grand Rapids: Kregel Publications, 1977), 315; R. C. H. Lenski, *The Interpretation of St. Matthew's Gospel* (Minneapolis: Augsburg Publishing House, 1943), 952-53, which points out that in Matt. 24:14 we are referred to "the end," and that like the Hebrew *dor,* translated *genea* in the LXX, the word can refer to a *kind* of people "that reproduces and succeeds itself in many physical generations."

[52]See William M. Alnor, *Soothsayers of the Second Advent* (Old Tappan, N.J.: Power Books, Fleming H. Revell Co., 1989), 194-95, where he refers to David Lewis's "Manifesto on Date Setting." Lewis takes Mark 13:33 as a key verse against all forms of date setting.

Lord's coming. After speaking of the creation's wait-ing "in eager expectation for the sons of God to be revealed," for "the creation itself will be liberated from its bondage to decay and brought into the glori-ous freedom of the children of God," the Bible goes on to say, "We know that the whole creation has been groaning as in the pains of childbirth right up to the present time. Not only so, but we ourselves, who have the firstfruits of the Spirit, groan inwardly as we wait eagerly for our adoption as sons, the redemption of our bodies. For in this hope we were saved. But hope that is seen is no hope at all. Who hopes for what he already has? But if we hope for what we do not yet have, we wait for it patiently" (Rom 8:19–25). The waiting "eagerly" and the waiting "patiently," al-though paradoxical, show it is good for us to be in the tension between working and watching, alert to the times yet not setting dates, in keeping with Jesus' instruction.

THE SOON COMING OF JESUS

In the early centuries of the Church the word "soon" (Gk. *tachu,* "quickly," KJV) did not cause a problem as it does for some today.[53] The word nor-mally means "quickly," "with speed," "without delay," "in a short time." However, it is probable that Jesus was referring to the manner of His coming, though it is also clear He wanted believers to live with a sense

---

[53]C. H. Dodd, in *The Interpretation of the Fourth Gospel* (Cambridge, England: Cambridge University Press, 1953), sug-gested that John no longer expected the *parousia* ("presence") of Christ in a Second Coming but wanted the Church to be con-tent with the "presence" of the Holy Spirit. However, the Gos-pel of John does not really teach this. John 14:3 and 21:22 speak of a personal return. The presence of the Holy Spirit is actually a pledge that Jesus will indeed come again. See Fison, *The Christian Hope,* ix–x; Alf Corell, *Consummatum est: Escha-tology and the Church in the Gospel of St. John,* trans. Order of the Holy Paraclete, Whitby (London: Society for the Promo-tion of Christian Knowledge, 1958), 89, 101.

of its imminency. When He comes He will come suddenly, "with speed" and "like a thief in the night" (1 Thess. 5:2). To the Early Church this meant they must stay on the alert, for the "owner of the house" may come back "in the evening, or at midnight, or when the rooster crows, or at dawn" (Mark 13:35). As a whole, they recognized they had a mission to accomplish and they understood God's patience, so they applied themselves "wholeheartedly to the task, and experienced no crisis over the Lord's delay."[54] Yet, at the same time, they lived in the light of the Lord's coming, waiting expectantly "for the blessed hope—the glorious appearing of our great God and Savior, Jesus Christ" (Titus 2:13).

THE PRESENT KINGDOM

It is significant, however, that John the Baptist, Jesus, and the disciples Jesus sent out proclaimed, "'The kingdom of heaven [or "of God"] is near'" (Matt. 3:2; 4:17; Mark 1:15; Luke 10:9,11).[55] "Near"

---

[54]Adrio Konig, *The Eclipse of Christ in Eschatology: Toward a Christ-Centered Approach* (Grand Rapids: William B. Eerdmans Publishing Co., 1989), 199. Konig sees 2 Pet. 3 as dealing with a minority who had a faulty version of imminence.

[55]A comparison of Matthew with Mark and Luke shows that the terms "kingdom of heaven" and "kingdom of God" are used interchangeably. See Robert L. Saucy, *The Case for Progressive Dispensationalism: The Interface between Dispensational and Nondispensational Theology* (Grand Rapids: Zondervan Publishing House, 1993), 19. The word "kingdom" (Gk. *basileia*) basically means "royal power," "royal rule," or "royal reign" and often refers to the king's authority rather than to his territory or subjects, though there must be a territory or realm where the king's rule operates. Cf. Herman Ridderbos, *The Coming of the Kingdom*, trans. H. de Jongste (Philadelphia: Presbyterian & Reformed Publishing Co., 1962), 19, 24-28. On the other hand, Matthew does use the "kingdom of heaven" to remind us that the Kingdom comes to us out of the heavenly realm, where realities are invisible and not subject to human dominion. See Carl F. H. Henry, "Reflections on the Kingdom of God," *Journal of the Evangelical Theological Society* 35:1 (March 1992): 43.

(Gk. *ēngiken*) is a Greek perfect tense and means "has come near and is still near."[56] The same word (*ēngiken*) is used of a time (the hour of betrayal) being near (Matt. 26:45) and of a person (Judas) being near (Matt. 26:46). James 5:8 uses it of the Lord's coming, and 1 Peter 4:7 uses it of "the end of all things" having come near.

When the Pharisees accused Jesus of driving out demons by Beelzebub, the prince of demons, Jesus declared, "'If I drive out demons by the Spirit of God, then the kingdom of God has come upon you'" (Matt. 12:28), meaning it was already present. God's royal power and authority was being manifested through Jesus and the Spirit. Jesus further explained that this was a manifestation of the "finger of God" (Luke 11:20), another way of speaking of the royal power and authority of God. Christ's first coming is clearly portrayed as a time of fulfillment. Jesus said, "'Blessed are the eyes that see what you see. For I tell you that many prophets and kings wanted to see what you see but did not see it, and to hear what you hear but did not hear it'" (Luke 10:23-24). They were "already tasting of the powers of the world to come," and so are all Christians through life in Christ and through the power of the Holy Spirit.[57]

It was with this in mind that Jesus told the Pharisees, "'The kingdom of God does not come with your careful observation, nor will people say, "Here it is," or, "There it is," because the kingdom of God is within [among] you'" (Luke 17:20-21). The Pharisees' "observation" included the calculation of dates and searching for signs.[58] Jesus rejected their speculation. Then, since He was speaking to Pharisees, the phrase

---

[56]Cf. Ridderbos, *Coming of the Kingdom*, 3-4.

[57]William Manson, "Eschatology in the New Testament," in *Eschatology,* Manson et al., 6.

[58]George Raymond Beasley-Murray, *Jesus and the Future: An Examination of the Criticism of the Eschatological Discourse, Mark 13 with Special Reference to the Little Apocalypse Theory* (London: Macmillan & Co., 1954), 175.

"within you" is probably better translated "among you." They needed to recognize who was in their midst.

THE KINGDOM TO COME

JEWISH EXPECTATIONS

Yet, though it was clear that the Kingdom, in the sense of God's power and rule, had broken into the world through the person and ministry of Jesus, it is also clear that this was different from first-century Jewish expectations and was just a preview of what was to come. After Jesus fed the five thousand, some of the Jews wanted to take Him by force and make Him their king (John 6:14–15). The vivid apocalyptic[59] prophecies of the contemporary pseudepigraphal book *The Assumption of Moses* were probably a factor in this. So were the political expectations of *The Psalms of Solomon* (ca. 48 B.C.).[60] Undoubtedly, the people thought that since Jesus could by a miracle feed a great crowd, He would have no trouble overcoming the Roman armies. But Jesus avoided this by withdrawing to a mountain by himself. As He told Pilate later, "'My kingdom is not of this world'" (John 18:36). It was not "of this world" with respect to its origin or its methodology. When it comes in its fullness it will be by a supernatural act.

On the Mount of Transfiguration, Peter, James, and John had a preview of the glory of Jesus that will be fully revealed and shared with His saints at His sec-

---

[59]"Apocalyptic" refers to visions that reveal a cataclysmic end to the present world and a blessed future in a new heaven and a new earth. See Richard E. Sturm, "Defining the Word 'Apocalyptic': A Problem in Biblical Criticism," in *Apocalyptic and the New Testament,* ed. Joel Marcus and Marion L. Soards, Journal for the Study of the New Testament Supplement Series 24 (Sheffield, England: Sheffield Academic Press, 1989), 21.

[60]J. H. Leckie, *The World to Come and Final Destiny,* 2d ed., rev. (Edinburgh, Scotland: T. & T. Clark, 1922), 42.

ond coming.[61] But the voice from heaven focused their attention on Jesus, and Jesus spoke of His coming sufferings, for the cross had to come before the crown (Matt. 17:1-8,12,22-23). The disciples, too, would have to suffer before they could reign with Him, and He gave them guidance about how to meet their tests and trials through the help of the Holy Spirit (Matt. 10:19-20). But they were not to forget the focus on the future reign with Christ. So Jesus taught them (and us) to pray, "'Your kingdom come'" (Matt. 6:10). He saw the Kingdom involving a future aspect—a kingdom and a reign on earth—which He would come back to accomplish.[62]

A VIVID EXPECTATION

Early Gentile Christians, like the Thessalonians, had "turned to God from idols to serve the living and true God, and to wait for his Son from heaven, whom he raised from the dead—Jesus, who rescues us from the coming wrath" (1 Thess. 1:9-10). "Wait" (Gk. *anamenein*) implies expectation. The gospel was already being spread in all directions. Thus, in view of Jesus' promise recorded in Matthew 24:14, some focused their attention on the time, and when some believers

---

[61]Bernard Ramm, "A Philosophy of Christian Eschatology," in *Last Things,* ed. H. Leo Eddleman (Grand Rapids: Zondervan Publishing House, 1969), 35.

[62]Clayton Sullivan points out that C. H. Dodd, in his "realized eschatology," which denied the reality of the Kingdom's involving a place and a future reign, was inconsistent and that by using the two-document theory of the Synoptic Gospels "excluded from his discussion a vast amount of synoptic data concerning the Kingdom." So did the "consistent eschatology" of Albert Schweitzer, Martin Dibelius, and Krister Stendahl, which suggested that Jesus thought the Kingdom was to come immediately, but that He was mistaken. Clayton Sullivan, *Rethinking Realized Eschatology* (Macon, Ga.: Mercer University Press, 1988), 3, 13, 16, 17, 24, 35, 61, 80, 117. Both "realized" and "consistent" theologies deny the future "renewal and fulfillment of the whole creation." Carl E. Braaten, *Eschatology and Ethics* (Minneapolis: Augsburg Publishing House, 1974), 11.

died, a fear arose that they would miss all the glory and blessing of Christ's return. Paul made it clear that they would miss nothing, for they would rise first and then "we who are still alive and are left will be caught up together with them in the clouds to meet the Lord in the air" (1 Thess. 4:15-17).

Paul did not tell them to cease waiting, to cease expecting. At that point Paul himself may have expected to be alive when Jesus returned.[63] However, he also looked forward to his resurrection (1 Cor. 6:14; 2 Cor. 4:14; Phil. 3:11), and he said, "I die every day" (1 Cor. 15:31), which means he risked his life every day. He dared to do so because of his assurance of future resurrection. Rather than merely expecting to be alive when Jesus returned, it seems he was focusing attention back on the Lord.[64] He recognized also that the Corinthians did not lack any spiritual gift and that this was related to their eagerly waiting "for our Lord Jesus Christ to be revealed" (1 Cor. 1:7). But this too was the result of God's grace given them in Christ Jesus, which meant in Him they were "enriched in every way" (1:4-5). In effect, their attention was to be on the Lord, not on the time.

Later, when Paul knew he would give his life as a witness (martyr) for Christ, his hope and assurance were not dimmed as he declared, "I have fought the good fight [the only fight worth fighting], I have finished the race, I have kept the faith. Now there is in store for me the crown of righteousness, which the Lord, the righteous Judge, will award to me on that day—and not only to me, but also to all who have longed for his appearing" (2 Tim. 4:7-8). The delay of that appearing did not bother Paul, for his faith and hope were fixed on Jesus, not on time. Yet, he en-

---

[63]Oscar Cullmann's idea that Paul changed his mind is refuted by Herman Ridderbos, *Paul: An Outline of His Theology,* trans. John R. De Witt (Grand Rapids: William B. Eerdmans Publishing Co., 1975), 491-92.

[64]Leon Morris, *New Testament Theology* (Grand Rapids: Academie Books, 1986), 88-89.

couraged a love for Christ that would inspire a continued longing for His return.[65]

THE TENSION BETWEEN "SOON" AND "NOT YET"

Actually, Jesus himself repeatedly warned His disciples that His coming would be delayed.[66] Delay is implied in the parables of the mustard seed (Luke
13:18-19), the seed growing (Mark 4:26-29), the sower (Luke 8:5-15), the weeds (Matt. 13:24-30), the tal-
ents (Matt. 25:14-30, note v. 19, "after a long time"),
and the ten virgins (Matt. 25:1-13, note v. 5, "a long
time"). Delay is also implied when the account of the
persistent widow ends with the question, "'When the
Son of Man comes, will he find faith on the earth?'"
(Luke 18:8).

Just before His triumphal entry into Jerusalem Jesus
gave the Parable of the Ten Minas because "the people thought that the kingdom of God was going to
appear at once [Gk. *parachrēma*, "immediately"]."
The parable (Luke 19:11-27) let them know that
there would be delay, yet at the same time they
would have to be on the alert, ready whenever He
might come. In the parable Jesus compared himself
to a man of noble birth who went to a "distant"
country to have himself appointed king and then to
return. This indicated He would be gone a long time.
Later, the disciples understood that the parable meant
that before Jesus could return as King He must ascend to heaven and be enthroned there (Heb. 12:2;
Rev. 3:21).

---

[65]Emil Brunner, *Eternal Hope,* trans. Harold Knight (Philadelphia: Westminster Press, 1954), 128.

[66]Some critics, such as E. Grasser, have theorized that statements of long delay were created by the later church and in-
serted into the Gospel record. This theory has been effectively
refuted by I. H. Marshall, *Eschatology and the Parables* (London: Theological Students' Fellowship, 1973), 15-21. He points
out also that "the root of criticism is simply the critics' refusal
to accept the possibility of a supernatural Jesus" (21).

Signs. During the last week before His crucifixion (as recorded in Matt. 24), the disciples pointed to the temple buildings in awe. When Jesus told them that not one stone of those buildings would be left on another, the disciples apparently jumped to the conclusion that such a destruction would bring Christ's return and the end of the age. So they asked, "'When will this happen, and what will be the sign of your coming and of the end of the age?'" Jesus, however, did not answer their question right away. He first turned their attention to what they would be facing in this age and warned against deceivers. He implied that we need to be careful about looking for signs, for the many false christs who would arise would undoubtedly use "signs" to deceive many. Some interpreters would try to make "wars and rumors of wars" into signs, but wars, famines, earthquakes, and the persecution of Christians would be just part of the age.

End-time signs should not be used as "an intriguing game of speculation." Rather, they should "produce radical change in the life . . . a deeper commitment to Jesus Christ, and a greater degree of nonconformity to the world system."[67] We need to emphasize this all the more as we see false prophets appearing and deceiving the people and as wickedness increases and the love of most grows cold. Only those who stand firm to the end will be saved (Matt. 24:13). The verb "to stand firm" is singular in the Greek, for Jesus wants each one of us to apply it to himself or herself.

The salvation in view is the full inheritance that Jesus will give to each believer when He comes again. It includes our new bodies and our reigning with Jesus in the Millennium. Keeping this wonderful promise before us will help us never to turn back to the world or to the old life. What Jesus wanted the disciples to see also was that this age would not be

---

[67]Keith M. Bailey, *Christ's Coming and His Kingdom* (Harrisburg, Pa.: Christian Publications, 1981), 27.

an ideal age. The fullness of the Kingdom has not yet come. Even the sufferings of this age are but the "beginning of birth pains," compared to the judgment that will come at the end of the age—judgment that will bring in the Kingdom (as Dan. 2:44-45 indicates).

Jesus also wanted them to see that they could not wait for ideal conditions before getting the gospel out. They must go out into the world with all its wars, rumors of wars, famines, earthquakes, false christs, and false teachers, and preach the gospel. They must live by faith in the midst of all these adverse events. Instead of being distracted by them, they must keep their confidence in God's revealed Word and their hope in Jesus as they carry out His great commission.

The fact, too, that "this gospel of the kingdom will be preached in the whole world as a testimony to all nations" before the end, the consummation, comes also indicates a considerable time (Matt. 24:14).[68] (The gospel of the Kingdom, it should be noted, is the same gospel that Jesus proclaimed, the same one He commissioned His disciples to teach and preach, the same one the apostle Paul preached to both Jews and Gentiles, for there is only one gospel [Acts 20:25; 28:23,31]. As Paul told the Galatians, "If we or an angel from heaven should preach a gospel other than

---

[68]Increasing the number of missionaries, the number of Bibles distributed, and the number of countries reached by the gospel does not mean we are hastening the date assigned by God to the end. When we do these things we are but doing what should be done in every generation. At the same time we must always stand firm, lifting up our heads, because our redemption is drawing near (Matt. 24:13; Luke 21:28). See Ewert, *Then Comes the End,* 35; Oscar Cullmann, *The Early Church,* ed. A. J. B. Higgins, trans. A. J. B. Higgins and S. Goodman (London: SCM Press, 1956), 157.

the one we preached to you, let him be eternally condemned" [Gal. 1:8].[69]

At the Last Supper when Jesus told His disciples, "'I will not drink of this fruit of the vine from now on until that day when I drink it anew with you in my Father's kingdom'" (Matt. 26:29), He indicated we must wait for the Kingdom.[70] "That day" is clearly a future day, the promised Day of the Lord when there will be judgment and restoration. "This fruit" indicates "that day" will be on this earth and the Father's kingdom will also be on this earth, not just in heaven.[71]

This Generation. Jesus never said how long He would be gone.[72] He did say, "'Now learn this lesson from the fig tree: As soon as its twigs get tender and its leaves come out, you know that summer is near. Even so, when you see all these things, you know that it is near, right at the door. I tell you the truth, this generation will certainly not pass away until all these things have happened'" (Matt. 24:32–34; Mark 13:28–30; Luke 21:29–32). Some today take this to mean that Jesus expected to return within a genera-

---

[69]Some have seen the fulfillment of Matt. 24:14 and Mark 13:10 in the angelic proclamation during the Tribulation (Rev. 14:6–7). However, Jesus was addressing His disciples and dealing with the Church Age, during which the grace of God is proclaimed. See Dale Moody, *The Hope of Glory* (Grand Rapids: William B. Eerdmans Publishing Co., 1964), 157.

[70]George Eldon Ladd, *Crucial Questions about the Kingdom of God* (Grand Rapids: William B. Eerdmans Publishing Co., 1952), 69.

[71]Even though many of the old hymns see nothing but the heavenly kingdom. See Geoffrey Wainwright, *Eucharist and Eschatology* (London: Epworth Press, 1971), 56, cf. 58–59.

[72]See Joachim Jeremias, *New Testament Theology,* trans. John Bowden (New York: Charles Scribner's Sons, 1971), 139. Jeremias says, "We have no saying of Jesus that postpones the end into the distant future." However, Jesus limited himself in such a way that He did not know the time, only that there would be delay.

tion, that is, within forty years.[73] But they give insufficient attention to what He immediately added: "'No one knows about that day or hour, not even the angels in heaven, nor the Son, but only the Father'" (Matt. 24:36; Mark 13:32). Consequently, other interpretations have been suggested.

Some take the word "generation" (Gk. *genea*) to mean "race," referring to the Jewish people as a race. The earliest meaning of the word refers to those descended from a common ancestor. Then the word came to mean "race" or "nation." Therefore, the verse's meaning would be that the Jewish people would not be wiped out by the calamities, the wars, famines, earthquakes, etc. This certainly has been true. Where are the other small nations that surrounded ancient Israel, such as the Moabites, Edomites, Ammonites, Hittites, Horites, Hivites, Jebusites, Philistines? They were scattered, intermarried with other peoples, and lost their identity. The Jews were scattered, intermarried, and have suffered many tribulations, but by God's providence have not lost their identity.[74]

The more common use of the word *genea* in the New Testament does refer to Jesus' contemporaries, the generation of people then living.[75] However, the Septuagint regularly translates the Hebrew *dor* in the Old Testament by *genea* where it "reveals a *kind* of men . . . the evil kind that reproduces and succeeds

---

[73]The Bible sometimes looks at a generation as one hundred years, but since the implication here is that His disciples would see this, forty years is more probable.

[74]John Miley, *Systematic Theology,* vol. 2 (New York: Hunt & Eaton, 1893; repr. Peabody, Mass: Hendrickson Publishers, 1989), 443.

[75]See Matt. 11:16; 12:41-42,45; 17:17; 23:36; Luke 7:31; 9:41; 11:29-32,50-51; 17:25; cf. Matt. 1:17; Acts 13:36; Heb. 3:10.

itself in many physical generations. . . . [N]ote Acts 2:40; Phil. 2:15; Heb. 3:10."[76]

Others take it that Jesus meant the final generation before the Tribulation, the generation that would see the intensification of wars, famines, earthquakes, and false teachings. Or, because the fig tree is often a symbol of Israel in the Old Testament, they take the coming out of the leaves of the fig tree to refer to the restoration of the State of Israel in 1948. However, as has already been mentioned, the phrase "this generation," when it refers to time in the rest of the New Testament, refers to the first-century generation that was alive at that time. Furthermore, the idea that the final generation began in 1948 has only led to confusion.

Still others suggest that the phrase "all these things" skips back to the original prediction of Jesus that brought the disciples' question—that not one stone of the temple would be left on another (Matt. 24:2; Mark 13:2). Therefore, "this generation" would refer to the time when the temple was destroyed by the Romans in A.D. 70, not to the second coming of Christ.[77] That prediction was fulfilled exactly. Nevertheless, Jesus also makes it clear that "the really important event is not the temple's ruin but the coming of the Son of man."[78]

A TIME KNOWN ONLY TO THE FATHER

Jesus will indeed return in power and great glory. However, no one but the Father in heaven knows the

---

[76]Lenski, *Interpretation of St. Matthew's Gospel*, 952–53. Lenski thus identifies the generation as the Jews who will continue through this age while a succession of signs takes place. Ridderbos also takes the generation as "the people of this particular disposition and frame of mind who are averse to Jesus and his words. . . . [T]he temporal meaning of *genea* recedes into the background or is ignored." Ridderbos, *Coming of the Kingdom*, 502.

[77]Moody, *Hope of Glory*, 178.

[78]Beasley-Murray, *Jesus and the Last Days*, 388.

time (Matt. 24:36; Mark 13:32-33). Perhaps God with-held this information to minimize the peril attendant on the delay of His return. For many are tempted to follow the example of the wicked servant in Matthew 24:45-51, who "says to himself, 'My master is staying away a long time,' and he then begins to beat his fel-low servants and to eat and drink with drunkards. The master of that servant will come on a day when he does not expect him and at an hour he is not aware of. He will cut him to pieces and assign him a place with the hypocrites, where there will be weep-ing and gnashing of teeth" (vv. 48-51).

It is better that we do not know the time of Christ's coming. God wants us to do His work. We are more likely to be faithful and enthusiastic in do-ing it if we know we must always be alert, ready at any time for His coming (Matt. 24:42; 25:13). This alertness should be "permanent and natural and quite unforced," involving "not only the mind but . . . the whole personality . . . always on the *qui vive,* never bored with doing nothing and never feverish with do-ing everything."[79]

Though Jesus again indicated that it would be a long time (Matt. 25:19), He repeatedly emphasized that His coming would be both sudden and unex-pected. "'So if anyone tells you, "There he is, out in the desert," do not go out; or, "Here he is, in the in-ner rooms," do not believe it. For as lightning that comes from the east is visible even in the west, so will be the coming of the Son of Man'" (Matt. 24:26-27). The following verse, "'Wherever there is a car-cass, there the vultures will gather,'" also refers to the suddenness of His coming and may mean simply "You will see it when it comes."[80] It also indicates judgment will come to the wicked just as vultures quickly come to a corpse.

---

[79]Fison, *Christian Hope,* 174.
[80]Jeremias, *New Testament Theology,* 123.

THE MEANING OF "WATCHING"

Faithful believers, however, will not be taken by surprise. They will be waiting, working, no matter how long the Lord's coming is delayed (Luke 12:35-38). Christians can be taken by surprise only if they let their hearts "be weighed down with dissipation, drunkenness and the anxieties of life." Then "that day will close on" them "unexpectedly like a trap" (Luke 21:34). Jesus warned, "'Be always on the watch, and pray that you may be able to escape all that is about to happen, and that you may be able to stand before the Son of Man'" (Luke 21:36). Paul also drew attention to how much we need these warnings (Rom. 13:11-14; 1 Cor. 6:9-10; 9:27; 10:11-12; 11:32; 16:22; Eph. 5:6-20).

But to be on the watch does not mean to keep looking into the heavens. After Jesus ascended, two angels said to the disciples, "'Why do you stand here looking into the sky? This same Jesus, who has been taken from you into heaven, will come back in the same way you have seen him go into heaven'" (Acts 1:11). This caused them to return to Jerusalem, where "they all joined together constantly in prayer, along with the women and Mary the mother of Jesus, and with his brothers" (1:14). They realized that being on the watch meant waiting for the gift promised by the Father, the baptism in the Holy Spirit (1:4), and being witnesses "to the ends of the earth" (1:8,22).

On the Day of Pentecost, Peter, speaking by the Spirit's gift of prophecy, referred to Joel's "afterward" as "the last days" (Acts 2:17; cf. Joel 2:28). By this he recognized that the whole Church Age is "the last days," for it is the last age before the return of Christ and the millennial age to come. Old Testament prophets saw "the last days" as days of judgment, restoration, and salvation (cf. Isa. 2:2-4,10-21; 4:2-6; 11:10-11; Hosea 2:21-23; Joel 2:23-27; Amos 9:11-15).

The New Testament simply recognizes the Church Age as the age of the Holy Spirit. Thus, Peter called for repentance and said of the gift of the Holy Spirit: "'The promise is for you and your children and for all who are far off—for all whom the Lord our God will call'" (Acts 2:38-39). "You and your children" would include all the Jews who would accept Jesus as their Messiah, Lord, and Savior. "All who are far off" would be the Gentiles (cf. Eph. 2:11-14,17), though Peter did not understand this until he was sent to the house of Cornelius (Acts 10:34-35,43). Reaching those who are "far off" also implies the passage of time and the delay of our Lord's coming.

Then after the healing of the crippled beggar at the Gate Beautiful of the temple, Peter declared that there would be times (plural) of refreshing coming from the Lord, that Jesus would come again, but that "he must remain in heaven until the time comes for God to restore everything, as he promised long ago through his holy prophets" (Acts 3:19-21). Peter's emphasis, however, was not on the time, but on God's purpose of refreshing and of blessing all the peoples of the earth. That blessing was coming first to the people Peter was speaking to, "by turning [them] from [their] wicked ways" (Acts 3:25-26). That this blessing of right living was to come to all peoples of the earth as they turned to Jesus again indicates time and delay. In fact, this delay was necessary so that people might be saved, for there is no other way of salvation except through Jesus Christ (Acts 4:12).

GOD'S VIEW OF TIME

By the time of Peter's second epistle scoffers were saying, "'Where is this "coming" he promised?'" (2 Pet. 3:4). But we have to remember that God does not look at time the way we do, nor is He limited by time. "With the Lord a day is like a thousand years, and a thousand years are like a day" (2 Pet. 3:8). God can do in a day what we might expect to take a thousand years. He can stretch out to a thousand years what we would like to see done in a day. He is also concerned about more people coming to repentance, allowing us to continue to carry forward the Great Commission (2 Pet. 3:9). It is good for us, therefore, to live in the tension between "soon" and "not yet," doing His business, carrying out the tasks He gives us to do, until He comes back (Mark 13:33–34; Luke 19:13).

Paul reinforces the warnings of Jesus by recognizing that the "day of the Lord will come like a thief in the night" (1 Thess. 5:2). Believers, however, will not be taken by surprise—not because they know the time of His coming, but because they are "day persons," living in the light of God's Word and expecting Jesus to return at any time (not "night persons" who belong to the darkness of evil). Consequently, they are alert and self-controlled, protected by faith and love as a breastplate, and the hope of salvation as a helmet (1 Thess. 5:4–9). Like the apostle Paul, they maintain an intense longing for Christ's appearing (2 Tim. 4:8) because they love and trust Him so much. Paul's hope was never "bound to a fixed date but to the gospel that pronounced the fulfillment of the Old Testament promises and called for trusting existence."[81]

A GUARANTEE OF FUTURE BLESSINGS

Paul also recognized that the outpouring of the Spirit was a sign that the new age had already begun, but it is only a foretaste, giving assurance of the

---

[81]Hans Schwarz, "Eschatology," in *Christian Dogmatics,* ed. Carl E. Braaten and Robert W. Jenson, vol. 2 (Philadelphia: Fortress Press, 1984), 498.

promised Kingdom blessings.[82] Thus, he refers to the baptism in the Holy Spirit as God's "seal of ownership on us" and "his Spirit in our hearts as a deposit [a first installment], *guaranteeing what is to come*" (2 Cor. 1:22). After speaking of the time when we will receive our new bodies, he reemphasizes, "God who has made us for this very purpose . . . has given us the Spirit as a deposit, *guaranteeing what is to come*" (2 Cor. 5:5).

Later Paul wrote to the Ephesians, "Having believed, you were marked in him [rather, "by Him," by Jesus the Baptizer] with a seal, the promised Holy Spirit, who is a deposit *guaranteeing our inheritance until the redemption of those who are God's possession*—to the praise of his glory" (Eph. 1:13–14). Then Ephesians 4:30 goes on to say, "Do not grieve the Holy Spirit of God, with whom you were sealed for the day of redemption."

The deposit (Gk. *arrabōn,* "earnest," KJV) is a "first installment," an actual part of the inheritance that guarantees we will receive a larger measure later when we receive our full inheritance[83]—that is, when Jesus returns and we receive our new bodies, changed into His likeness (Rom. 8:23; 1 Cor. 15:51–52). The "seal of ownership" is also related to the thought of 1 John 3:2, "Now we are children of God, and what we will be has not yet been made known. But we know that when he appears, we shall be like him, for we shall see him as he is."

In the midst of the corruption, decay, and death that mark "the present evil age" (Gal. 1:4), we also have dying bodies with many limitations; we share many of the difficulties, problems, and sorrows com-

---

[82]Ralph P. Martin, "The Spirit in 2 Corinthians in Light of the 'Fellowship of the Holy Spirit' in 2 Corinthians 13:14," in *Eschatology and the New Testament,* ed. W. Hulitt Gloer (Peabody, Mass.: Hendrickson Publishers, 1988), 119, cf. 127.

[83]Charles Webb Carter, *The Person and Ministry of the Holy Spirit: A Wesleyan Perspective* (Grand Rapids: Baker Book House, 1974), 302.

mon to humankind (1 Cor. 4:9-13; 2 Cor 4:8-10; 6:1-10). Yet at the same time, in and through the Holy Spirit, we enjoy the actual beginning of our inheritance—the "firstfruits" (Rom. 8:23; cf. 1 Cor. 2:9-10; 2 Cor. 4:7)—including the gifts and blessings of the Spirit.[84] These enable us to demonstrate the power, rule, and life of God even in this present life on earth.[85]

REVIVALS AVAILABLE

Besides this, we can have special "times of refreshing," as Acts 3:19 indicates. Such times give us spiritual victories as the Holy Spirit transforms and conforms our lives "to the model of the future consummation." They also encourage us to live in hope, knowing that complete deliverance, the consummation of our salvation, is coming.[86]

Church history shows too that God has indeed sent times of refreshing whenever there was genuine repentance that included a change of attitude toward God, Christ, and the Bible. Acts 3:19-20 indicates that we can have more of these times of refreshing right down to the time Jesus comes again. Therefore, our attention should be on the positive assurances of God's promises rather than on the negative aspects of the course of this age. It is true that in the last days there will be terrible times, times hard to live in (2 Tim. 3:1). It is also true that "evil men and impostors will go from bad to worse, deceiving and being deceived" (3:13). We see these things happening, and they should increase our longing for the soon return

---

[84]French L. Arrington, *Paul's Aeon Theology in 1 Corinthians* (Washington, D.C.: University Press of America, 1978), 119, 133.

[85]Stanley M. Horton, *What the Bible Says about the Holy Spirit* (Springfield, Mo.: Gospel Publishing House, 1976), 236-37; Travis, *The Jesus Hope,* 96.

[86]Neill Quinn Hamilton, *The Holy Spirit and Eschatology in Paul,* Scottish Journal of Theology Occasional Papers, no. 6 (Edinburgh, Scotland: Oliver & Boyd, 1957), 87, 89.

of our Lord. But let us claim the promised refreshing as we study and proclaim the Scriptures so that we "may be thoroughly equipped for every good work" (3:17), doing those good works even in the midst of the darkness and perils of the last days.[87]

BEING DIFFERENT FROM THE WORLD

It may be also that we need to create a Christian subculture. If we are to escape from the wrath to come (Rom. 5:9; 1 Thess. 5:9), we must avoid those things that bring God's wrath and warn others by example and by loving warnings (cf. Jude 21–23). For, in today's world, the buildup of sins that call for divine judgment surely indicates that the wrath revealed in the Book of Revelation is soon to come.

After talking about loving your neighbor as yourself, Paul went on to say,

Do this, understanding the present time. The hour has come for you to wake up from your slumber, because our salvation is nearer now than when we first believed. The night is nearly over; the day is almost here. So let us put aside the deeds of darkness and put on the armor of light. Let us behave decently, as in the daytime, not in orgies and drunkenness, not in sexual immorality and debauchery, not in dissension and jealousy. Rather, clothe yourselves with the Lord Jesus Christ, and do not think about how to gratify the desires of the sinful nature [or the flesh] (Rom. 13:9,11–14).

Similarly, Paul reminds us of the judgment that came on the Israelites who indulged in pagan revelry, committed sexual immorality, tested the Lord, and

---

[87]Adrio Konig suggests that since "the New Testament names Jesus himself as the Last, the End, and the Omega," that though it is natural and "correct to say that every tick of the clock brings us nearer to the end (i.e., to Christ's return)[,] . . . it is equally true that we now live in the end (i.e., in communion with Jesus, who is the end [the accomplished goal])." *Eclipse of Christ*, 6, 26.

grumbled. "These things happened to them as examples and were written down as warnings for us, on whom the fulfillment of the ages has come" (1 Cor. 10:11). Surely, if these warnings were appropriate for the Corinthians two thousand years ago, they are even more applicable today. His coming is indeed nearer than when we first believed!

STUDY QUESTIONS

1. Why is the doctrine of the imminence of Christ's coming important to consider when dealing with the time of the Rapture?

2. Why are there so many differences of opinion about the time of the Rapture?

3. What are the chief arguments usually presented against the pretribulationist view, and how can they be answered?

4. What other Scripture passages fit with the pretribulationist view?

5. What evidences show we are now in what the Bible calls "the last days"?

6. What are the reasons we should not attempt to set dates for the Rapture?

7. Why is it a good thing that we do not and cannot know the time of the Rapture?

8. How is God's view of time different from ours?

9. How does the picture of the Holy Spirit as a "first installment" and a "seal" relate to our hope of Christ's return?

10. How much do we need revival today, and how will being different from the world contribute to receiving times of refreshing?

Chapter Five

Millennial Views

One of the exciting things in the Book of Revelation is the promise in chapter 20 that Satan will be bound and locked up in the abyss for a thousand years. No longer will he be able to deceive the nations as he did through the Antichrist and his false prophet. This thousand-year period is called the Millennium, from the Latin *mille,* "thousand," and the New Latin *ennium,* from the Latin *annus,* "year." (Just as "biennium" means a period of two years, so "millennium" means a period of a thousand years.)

THREE VIEWS

The views of the Millennium most common among evangelicals are the premillennial, amillennial, and postmillennial views. Premillennialists believe our Lord Jesus Christ will return before the Millennium to reign as Priest-King on the earth for a thousand years of blessing and peace, fulfilling Bible prophecy literally. Amillennialists spiritualize those prophecies and say there is no golden age, or Millennium, on earth—not before Christ's return, not after He returns.[1] They channel "all Old Testament prophecies into the ministry of the crucified and risen and exalted Jesus . . . at a price—that of forfeiting historical facets of the king-

---

[1]Stanley J. Grenz, "The Deeper Significance of the Millennial Debate," *Southwestern Journal of Theology* 36:2 (Spring 1994): 19.

dom."[2] They argue that Satan was bound at the cross, so that his power is restricted and he cannot hinder the spread of the gospel or keep believers from having victory over evil through Christ. They identify the Millennium with the present restraint of evil mentioned by Paul (2 Thess. 2:6-7).[3]

Most amillennialists take "thousand" as a symbolic number indicating the completion of whatever time period there is between the first and second comings of Christ. Some apply this to the believers' spiritual reign with Christ on the earth (that is, in their inner spiritual life) during the Church Age.[4] Others apply it to what believers are enjoying after death in heaven during the present time.[5] Or they limit it to "a reign of martyrs in paradise to indicate victory even while the Church flees to the wilderness."[6] All their arguments are very subjective;[7] none of them gives proper consideration to what Revelation 20:1-4 actually says. Most amillennialists will agree with premillennialists, however, that things will get worse on

---

[2]Carl F. H. Henry, "Reflections on the Kingdom of God," *Journal of the Evangelical Theological Society* 35:1 (March 1992): 40.

[3]Sydney H. T. Page, "Revelation 20 and Pauline Eschatology," *Journal of the Evangelical Theological Society* 23:1 (March 1980): 33-36.

[4]Oswald T. Allis, *Prophecy and the Church* (Philadelphia: Presbyterian & Reformed Publishing Co., 1945), 70; Grenz, "Deeper Significance," 18.

[5]Anthony A. Hoekema, *The Bible and the Future* (Grand Rapids: William B. Eerdmans Publishing Co., 1979), 230-33; Floyd Hamilton, *The Basis of Millennial Faith* (Grand Rapids: William B. Eerdmans Publishing Co., 1942). This view was first popularized by F. Duesterdieck (1859) and Theodor Kliefoth (1874); John F. Walvoord, *The Blessed Hope and the Tribulation: A Historical and Biblical Study of Posttribulationism* (Grand Rapids: Zondervan Publishing House, 1976), 14.

[6]Everett I. Carver, *When Jesus Comes Again* (Phillipsburg, N.J.: Presbyterian & Reformed Publishing Co., 1979), 299.

[7]Robert L. Thomas, "A Hermeneutical Ambiguity of Eschatology: The Analogy of Faith," *Journal of the Evangelical Theological Society* 23:1 (March 1980): 47.

Chapter 5
Millennial
Views

earth before Jesus returns. They differ, however, by saying that the return of Christ will bring a general resurrection and a general judgment of both the righteous and the wicked at the same time.

Postmillennialists also claim Satan was bound at the cross, though some consider the binding as a process that is still going on. They treat the thousand-year period as an extension of the Church Age in a new dimension that will bring a great spread of the gospel so that "Christ will return to a truly Christianized world."[8] They also take the number "thousand" as a symbol for whatever time it takes to Christianize the world. On the basis of the Great Commission (Matt. 28:18–20) and the promise of the Spirit's powerful work (Luke 24:49; John 16:7–11), they claim that the "divinely instituted agencies for the evangelization of the world" carry "divine guaranties of success."

They say, therefore, that not until after the world as a whole is converted and there is a long period of peace, blessing, and righteousness will Christ return for a general resurrection and a general judgment of both the righteous and the wicked.[9] Thus, they also argue that those who do not believe the world will be taken over by the Church before Christ's return do not believe in the power of the gospel.[10]

---

[8]Loraine Boettner, "Postmillennialism," in *The Meaning of the Millennium: Four Views*, ed. Robert G. Clouse (Downers Grove, Ill.: InterVarsity Press, 1977), 118. See also J. Marcellus Kik, *An Eschatology of Victory* (Nutley, N.J.: Presbyterian & Reformed Publishing Co., 1971), 4.

[9]Loraine Boettner, *The Millennium* (Philadelphia: Presbyterian & Reformed Publishing Co., 1957), 14. Some allow for a brief resurgence of apostasy and evil just before Jesus comes again. Ibid., 69.

[10]John Miley claimed that premillennialism automatically discouraged the evangelization of the world and brought detriment to the interests of Christianity. See his *Systematic Theology*, vol. 2 (New York: Hunt & Eaton, 1893; repr. Peabody Mass.: Hendrickson Publishers, 1989), 446–47. The history of modern missions shows the reverse is true.

Augustus Strong modified this view somewhat, stating that Christ would come spiritually at the beginning of the thousand years and would then reign in a spiritual sense with His saints to advance His kingdom. Then, after the thousand years, He would return visibly and literally to bring a final resurrection of both the righteous and the wicked, followed by a general judgment.[11]

Recent modifications have been made by theonomists, "kingdom now," and "dominion" (or "reconstruction") proponents, who say that the Church must subdue education, the arts, the sciences, government, the financial systems, and every other realm of human life, bringing it all under God's dominion so true peace, goodness, justice, and righteousness prevail everywhere before Jesus will return.[12] Like other postmillennialists they have no room for the fulfillment of prophecies to Israel. Some say that "Israel as the Covenant People . . . was to be destroyed, finally and irrevocably," and "the Kingdom . . . established *progressively* throughout history."[13]

There is, however, little evidence of any such prospect of progress in this present world of increasing violence and poverty. Jesus, in the Parable of the Wheat and the Weeds, said, "'Let both grow together until the harvest'" (Matt. 13:30). Then He interpreted this by saying, "'The harvest is the end of the age'" (v. 39). The harvest therefore is a cataclysmic event that does not allow for the gradual conversion of the

---

[11]Augustus Hopkins Strong, *Outlines of Systematic Theology* (Philadelphia: Judson Press, 1908), 263–64; William W. Stevens, *Doctrines of the Christian Religion* (Nashville: Broadman Press, 1967), 383–84.

[12]Charles C. Ryrie, *Basic Theology* (Wheaton, Ill.: Victor Books, 1986), 444. Ryrie notes that some theonomists are former amillennialists.

[13]David Chilton, *Paradise Restored: A Biblical Theology of Dominion* (Tyler, Tex.: Reconstruction Press, 1985), 73, 80. Chilton also says, "The Great Tribulation ended with the destruction of the temple in A.D. 70" (88, 93).

world as a whole. The hope for the Christianization of the world led liberals to develop the so-called social gospel, and that has failed and will continue to fail. The millennial kingdom can be brought in only through God's judgment followed by His divine gracious action.

Because premillennialists recognize this, critics call them pessimistic.[14] Actually, premillennialists believe in the power of the gospel. They recognize, however, that Jesus was being realistic in Matthew 24:4–14. He was telling His disciples that they could not wait for ideal conditions before spreading the gospel. We must go out into the world the way it is, with all its wars, rumors of wars, famines, and earthquakes, and tell the good news of salvation through Christ. He was realistic also when He gave the Parable of the Sower. Some of the seed would not produce the hoped-for results; not everyone would believe the gospel. But there would be good ground, producing much fruit (Matt. 13:1–8,18–23). There will be some "from every tribe and language and people and nation. . . . And they will reign on the earth" (Rev. 5:9–10). This kind of realism has spurred premillennialists into some of the greatest and most successful missionary endeavors of modern times. Pentecostal premillennialists have had the further help of the gifts of the Spirit, which are given to build the Church both spiritually and numerically.[15]

On the other hand, some premillennialists have allowed the fact of future judgment to cause them to have little or no concern about the environment and stewardship of the gifts God has placed in the natural world. More recently, however, many, along with other evangelicals, have responded to the environmental crisis, recognizing that until Jesus comes we

[14]Grenz, "Deeper Significance," 19.
[15]Stanley M. Horton, *What the Bible Says about the Holy Spirit* (Springfield, Mo.: Gospel Publishing House, 1976), 224, 282–83.

must accept the ecological responsibility laid on humankind in the beginning when God said to "subdue" the earth (that is, bring it under proper control) and "rule" over, or govern, animal life (that is, in such a way as to care for and protect it [Gen. 1:28]).[16]

EARLY MILLENNIALISM

The Bible is very clear that our Lord Jesus Christ will return to reign on the earth as King of kings and Lord of lords. The Early Church looked forward to His return to establish His kingdom and to reign in Jerusalem as the heir of David's throne. They took literally Jesus' promise that the twelve apostles would sit on twelve thrones judging and ruling the twelve tribes of a restored Israel (Matthew 19:28).

The Thessalonian believers who "turned to God from idols to serve the living and true God, and to wait for his Son from heaven" (1 Thess. 1:9-10), could identify with the new song of Revelation 5:9-10 which celebrated not only redemption by the blood of the Lamb but also coronation by Christ, as kings and priests who "will [in the future] reign *on the earth.*" Through the first century many suffered persecution, but they believed that "if we endure, we will also reign with him" (2 Tim. 2:12). The picture of Christ's ultimate victory in the Book of Revelation added the assurance of a thousand years of millennial reign before the last judgment and the coming of the new heavens and new earth prophesied by Isaiah (65:17; 66:22).

---

[16]See Erich Sauer, *The King of the Earth* (Grand Rapids: William B. Eerdmans Publishing Co., 1962), 9; Francis Schaeffer, *Pollution and the Death of Man: The Christian View of Ecology* (Wheaton, Ill.: Tyndale House Publishers, 1970); William B. Radke, *Project Earth: Preserving the World God Created* (Portland, Oreg.: Multnomah Press, 1991); Calvin B. DeWitt, "Christian Environmental Stewardship: Preparing the Way for Action," in *Perspectives on Science and Christian Faith* 46:2 (June 1994): 80-89.

From Asia Minor, then, premillennial concepts quickly spread.[17] They are reflected in the writings of Papias (60-130), Justin Martyr (100-165), Irenaeus (130-202), Tertullian (160-230), and others. Justin Martyr expected the literal fulfillment of Isaiah 65:18-24. Irenaeus[18] took Isaiah 11 and 65 literally and protested against those who spiritualized these passages. Tertullian looked for a promised Kingdom on earth after the resurrection.[19] Some did go to an extreme. The Gnostic heretic Cerinthus pictured the Millennium as a time of unbridled gratification of fleshly desires. But the Church as a whole rejected that idea even when considering belief in an earthly Millennium "an unquestioned article of orthodoxy," or right doctrine, built on Old Testament prophecies but confirmed by and dependent on the New Testament.[20]

Until the middle of the second century most Christians held to the hope that Christ would return and they would reign with Him for a thousand years. As time went on, the hope of some grew cold. Yet many in the Early Church still emphasized Christ's millennial reign on earth. They were sometimes called "chiliasts," from the Greek *chilioi,* "thousand." Methodius of Olympus (d. 311) taught a Millennium on earth celebrating a fulfillment of the Feast of Tabernacles. Apollinarius of Laodicea (310-90) thought, however, that during the Millennium believers would need to keep the Law. A few others in the third and fourth centuries, such as Commodianus, Victorinus, and Lactantius, held to some sort of Millennium on earth.

Then concern over Christology turned attention away from the future hope. Origen (ca. 185-ca. 254),

---

[17]Larry V. Crutchfield, "The Apostle John and Asia Minor as a Source of Premillennialism in the Early Church Fathers," *Journal of the Evangelical Theological Society* 31:4 (December 1988): 412, 427.

[18]*Against Heresies,* v: 32-35.

[19]*Against Marcion,* III, chap. 24.

[20]J. N. D. Kelly, *Early Christian Doctrines,* 2d ed. (New York: Harper & Row, Publishers, 1960), 472.

influenced by Greek philosophy and the Jewish philosopher Philo, popularized an allegorical method
that led to spiritualizing the future Kingdom and interpreting it to be the present Church Age.[21] Consequently, he denied that there will be any future
millennial age or millennial kingdom. Dionysius of Alexandria (200–265) also denied a literal millennial
kingdom, and Eusebius of Caesarea (260–339) interpreted all prophecies in a mystical or symbolic way.

THE RISE OF AMILLENNIALISM

After Emperor Constantine[22] made Christianity the
official religion of the Roman Empire, a change began
to take place. The pastors and superintendents of the
churches no longer took the role of servant leaders.
Instead, they followed the pattern of the Roman Empire. When the capital of the empire was moved from
Rome to Constantinople, this left a vacuum in Rome,
and the bishop of Rome stepped into the gap to take
political leadership and made his seat a throne. Many
bishops then began to look at their churches as power bases. The attention was soon on earthly power
and authority rather than on the blessed hope of the
Church. As a result, amillennialism arose as a denial
of any future kingdom of God on earth.

Jerome (347–420), who translated the Bible into
Latin, called a literal Millennium a Jewish idea, spiri-
tualized the Book of Revelation, and identified the
Church Age with the Millennium.[23]

---

[21]Hans Schwarz, *On the Way to the Future: A Christian View
of Eschatology in the Light of Current Trends in Religion, Philosophy, and Science*, rev. ed. (Minneapolis: Augsburg Publishing House, 1979), 175. Origen held that there were three levels
of interpretation: the natural, the moral, and the spiritual.

[22]Constantine reigned 306–37.

[23]Harold W. Hoehner, "Evidence from Revelation 20," in *A
Case for Premillennialism: A New Consensus*, ed. Donald K.
Campbell and Jeffrey L. Townsend (Chicago: Moody Press,
1992), 241–42.

Augustine, bishop of Hippo in North Africa from 396 to 430, influenced by Tyconius (d. 400) and using a figurative rather than a literal approach, contended that the Millennium began with the first coming of Christ and that each baptism is a "first resurrection"—where the soul is raised from spiritual death and reigns with Christ in spiritual life; he considered each baptism a continuation of the Millennium. Much of the amillennial system of today is already described in his *City of God* (Books 20 through 22).[24] He took the thousand years as a figure of perfection, ten cubed, and considered it the fullness of whatever time there will be. Like many of the so-called church fathers of that period, he was more influenced by the pagan Greek philosophy of Plato (427–347 B.C.) than by the Bible.[25] He emphasized the church as the kingdom of God, considering those on thrones (Rev. 20:4) to be the present rulers of the Catholic Church, which he designated as the camp of the people of God (Rev. 20:9). He took the binding of Satan (Rev. 20:2–3) to mean that Satan is not allowed to exercise his full powers during the present age. He made the church take the place of the Roman Empire, with the church supreme over the world. Soon, however, the only kingdom many were concerned about was whatever kingdom they could build for themselves using the people as their servants. The application to our day is obvious.

GOD'S KINGDOM

By the fifth century the kingdom of God and the visible hierarchical church were identified with each

---

[24]His views were endorsed by Pope Gregory the Great (590–604). See Joseph Pohle, *Eschatology, or the Catholic Doctrine of the Last Things: A Dogmatic Treatise,* English version by Arthur Preuss (Westport, Conn.: Greenwood Press, Publishers, 1971; repr. from 1917), 158.

[25]Dale Moody, *The Hope of Glory* (Grand Rapids: William B. Eerdmans Publishing Co., 1964), 16.

other, with the church giving out the judgments. As a result, the future Kingdom and the final judgments were no longer emphasized.[26] Then in the latter part of the Middle Ages, the Roman church believed it was building the eternal city of God here on earth.[27] Most closed their eyes to the evil that was rampant. Few gave any evidence of believing that God has a plan or that He will establish the future Kingdom by His own act.[28] Only occasionally did the belief in a future Millennium flare up, usually in protest against hierarchical authority. An important example came through the teaching of Joachim of Floris (Flora, Fiore) in Calabria, in the heel of the Italian peninsula (1145–1202).[29] He believed in an age of the Father, an age of the Son, and taught that these were to be followed by the age of the Holy Spirit beginning in 1260. He stirred many to godly living and spiritual worship.[30]

The Reformation brought a new emphasis on the authority of the Bible and the activity of the living

---

[26]Louis Berkhof, *Systematic Theology,* 4th ed., rev. (Grand Rapids: William B. Eerdmans Publishing Co., 1941), 663. There was a brief flare-up of an expectation of the end of the world just before the year 1000 due to the teaching of some church fathers that the earth was created about 5000 B.C. and to the idea in Barnabas (15:4) that six thousand years after creation there would be a final sabbath rest. Cf. William Manson, G. W. H. Lampe, T. F. Torrance, and W. A. Whitehouse, *Eschatology* (Edinburgh, Scotland: Oliver & Boyd, 1953), 31.

[27]R. P. C. Hanson, *The Attractiveness of God: Essays in Christian Doctrine* (Richmond, Va.: John Knox Press, 1973), 194; Manson et al., *Eschatology,* 37.

[28]Stephen Travis, *The Jesus Hope* (Downers Grove, Ill.: Inter-Varsity Press, 1974), 54.

[29]Berkhof, *Systematic Theology,* 663. See Jacques Le Goff, *The Birth of Purgatory,* trans. Arthur Goldhammer (Chicago: University of Chicago Press, 1984), 83. Joachim proposed that the Millennium would begin about 1260 and that the world would then be converted. See Ryrie, *Basic Theology,* 443.

[30]Moody, *Hope of Glory,* 17.

God in history, the God who will judge humankind.[31]
However, with respect to the last things, the attention was given to the glorification of believers, and there was little mention of the consummation of the age and the final state.[32] Amillennialism was carried over into the Protestant churches after the Reformation. Most had no room in their theological systems for any restoration of Israel on earth. Therefore, they spiritualized the Kingdom prophecies of the Old Testament and applied them to the Church.[33] They declared that Israel, by rejecting Christ, had forfeited all of the promises God had given to it, and its role or mission had been taken over by the Church. Some saw a future salvation of the Jews and their incorporation into the Church, but without their having any special place in God's plan.

THE BOOK OF REVELATION

Amillennialists also spiritualized the Book of Revelation and claimed that Satan was bound at the cross, so that whatever Millennium there might be is going on now (either spiritually on earth or else in heaven). They taught that when Christ returns there will be a general judgment of both the righteous and the wicked at the same time. Then Jesus will immediately establish His eternal kingdom and reign in the New Jerusalem, with no Millennium in between.

The Geneva Bible (1560) in its notes on the Book of Revelation, however, put the binding of Satan at Christ's birth and claimed Satan was loosed in the time of Pope Sylvester (999–1002). Some said he was loosed in the time of Pope Gregory VII (1073–85), and some said in 1300. In each case, they believed they were living in the "short time" of Revelation

---

[31]T. F. Torrance, "The Eschatology of the Reformation," in *Eschatology*, Manson et al., 38.

[32]Manson et al., *Eschatology*, 38; Berkhof, *Systematic Theology*, 663.

[33]Ryrie, *Basic Theology*, 449.

20:3. Protestants were teaching also that Gog and Magog were the pope and Mohammed, and that the Roman Catholic Church was about to be destroyed.

THE PLACE OF ISRAEL

One of the chief proponents of amillennialism in the middle of the twentieth century was Oswald Allis of Westminster Seminary. In his book *Prophecy and the Church,* he pointed to the extremes of some dispensationalists, said those extremes are wrong, and indicated that therefore amillennialism is correct.[34]

Since the amillennial system has no room for any restoration of national Israel, amillennialists deny that national Israel is in any sense God's chosen people.[35] Most of them say that what has happened in Israel since 1948 is irrelevant. Some go even further. One amillennialist pastor in Springfield, Missouri, told me he hates the Jews. He thought he had a right to hate them, for he considers them enemies of the Church. But did the apostle Paul hate the Jews who had not accepted Christ, even though they persecuted him and threatened his life? Not at all! In fact, he would have been willing to spend eternity in hell if that would have guaranteed their salvation. He knew that was not possible, but that is how much he loved them (Romans 9:1-5).

In seventeenth-century England, belief in a Millennium became more popular, especially among Puritans trained by Joseph Meade.[36] He recognized that Old Testament prophets did not see the time gap between the first and second comings of Christ. Many, however, still believed the Millennium was already

---

[34]Oswald T. Allis, *Prophecy and the Church,* entire book.

[35]Jay E. Adams, *The Time Is at Hand* (Philadelphia: Presbyterian & Reformed Publishing Co., 1974), 3. Adams also considers the Millennium "a present reality," ibid., 9.

[36]Wilber B. Wallis, "Eschatology and Social Concern," *Journal of the Evangelical Theological Society* 24:1 (March 1981): 5.

fulfilled in the history of the Church. Part of the reason was the fact that those who did preach the second coming of Christ to bring in the Millennium hurt their cause by making computations that put His return between 1640 and 1660.[37]

THE RISE OF POSTMILLENNIALISM

In the eighteenth century, postmillennialism began to be popular. The defeat of the Spanish Armada in 1588 caused many to think that the papal antichrist could be defeated and that Protestants could bring a Millennium before Christ's return. Daniel Whitby (1638-1726) then popularized the view that Christ would not return until after a millennium of progress brought the world under the authority of the gospel.[38] Jonathan Edwards (1703-58) looked for a victory over the Antichrist (the Roman Catholic Church), Islam, and paganism and the conversion of the Jews, all to be accomplished by the outpouring of the Holy Spirit in a mighty revival. This would bring in a long period of spiritual prosperity for the Church. Then Satan would again threaten the Church and Christ would come in judgment to bring in the eternal Kingdom.[39]

Postmillennialism became dominant in nineteenth-century America and fit in with the then current phi-

---

[37]Bryan W. Ball, *A Great Expectation: Eschatological Thought in English Protestantism to 1660,* vol. 12 in *Studies in the History of Christian Thought,* ed. Heiko A. Oberman (Leiden, Netherlands: E. J. Brill, 1975), 1-4, 19-23.

[38]Wallis, "Eschatology," 4-5. Whitby's view was not only that the world would be converted, but also that converted Jews would reign over the world from Jerusalem, the pope and the Turks would be defeated, and there would be a thousand years of peace and righteousness before Jesus returned. See Ryrie, *Basic Theology,* 443.

[39]Jonathan Edwards, *The History of Redemption* (Marshallton, Del.: The National Foundation for Christian Education, [1773]), 305-28.

losophies of automatic progress. "The campaigns for Sabbath reform, temperance, and antislavery were all part of the program to prepare the nation for the advent of the great millennial age."[40] Some, such as Charles Hodge and Benjamin B. Warfield, were Bible believers.[41] Others tended to take a liberal approach and even identified their views with a theistic evolutionism.[42]

THE RISE OF DISPENSATIONALISM

By the end of the century, however, summer Bible conferences were spreading the hope of a future Millennium again.[43] With this came the spread of dispensationalism, whose literal interpretation of prophecy is in extreme contrast to the figurative interpretations of postmillennialists and amillennialists, as well as those of liberals and existentialists.[44] It also rejected the idea that the Church had replaced Israel in God's plan and taught that God had two plans, one for national Israel and another for the Church.

Many taught that Jesus in His first coming offered a kingdom to Israel and gave the Sermon on the Mount as the laws of the kingdom, as "the law of Moses

---

[40]George M. Marsden, *The Evangelical Mind and the New School Presbyterian Experience* (New Haven, Conn.: Yale University Press, 1970), 185–86.

[41]Charles Hodge, *Systematic Theology,* vol. 3 (New York: Charles Scribner's Sons, 1895), 790–880.

[42]Walvoord, *Blessed Hope,* 14.

[43]Craig A. Blaising, "Introduction," in *Dispensationalism, Israel and the Church: The Search for Definition,* ed. Craig A. Blaising and Darrell L. Bock (Grand Rapids: Zondervan Publishing House, 1992), 16–22.

[44]Thomas N. Finger, *Christian Theology: An Eschatological Approach,* vol. 1 (Nashville: Thomas Nelson Publishers, 1985), 110.

raised to its highest power."[45] They taught also that the kingdom was rejected and postponed, with the Church Age interjected as a parenthesis in God's plan. At the end of the Church Age, Jesus will return to establish a kingdom for Israel. This kingdom is referred to as the "kingdom of heaven" in contrast to the "kingdom of God," though a comparison of the Gospels shows that these terms are used interchangeably.[46]

Further, the Church is identified as a heavenly people, Israel as an earthly people. The promise that the seed of Abraham will be like the stars of heaven (Gen. 15:5) and the sand of the sea (Gen. 32:12) (or the dust of the earth [Gen. 28:14]) is taken to mean that the Church is like the stars, and Israel like the sand or the dust. However, Moses made it clear that when Israel was about to enter the Promised Land they were already like the stars of heaven in number (Deut. 1:10; 10:22).[47] And Paul, in Romans 11:17-25, indicated there is only one olive tree. The Gentile believers have been grafted into it, and Israel's rejection

---

[45]Charles L. Feinberg, *Premillennialism or Amillennialism?* 2d ed. (Wheaton, Ill.: Van Kampen Press, 1954), 64. Ladd points out that "when Christians will not use the Lord's prayer because it is given for the kingdom age and not for the present age, we must test carefully the validity of the position." George Eldon Ladd, *Crucial Questions about the Kingdom of God* (Grand Rapids: William B. Eerdmans Publishing Co., 1952), 106.

[46]Feinberg identified the kingdom of heaven as having Israel alone in view while the kingdom of God is "universal in scope and outreach." *Premillennialism,* 288-89. Other dispensationalists admit that "no distinction between these expressions is intended by the biblical writers." Robert L. Saucy, *The Case for Progressive Dispensationalism: The Interface between Dispensational and Nondispensational Theology* (Grand Rapids: Zondervan Publishing House, 1993), 19.

[47]Only about six thousand stars are visible to the naked eye, and Israel was far beyond that number.

is not complete, nor is it final.[48] They will be grafted back in again to the same olive tree, the same continuing plan of God, that the Gentiles have been grafted into.[49]

It is in this context also that we must understand Paul's statement that "all Israel will be saved" (Rom. 11:26). They must be saved by grace through faith in the risen Lord Jesus Christ, "for there is no other name under heaven given to men by which we must be saved" (Acts 4:12; cf. Eph. 2:8). God raised Jesus from the dead and exalted Him to His own right hand as Prince and Savior "that he might give repentance and forgiveness of sins to Israel" (Acts 5:30-31). There is no other way of salvation, so Israel must come by grace through faith in the risen Jesus. Furthermore, Paul had already said that "not all who are descended from Israel are Israel" (Rom 9:6). A great number of Jews may be saved during the Tribulation (Deut. 4:30-31; Hos. 5:14 through 6:3; Rev. 7:1-8). Those who do not believe in Jesus will probably join the armies of the Antichrist and be destroyed when Jesus returns in glory (cf. Isa. 10:20-23; Ezek. 20:34-38; Zech. 13:8-9). The believers, along with the godly people of Israel in ancient times, will be the "all Israel" who will be saved.

Some dispensationalists even interpret Jeremiah 31:31 as a new covenant for Israel distinct from an unpredicted new covenant given to the Church, though the New Testament makes no such distinction. There is only one new covenant, the covenant put into effect by the death of Jesus on Calvary's cross (Heb. 9:14-15; 12:24).

---

[48]Charles M. Horne, "The Meaning of the Phrase 'And thus all Israel will be saved' (Romans 11:26)," *Journal of the Evangelical Theological Society* 21:4 (December 1978): 330.

[49]Some recent dispensationalists recognize that God has one unified plan that includes both Israel and the Church and that both "ultimately have a heavenly hope together in the heavenly Jerusalem." Saucy, *Case for Progressive Dispensationalism*, 24.

Some have gone so far as to say that prophecies given to the Jews have no bearing on God's plan for the Church. For example, some say that Joel 2:28–32 was just for the Jews and was not fulfilled on the Day of Pentecost when the believers (who were already the Church) were baptized in the Spirit. One writer goes so far as to say that Peter did not really mean "this is what was spoken by the prophet Joel." What Peter really meant was "this is something like that."[50] But Peter's statement could not be put more strongly. Joel's prophecy was indeed fulfilled on the Day of Pentecost, and both Joel and Peter indicate a continuing fulfillment from the Day of Pentecost until the end of the age. It should not seem strange, therefore, that some Old Testament prophecies of end-time events will have fulfillment that involves both Israel and the Church.

Clearly, God will be faithful to His promises to national Israel without splitting Israel and the Church into two peoples and two plans.[51] To accept this, many dispensationalists today have modified the classic dispensational view.

LIBERAL VIEWS

Liberals, who were really antisupernaturalists, under the influence of the philosophers Immanuel Kant, Albrecht Ritschl, Georg W. F. Hegel, and Friedrich Schleiermacher, deleted from the social gospel they preached any future divine intervention.[52] To them the kingdom of God was something human beings could create by their own wisdom without any help

weird!

---

[50]Arno C. Gaebelein, *The Holy Spirit in the New Testament* (New York: Our Hope, n.d.), 34.

[51]Walter C. Kaiser, Jr., "The Davidic Promise and the Inclusion of the Gentiles (Amos 9:9–15 and Acts 15:13–18): A Test Passage for Theological Systems," *Journal of the Evangelical Theological Society* 20:2 (June 1977): 110.

[52]Helmut Thielicke, *The Evangelical Faith*, trans. G. W. Bromiley, vol. 1 (Grand Rapids: William B. Eerdmans Publishing Co., 1974), 125.

from above. Religion was treated as mere human feelings or moral aspirations, while God as the source and the giver of eternal hope was ignored. Christian ethics would Christianize the world. This antisupernaturalism reached a climax with Albert Schweitzer and Rudolf Bultmann. Schweitzer stripped the biblical presentation of Jesus to make Him a mere man who mistakenly thought the end would come in His own lifetime. Schweitzer took "astonishing liberties with the historical evidence."[53] So did Bultmann when he excised miracles from the Bible, focused only on the individual and this present existence, rejected the Bible's linear view of history,[54] and treated the biblical hope as mere human speculation or Jewish apocalypticism.[55]

EXISTENTIALISM

Also, in Europe, existentialism, by its focus on the human, ignored "the cosmic dimensions of Scripture" and provided an escape from any concern over the past or future.[56] Among existentialists the neoortho-

[53]J. H. Leckie, *The World to Come and Final Destiny*, 2d ed., rev. (Edinburgh, Scotland: T. & T. Clark, 1922), 42.

[54]Against Bultmann see the defense of linear history in Oscar Cullmann, *Christ and Time*, rev. ed., trans. Floyd V. Filson (Philadelphia: Westminster Press, 1964), 96, 105. See James Barr, *Biblical Words for Time*, 2d ed., rev. (Naperville, Ill.: Alec R. Allenson, 1969), 12–180, for criticisms of Cullmann's overstatements.

[55]Bultmann treated eschatology as "mythological" and considered the miraculous obsolete and unacceptable. See comments by Emil Brunner, *Eternal Hope*, trans. Harold Knight (Philadelphia: Westminster Press, 1954), 214; Millard J. Erickson, *Christian Theology* (Grand Rapids: Baker Book House, 1985), 1159.

[56]Zachary Hayes, *What Are They Saying about the End of the World?* (New York: Paulist Press, 1983), 7; Carl E. Braaten, *Eschatology and Ethics* (Minneapolis: Augsburg Publishing House, 1974), 15, 16; Hendrikus Berkhof, *Well-Founded Hope* (Richmond, Va.: John Knox Press, 1969), 12. Finger argues that "Israel's 'ingrafting' is another indication" that the existential view of our future hope is not biblical. Finger, *Christian Theology*, vol. 1, 170.

dox attempted to reclaim orthodox doctrines while at the same time treating the Bible as a merely human record. In Switzerland Karl Barth emphasized the sovereignty of God and "restored eschatology to its pervasive place in theology."[57] In England C. H. Dodd popularized the idea that the kingdom of God had fully come "once and for all" in the ministry of Jesus, and that the writers of the New Testament misunderstood His teachings and developed an expectation that He would return.[58] A modification called "inaugurated eschatology," by R. P. Fuller, taught that Jesus looked back to the coming of the Kingdom. Fuller also explained away the New Testament record that shows He looked forward to a future Kingdom.[59]

[57]Charles Mwakitwile, "The Eschatology of Karl Barth," *Southwestern Journal of Theology* 36:2 (Spring 1994): 25.

[58]I. H. Marshall, *Eschatology and the Parables* (London: Theological Students' Fellowship, 1973), 13; J. E. Fison, *The Christian Hope: The Presence and the Parousia* (London: Longmans, Green & Co., 1954), ix-x. In a letter to Dr. George Beasley-Murray, Dodd admitted that Jesus may have used apocalyptic language, but "certainly in a symbolic sense." George Raymond Beasley-Murray, *Jesus and the Future: An Examination of the Criticism of the Eschatological Discourse, Mark 13 with Special Reference to the Little Apocalypse Theory* (London: Macmillan & Co., 1954), 100. Dodd dismissed the *parousia,* disposed of the apocalyptic elements in the New Testament as Jewish influence, and imported "a Platonic conception of time" that has no place for God, Christ, or the Holy Spirit acting in a future age. For a critical evaluation of Dodd's theology see Neill Quinn Hamilton, *The Holy Spirit and Eschatology in Paul,* Scottish Journal of Theology Occasional Papers, no. 6 (Edinburgh, Scotland: Oliver & Boyd, 1957), 54-60; Clayton Sullivan, *Rethinking Realized Eschatology* (Macon, Ga.: Mercer University Press, 1988), vii, 4, 34-70.

[59]Marshall, *Eschatology and the Parables,* 14; Hanson, *The Attractiveness of God,* 190. Others who deny the traditional views of God, Christ, and eschatology include Paul Tillich (individuals are estranged from God as the ground of being), Schubert M. Ogden (neoclassical theism, process theology), Gordon Kaufmann (God is the evolutionary process that moves humanity toward the kingdom of God on earth), Edward Farley (the nature of faith and the church is ever changing), Robert P. Scharlemann (revelation is impossible in language).

There have been several reactions to Bultmann. One of the most prominent has been Jürgen Moltmann's theology of hope. He emphasized that "Christianity . . . is hope, forward looking and forward moving, and therefore also revolutionizing and transforming the present."[60] At the same time he looked, not for a future apocalyptic day, but for Christ's coming imminently toward man. We are not to wait passively for His return, but rather we must suffer in order to become one "with those who are not liberated." We must "make peace in the areas of poverty and exploitation, violence and oppression, and the destruction of the environment."[61]

LIBERATION THEOLOGY

Existentialism then—along with the political theology of the Roman Catholic John Baptist Metz—inspired the development of liberation theology, which sees the kingdom of God as a metaphor and seeks to make radical political and social change in the present. On the basis of current social theories, this theology teaches that truth is found only in the midst of concrete historical events where people are involved in attempting to change the world.[62]

---

[60]Jürgen Moltmann, *Theology of Hope: On the Ground and the Implications of a Christian Eschatology,* trans. James W. Leitch, from the 5th German ed. (New York: Harper & Row, Publishers, 1967), 16. Koch points out that Moltmann separates this hope from history and "in the end tears salvation and creation apart." Klaus Koch, *The Rediscovery of Apocalyptic,* trans. Margaret Kohl (Naperville, Ill.: Alec R. Allenson, n.d.), 107–8. Randall E. Otto, "God and History in Jürgen Moltmann," *Journal of the Evangelical Theological Society* 35:3 (September 1992): 379, 384, also points out that Moltmann denies the supernatural, does not view the Bible's history as real history, and denies the Bible's view of the fulfillment of the hope it presents. Moltmann also imposes on the Bible "a view of history derived from revisionist Marxism."

[61]Joe Davis, "The Eschatology of Jürgen Moltmann," *Southwestern Journal of Theology* 36:2 (Spring 1994): 27.

[62]Finger, *Christian Theology,* 74–77; Hayes, *What Are They Saying?* 10–11; Schwarz, *On the Way,* 107.

Though Christians have a responsibility to do what they can for others in a sacrificial way, there is, however, no scriptural basis for New Testament believers to become involved in political change by means of armed revolution. No political utopia is possible by such means. Israel was not delivered from Egypt by arming themselves or committing terrorist acts. The millennial kingdom will not come through human effort. God brought Israel out of Egypt by direct, divine intervention. The Bible shows that our only hope, our sure hope, for a new world order is that God will intervene, bring judgment on the present world system, and send Jesus back to earth again to establish His rule and make David's throne eternal (2 Sam. 7:11–13; Ps. 89:20–37; Isa. 9:7).

Chapter 5
Millennial
Views

KEY ISSUES FOR PREMILLENNIALISTS

The key issues that separate premillennialists from postmillennialists and amillennialists are (1) the hermeneutic: literal or figurative; (2) the binding of Satan: after the Tribulation or at the Cross; (3) the nature of the first resurrection: at the time of the Rapture or at conversion; (4) the judgments: the judgment seat of Christ before the Millennium, and the Great White Throne Judgment after the Millennium, or one general judgment after a general resurrection of both the righteous and the wicked; (5) the place of Israel: Israel's literal restoration in the Millennium or its deletion from God's plan forever; and (6) the reign of Christ and the saints "on the earth": after Christ returns or in the present age.

LITERAL INTERPRETATION

When referring to literal interpretation, we have in mind seeking the meaning of a passage in its context, and not just within the context of the passage itself, but also within the book it is a part of and within the Bible as a whole. For example, the serpent in Genesis 3:1 is identified as an animal. It was a literal serpent.

But that does not mean it was only a serpent.[63] As we read on we see that it was more than a serpent, having knowledge and ability that no ordinary serpent would have. Then as we go to Revelation 12:9 and 20:2 we find that this serpent is identified as "the devil, or Satan." From the Bible as a whole it is clear that only God can create. It is also clear that Satan and his demons, as spirit beings, can manifest themselves only by taking possession of some living being that has a body. Therefore, Satan must have taken possession of a serpent.

Similarly, we recognize that the Bible often uses symbols, but those symbols have a meaning and represent a reality. The Antichrist is called a beast, but he will be a real person. We also recognize that the fact that the Book of Revelation uses symbols does not mean everything in the book is symbolic. Items that are clearly literal include, for example, the blood of Jesus (5:9), the saints reigning on the earth (5:10), the tribes of Israel (7:5-8), Christ's crucifixion (11:8), and the earthquake greater than any since humanity has been on the earth (16:18). Many other things, such as the Great White Throne and the New Jerusalem, should also be taken literally.[64]

To be consistent, those who do not accept a literal interpretation of the Millennium should also "spiritualize"[65] the Second Coming. Some do make it "the mere continued presence of Jesus with His beloved at

---

[63]Elliott E. Johnson, "Premillennialism Introduced: Hermeneutics," in *A Case for Premillennialism: A New Consensus,* ed. Donald K. Campbell and Jeffrey L. Townsend (Chicago: Moody Press, 1992), 17.

[64]Stanley M. Horton, *The Ultimate Victory* (Springfield, Mo.: Gospel Publishing House, 1991), 314.

[65]This method of "spiritualizing" Scripture takes things figuratively or allegorically, looking for hidden, mystical meanings, and "has nothing to do with spirituality or being spiritual." Paul Lee Tan, *The Interpretation of Prophecy* (Rockville, Md.: Assurance Publishers, 1974), 33.

all times."[66] But, as Bernard Ramm indicates, there are too many passages that call for Christ's literal return.[67] Hebrews 9:27-28 is clear: "Just as man is destined to die once, and after that to face judgment, so Christ was sacrificed once to take away the sins of many people; and he will appear a second time, not to bear sin, but to bring salvation to those who are waiting for him." Christ Jesus is our hope (1 Tim. 1:1), and His literal return to bring the fullness of our salvation calls for a literal resurrection, a literal Millennium, and a literal Kingdom on earth.

THE BINDING OF SATAN

John's vision of war in heaven shows Satan defeated and "hurled to the earth, and his angels with him" (Rev. 12:7-9). After that, Satan will no longer be able to enter the heavenlies, although he will still have power on earth for a short time. Then after the final defeat of the Antichrist, Satan will be bound for a thousand years.[68]

Some have identified the binding of Satan with Constantine's edict stopping persecution of the Church and making Christianity the official religion of the Roman Empire. However, persecution did occur again, evil became worse in the Dark Ages that followed, and the Roman church itself in the Inquisition became the persecutor of true believers.

Most amillennialists and postmillennialists relate the binding of Satan to Christ's victories over Satan during His ministry and at the cross. They make the binding a matter of limiting Satan's powers rather than his total confinement. They quote Matthew 12:28-29, "'If I drive out demons by the Spirit of God, then the kingdom of God has come upon you.

---

[66]Bernard Ramm, "A Philosophy of Christian Eschatology," in *Last Things*, ed. H. Leo Eddleman (Grand Rapids: Zondervan Publishing House, 1969), 33.

[67]Ibid.

[68]Horton, *Ultimate Victory*, 176-77.

Or again, how can anyone enter a strong man's house and carry off his possessions unless he first ties up the strong man? Then he can rob his house.'" This driving out of demons is not a total binding of Satan but a restriction of his power in specific cases. Satan and his demons continue to be active on earth (Acts 16:16,18).

They also refer to Colossians 2:13–15 where Jesus "forgave us all our sins, having canceled the written code, with its regulations, that was against us and that stood opposed to us; he took it away, nailing it to the cross. And having disarmed the powers and authorities, he made a public spectacle of them, triumphing over them by the cross." Certainly the Cross was a defeat for Satan, but the final effects of that are not yet seen on earth. Satan is still active, although he has never been able to go further than God's sovereignty has allowed (see Job 1:12; 2:6).

If Revelation 20:1–3 refers to what happened at the cross, then the binding was indeed only partial. Satan still is "the ruler of the kingdom of the air, the spirit who is now at work in those who are disobedient" (Eph. 2:2). Satan can also hinder Christians (1 Thess. 2:18). For that reason, we must resist him, "standing firm in the faith," for he still "prowls around like a roaring lion looking for someone to devour" (1 Pet. 5:8–9; cf. Eph. 6:11–12,16). When Ananias failed to resist him, Satan filled his heart so that he lied to the Holy Spirit (Acts 5:3). Clearly, Satan still has power on earth and can be bound only in individual cases.

Most amillennialists and postmillennialists do recognize that the return of Jesus in triumph and the judgment of the Antichrist and the false prophet (Rev. 19:11–21) are future.[69] But they are inconsis-

---

[69]Some do not believe in a literal return of Jesus and interpret Rev. 19:11–16 "as a highly symbolic portrayal of the witness of the word of God in the world through the church. This interpretation seems impossible. The theme of Revelation is the return of the Lord to consummate His redemptive work." George Eldon Ladd, "Historic Premillennialism," in *The Meaning of the Millennium,* ed. Clouse, 33.

tent in placing the binding of Satan (Rev. 20:1-3) at the cross in the past. It is only logical that Jesus in His return will deal not only with the Antichrist and his armies, but also with Satan who will indwell the Antichrist and give him his authority.

Amillennialists say Satan is bound only in the sense that he cannot now deceive the nations. But nations are made up of individuals, many of whom are now being deceived by Satan. Actually, it is clear that the binding of Satan (Rev. 20:2) is total. The "angel . . . out of heaven" not only binds Satan, but also throws him into the abyss and locks and seals "it over him, to keep him from deceiving the nations anymore until the thousand years" are ended. Then "Satan will be released from his prison and will go out to deceive the nations in the four corners of the earth" (Rev. 20:7-8).

Clearly, during the thousand years Satan is totally imprisoned and is not on the earth, nor is he free to go about deceiving the nations. "Nations" (Gk. *ethnē*) means peoples, rather than nationalistic states, and often refers to Gentiles or pagans. In Revelation 20:3 Satan is not able to deceive people on the earth, and in 20:8 he again deceives people on the earth. In effect, no one is deceived by Satan during the thousand years of the Millennium. This fits the premillennial view.

THE FIRST RESURRECTION

Amillennialists and postmillennialists identify the first resurrection with the new birth and the new life given by the Spirit. They say that "over these spiritually raised ones . . . the second death, or eternal punishment, has no power."[70] They draw attention to Romans 6:3-4: "Don't you know that all of us who were baptized into Christ Jesus were baptized into his death? We were therefore buried with him

---

[70]Stevens, *Doctrines,* 383.

through baptism into death in order that, just as Christ was raised from the dead through the glory of the Father, we too may live a new life." But, in this context, the Bible is talking about dying to sin and living in righteousness. So "count yourselves dead to sin but alive to God in Christ Jesus" (Rom. 6:11). This is an application to our present life, which does not deny the promise of a literal resurrection of the body, as 1 Corinthians 15 makes clear. Some amillennialists take the phrase "I saw the souls of those who had been beheaded" (Rev. 20:4) to mean that John saw nothing but souls, and they were simply reigning in heaven, not on earth. But John also observed in 20:4 that "they came to life."

That the sentence "They came to life and reigned with Christ a thousand years" refers to bodily resurrection, not spiritual resurrection, is also confirmed by the fact that "the rest of the dead did not come to life until the thousand years were ended" (20:4,5).[71] The "rest of the dead" are the unsaved. If coming to life in verse 4 refers to spiritual resurrection at the new birth, then verse 5 must mean that after the thousand years "the rest of the dead" are the spiritually dead, and they are all given a second chance and are all saved. But "the rest of the dead" are actually brought before the Great White Throne and are cast into the lake of fire (Rev. 20:11-15).

Revelation 20:4 deals with two groups of people. The first group sits on thrones to judge (that is, "rule," as the word so often means in the Old Testament). The message to all the churches (Rev. 3:21-22) indicates this group comprises all the believers from the Church Age who remain faithful, being overcomers, that is, conquerors, winners (Rev. 2:26-27; 3:21; see also 1 John 5:4). Among them, as Jesus

---

[71]Amillennialists have to make *ezēsan* ("they came to life") mean coming to life spiritually (by being born again) in Rev. 20:4 and make the identical word mean something else in verse 5.

promised, are the twelve apostles judging (ruling) the twelve tribes of Israel (Luke 22:30); for Israel, restored, cleansed, filled with God's Holy Spirit, will undoubtedly occupy all the land promised to Abraham (Genesis 15:18).[72]

In addition to the overcomers from the Church Age, John saw "souls," that is, living individuals who have been martyred during the Tribulation (Rev. 6:9–11; 12:15).[73] These two groups are joined to reign with Christ for the thousand years.

Then Revelation 20:5 makes the plain (but parenthetical) statement about "the rest of the dead." These include all who are not in the two groups mentioned in verse 4. That is, they include all who died in their sins apart from the saving grace of God. They will not be resurrected until after Christ's millennial reign.

"This is the first resurrection" (v. 5) means that those mentioned in verse 4 complete the first resurrection.[74] Jesus spoke of two resurrections (John 5:29): the first, the resurrection of life for those who have done the good God meant for them to do in accepting Christ and living for Him; and the second, the

---

[72]In the Millennium, as Bruce Ware puts it, "Israel and the church are in fact one people of God[,] . . . one by faith in Christ and common partaking of the Spirit, and yet distinct insofar as God will yet restore Israel as a nation to its land . . . [under] one new covenant." Ware, "The New Covenant and the People(s) of God," in *Dispensationalism, Israel and the Church,* ed. Blaising and Bock, 97.

[73]It is possible that John intends to also include Christian martyrs such as Stephen, James, Antipas, and others, as well as the martyrs whose souls were under the altar (Rev. 6:9–11), who probably include those of the Old Testament (Matt 23:35; Heb. 11:35–37). J. Webb Mealy, *After the Thousand Years: Resurrection and Judgment in Revelation 20,* Journal for the Study of the New Testament Supplement Series 70 (Sheffield, England: Sheffield Academic Press, 1992), 110–11.

[74]"Resurrection" (Gk. *anastasis*) clearly refers to bodily resurrection in forty other passages in the New Testament. One passage, Luke 2:34, is a possible exception, though it too may refer to bodily resurrection.

resurrection of judgment for those who, through unbelief, have done evil. But just as the Old Testament
prophets did not show the time difference between
Jesus' first and second comings, so Jesus in John 5:29
did not show the time difference between the two
resurrections. His purpose was to encourage people
to live for God, so the time difference between the
two was not relevant to what He was teaching.

First Corinthians 15:20,23 gives us more insight as
Paul compares the first resurrection to a harvest. The
resurrected Christ is the "firstfruits of the harvest."
The main body of the harvest comes "in [its] own
turn" at the time of His coming to meet us in the
air.[75] Then the gleanings of the harvest will be those
martyred during the Tribulation; they will make the
first resurrection complete. The first resurrection is
also called the "better resurrection" (Heb. 11:35),
"the resurrection of the righteous" (Luke 14:14), and
is the resurrection from the dead that the apostle
Paul looked forward to, with the implication that
some will not attain it (Phil. 3:11). Those resurrected
are identified as "blessed" (Rev. 20:6), for they will
enjoy the fullness of God's blessing. They are "holy,"
that is, dedicated to God and His will. Because their
resurrection is like Christ's resurrection, they rise to
die no more (cf. John 11:24-25; 1 Cor. 15:43-54).
The "second death" (the lake of fire) will therefore
have no power over them.

Paul taught a specific resurrection of those who belong to Christ when He comes (1 Cor. 15:23). Paul's
hope (Phil. 3:11) was literally the "outresurrection
[tēn exanastasin] out from among the dead *[tēn ek
nekron]*." This also implies that since Paul expected
to arise "out from among the dead," some of the dead
will be left in their graves after the believers are
raised and caught away to meet the Lord in the air.

---

[75]The Old Testament saints will be included in the main body
of the harvest (Isa. 26:19-21; Ezek. 37:12-14; Dan. 12:2-3).

Some have taken the phrase *eita to telos,* "then the end will come," to mean the end comes immediately after the resurrection, leaving no room for a Millennium. However, Paul uses *eita* to indicate "distinct events separated by periods of time."[76] "The end" is an end period after which Jesus "hands over the kingdom to the Father." A period of time is indicated, which gives room for the Millennium and the reign of Christ (1 Cor. 15:25).

THE JUDGMENTS

The idea of a general judgment is tied closely to the idea of a general resurrection, with both the righteous and the wicked raised and then judged at the same time. Jesus did declare that the Father had given Him authority to judge. Then He said, "'Do not be amazed at this, for a time is coming when all who are in their graves will hear his voice and come out— those who have done good will rise to live, and those who have done evil will rise to be condemned'" (John 5:27–29). Paul at Athens said God "has set a day when he will judge the world with justice by the man he has appointed. He has given proof of this to all men by raising him from the dead" (Acts 17:31).

The Day of the Lord, or the Day of Judgment, however, is more than a twenty-four-hour day, for it includes the whole period from the Rapture to the Great White Throne Judgment. The rebellion and the revelation of the Antichrist appear on that "day." Paul also declared his hope in God "that there will be a resurrection of both the righteous and the wicked" (Acts 24:15). These passages, however, are talking about the fact of resurrection and judgment. Other passages clearly distinguish between the two resurrections and the two judgments.[77]

---

[76]D. Edmond Hiebert, "Evidence from 1 Corinthians 15," in *A Case for Premillennialism,* ed. Campbell and Townsend, 230–31.

[77]See pp. 52–53, 77, 81, 87, 166, 187–88, 222–24.

THE PLACE OF ISRAEL

For over a hundred years before Israel became a nation in 1948, premillennialists were predicting that
the Jews would be restored to the land God gave
them. "Premillennialists built bridges between Christians and Jews, engaged in sincere and unprejudiced
Jewish evangelism, condemned European anti-
Semitism, and in general stood for Jewish rights when
few others seemed to care."[78]

Replacement Theology. Amillennialists and postmillennialists, on the other hand, teach that the Church
has replaced Israel in God's plan, and that the Old
Testament prophecies dealing with the future restoration and glory of national Israel must be spiritualized
and applied to the Church as "the Israel of God" (Gal.
6:16).[79] They draw attention, for example, to passages such as the Parable of the Tenants, where the
tenants kill the son of the owner of the vineyard and
Jesus says, "'Have you never read in the Scriptures: "The stone the builders rejected has become
the capstone; the Lord has done this, and it is marvelous in our eyes"? Therefore I tell you that the kingdom of God will be taken away from you and given
to a people who will produce its fruits'" (Matt.
21:42–43). This need not be taken as a total rejection
of Israel, however, for Matthew goes on to say that
the chief priests and the Pharisees knew Jesus was
talking about them, in contrast to the crowd, the people who held that Jesus was a prophet (21:45–46).

---

[78]Timothy P. Weber, "A Reply to David Rausch's 'Fundamentalism and the Jew,'" *Journal of the Evangelical Theological Society* 24:1 (March 1981): 67.

[79]Since Paul everywhere else uses "Israel" to designate the
Jews or the Jewish nation, he must be speaking of Jewish Christians here. They needed this exhortation about circumcision.
See Ernest DeWitt Burton, *A Critical and Exegetical Commentary on the Epistle to the Galatians,* International Critical Commentary (Edinburgh, Scotland: T. & T. Clark, 1921), 358.

Not long afterward Jesus wept over Jerusalem, that is, over its people, and told them their house was left to them desolate. "House" can mean city, household, or a nation descended from a common ancestor. In this context Jesus is still talking to the people or nation, and He adds, "'You will not see me again until you say, "Blessed is he who comes in the name of the Lord"'" (Matt. 23:37-39). In other words, Jesus looked ahead to a spiritual restoration of the people of Israel.

It is true that both the Old and New Testaments show that Gentile believers will share with Israel in the future glories of the Messiah's reign.[80] But this does not mean the Church replaces Israel. Paul, using the figure of the olive tree, says that only "*some* of the branches have been broken off" and Gentiles "have been grafted in among the others and now share in the nourishing sap from the olive root" (Rom. 11:17). But this does not remove the distinction between Israel and the Church. Though salvation has always been by grace through faith, and the Jews no longer have any advantage or distinction with respect to salvation, yet Paul still recognizes "Jews and Gentiles as distinct ethnic groups in his letters (Rom. 1:16; 9:24; 1 Cor. 1:24; 12:13; Gal. 2:14,15)."[81] Furthermore, the term "Israel" in the New Testament is not used of Gentiles. The citizenship shared by Jewish and Gentile believers is that of the heavenly Jerusalem to come (Eph 2:19; Phil. 3:20; Heb. 12:22-24). Until then we must look for further fulfillments of prophecies given to Israel.

Prophecies for Israel. The Bible again and again declares that God will reveal himself in connection with His dealings with the nation of Israel. Many of the Old Testament prophecies apply specifically to Israel and are stated in such a way that they cannot be ap-

---

[80]See chap. 6.
[81]Carl B. Hoch, Jr., "The New Man of Ephesians 2," in *Dispensationalism, Israel and the Church*, ed. Blaising and Bock, 118.

plied to any other people. Ezekiel 36 and 37 are good examples. Ezekiel places great emphasis on the importance of God's name, which is identified with His holy nature and character. God declares:

> "It is not for your sake, O house of Israel, that I am going to do these things, but for the sake of my holy name, which you have profaned. . . . I will show the holiness of my great name, which has been profaned among the nations, the name you have profaned among them. Then the nations will know that I am the LORD, declares the Sovereign LORD, when I show myself holy through you before their eyes. For I will take you out of the nations; I will gather you from all the countries and bring you back into your own land. I will sprinkle clean water on you, and you will be clean. . . . I will give you a new heart and put a new spirit in you. . . . And I will put my Spirit in you. . . . You will live in the land I gave your forefathers; you will be my people, and I will be your God. . . . Then you will remember your evil ways and wicked deeds, and you will loathe yourselves for your sins and detestable practices. I want you to know that I am not doing this for your sake, declares the Sovereign LORD" (Ezek. 36:22-32).

God confirmed this in a vision. The Spirit of the LORD set Ezekiel in the middle of a great, wide valley full of dry bones (37:1-2). The Lord asked him, "'Can these bones live?'" Ezekiel did not want to say, "It does not look possible," so he replied, "'You alone know.'" Then God commanded him to prophesy to the bones, and by the power of the prophetic word, the bones came together, "tendons and flesh appeared on them and skin covered them, but there was no breath in them" (37:7-8). Then God commanded Ezekiel to prophesy again, and by a further action of the prophetic word, "breath entered them; they came to life and stood up on their feet—a vast army" (37:10).

God himself gave the interpretation of the vision. "'These bones are the whole house of Israel. They say, "Our bones are dried up and our hope is gone;

we are cut off." Therefore prophesy and say to them: "This is what the Sovereign LORD says: O my people, I am going to open your graves and bring you up from them; I will bring you back to the land of Israel. . . . I will put my Spirit in you and you will live, and I will settle you in your own land"'" (37:11–14).

Though Israel had profaned God's name, God promised to restore them to their own land, not for their sake but for His holy name's sake. Thus, it is clear that Israel could do nothing to stop the fulfillment of this prophecy. The promise of their restoration is unconditional. It is based on God's promise and covenant given to Abraham (Gen. 15:18–20; 17:8; cf. Neh. 9:7–8); the promise of the land is specific and "cannot be singled out from the other aspects of the Abrahamic promise as only temporary or a type of something 'spiritual' or 'heavenly.'"[82]

Ezekiel 36 also indicates they will come back to the land first in unbelief. Then, after they are in the land, God will bring about a spiritual restoration and put His Spirit in them. Chapter 37 confirms this by indicating that the bones come together without life, so Israel comes together without spiritual life. Then God does a further work. As in the case of most Old Testament prophecies, the time span is not in view. We do not know how long it will be after the restoration in unbelief that the spiritual restoration will come, but

---

[82]Saucy, *Case for Progressive Dispensationalism*, 44; T. V. Farris, *Mighty to Save: A Study in Old Testament Soteriology* (Nashville: Broadman Press, 1993), 72.

come it will. God's whole being is behind His promise here.[83]

The many Old Testament prophecies that concern Israel and the Promised Land have in no way been fulfilled in the Church, as some claim they have. God still has a place for Israel in His plan. He will make Israel a blessing to us all during the Millennium.

New Testament Recognition of Israel. In the New Testament, Zechariah, "filled with the Holy Spirit," prophesied "'salvation from our enemies and from the hand of all who hate us—to show mercy to our fathers and to remember his holy covenant, the oath he swore to our father Abraham: to rescue us from the hand of our enemies and to enable us to serve him without fear in holiness and righteousness before him all our days'" (Luke 1:67-75). That oath to Abraham was unconditional (Gen. 15:9-17) and also included the land (Gen. 15:18-21).[84]

Simeon, "moved by the Spirit," identified Jesus as "a light for revelation to the Gentiles and for glory to [God's] people Israel" (Luke 2:27,32). Thus, he saw that Israel would still have a special place and a special glory. Isaiah saw that light of the Lord shining

---

[83]Some amillennialists teach that the prophecies of Ezek. 36 and 37 were fulfilled when the Jews were sent back from Babylon to the land of Israel by Cyrus in fulfillment of Jeremiah's prophecy of the seventy years of exile. However, the very fact that they had Jeremiah's prophecy shows that their hope had not yet become "very dry," nor was their hope gone. Neither were they scattered in "all the countries" (36:24). But during the centuries following the destruction of Jerusalem in A.D. 70, the Jews were scattered in all directions. During the Middle Ages they were cast out of practically every country in Europe at one time or another. Then they could certainly say, "Our bones are dried up and our hope is gone; we are cut off" (37:11).

Their return to Israel in the twentieth century was primarily in unbelief. Political Zionism stirred the Jews to seek a homeland. But God will yet bring a spiritual restoration.

[84]Robert B. Chisholm, Jr., "Evidence from Genesis," in *A Case for Premillennialism,* ed. Campbell and Townsend, 40.

forth from Jerusalem in the restored land when he prophesied,

> Many people will come and say, "Come, let us go up to the mountain of the LORD, to the house of the God of Jacob. He will teach us his ways, so that we may walk in his paths." The law *[instruction]* will go out from Zion, the word of the LORD from Jerusalem. He will judge between the nations and will settle disputes for many peoples. They will beat their swords into plowshares and their spears into pruning hooks. Nation will not take up sword against nation, nor will they train for war anymore. Come, O house of Jacob, let us walk in the light of the LORD (Isa. 2:3-5).

Accordingly, people will come to the restored land, and in view of that, Isaiah urged his people to walk in the light of the Lord even in their day.

If Jesus wanted us to believe that the Church had replaced Israel, He had the perfect opportunity to say so when the disciples asked, "'Lord, are you at this time going to restore the kingdom to Israel?'" (Acts 1:6). They undoubtedly had in mind the kingdom prophesied in Daniel 7:27, "'Then the sovereignty, power and greatness of the kingdoms under the whole heaven will be handed over to the saints, the people of the Most High. His kingdom will be an everlasting kingdom, and all rulers will worship and obey him.'" The disciples would understand "the saints" in that context as Israel. They would also have in mind the covenant given to David, since they recognized Jesus as the promised greater Son of David.

Jesus, however, did not say the kingdom would not be restored to Israel. He simply focused on the time. In effect, the kingdom would be restored to Israel in the Father's good time. But until then they were to be witnesses to Jesus.

Paul emphatically says, "God did not reject his people, whom he foreknew" (Rom. 11:2). Theirs is still the covenants and the promises (Rom. 9:4). During the present time there is a faithful remnant who have accepted Christ. Though the major part of the nation of Israel rejected Christ, this was not due to God's decree but the result of their own unbelief and disobedience (Rom. 10:3). "God is dealing with believing and unbelieving people, and not with puppets."[85] Further, they are still a holy people (Rom. 11:16), and this rejection is not only partial but also temporary. After the ingathering of Gentile believers, multitudes of Jews will be converted toward the end of this age (Rom. 11:25-26). God's own faithfulness to His promises guarantees this.[86] The future miraculous salvation of Israel, however, does not mean that we should neglect seeking the salvation of Jews today. The gospel is still "the power of God for the salvation of everyone who believes: first for the Jew, then for the Gentile" (Rom. 1:16). Christ himself became "a servant of the Jews on behalf of God's truth, to confirm the promises made to the patriarchs [Abraham, Isaac, and Jacob] so that the Gentiles may glorify God for his mercy" (Rom. 15:8-9).

The Book of Hebrews also makes it clear that Israel is still a concern of Christ Jesus, for He "died as a ransom to set them free from the sins committed [by Israel] *under the first covenant*" (Heb. 9:15). "It is not angels he helps, but Abraham's descendants. For this reason he had to be made like his [Jewish] brothers in every way, in order that he might become a merciful and faithful high priest in service to God, and that he might make atonement for the sins of the people

[85]Gunter Wagner, "The Future of Israel: Reflections on Romans 9-11," in *Eschatology and the New Testament*, ed. W. Hulitt Gloer (Peabody, Mass.: Hendrickson Publishers, 1988), 81.

[86]See the discussion on "Israel in God's Plan of Salvation" and on Romans 11 in *The Full Life Study Bible*, ed. Donald Stamps (Grand Rapids: Zondervan Publishing House, 1992), 1748-53.

[that is, of Israel]" (Heb. 2:16-17).[87] Therefore, even though some Jews rejected Jesus, Jesus did not reject Israel as a nation. He died for them. Their restoration will glorify God and let the world see how great is His love and faithfulness, how marvelous is His redemption. He is a personal God who acts in history. He is not just a mere concept of love, a mere impersonal force.

CHRIST'S REIGN ON THE EARTH

Most amillennialists and postmillennialists say there is no promise of a future reign with Christ on the earth. They spiritualize Revelation 5:10, and, even though all but a few late manuscripts have the future tense ("they will reign on the earth"), they interpret it to mean a spiritual reign during the present age. William Barclay, for example, calls it "the secret of victorious living under any circumstances . . . victory over self, victory over circumstance, and victory over sin."[88]

The angel who binds Satan comes down out of heaven to bind Satan (Rev. 20:1), and the release of Satan allows him to "go out to deceive the nations in the four corners of the *earth*" (Rev. 20:7-8), yet some say the scene in Revelation 20:4-6 takes place in heaven. Certainly the context does not bear this out. The reign of Christ during the Millennium is on the earth.[89] It will be a universal reign "from sea to sea and from the River [Euphrates] to the ends of the earth" (Ps. 72:8; Zech. 9:10).

---

[87]Charles P. Anderson, "Who Are the Heirs of the New Age in the Epistle to the Hebrews?" in *Apocalyptic and the New Testament,* Journal for the Study of the New Testament Supplement Series 24, ed. Joel Marcus and Marion L. Soards (Sheffield, England: Sheffield Academic Press, 1989), 268.

[88]William Barclay, *The Revelation of John,* 2d ed., vol. 1 (Philadelphia: Westminster Press, 1960), 225.

[89]Chap. 6 discusses the millennial reign in more detail.

STUDY QUESTIONS

1. In what ways are the teachings of amillennialists and postmillennialists alike and in what ways are they different?

2. What are the chief points on which amillennialists and premillennialists differ, and on which do they agree?

3. What are the chief points on which postmillennialists and premillennialists differ, and on which do they agree?

4. What was the usual view of the Millennium in the first two centuries of church history?

5. What brought about the rise of amillennialism and what were the results of its spread?

6. Why did postmillennialism become popular in the eighteenth and nineteenth centuries?

7. What were the teachings of early dispensationalists with regard to Israel and the Church, and to what extent have many dispensationalists modified those views today?

8. How do you define a "literal" interpretation of the Bible and its prophecies?

9. What are the reasons for believing that Satan is yet to be bound and cast into the abyss?

10. What are the reasons for believing that God will bring a literal fulfillment to the prophecies concerning Israel that are still future?

11. What is the importance of the fact that we will reign with Christ *on the earth* during the Millennium?

Chapter Six

The Millennial Kingdom

Revelation 20:1-3 and 7-10 deal with the judgment of Satan. He will be imprisoned in the abyss for a thousand years. The abyss will be locked and sealed over him, so that he will have no possibility of any activity on earth during that period. Then he will be released for a short time before his eternal judgment in the lake of fire.

In between, in Revelation 20:4-6, the Bible speaks of those who are priests of God and of Christ and who reign with Him for a thousand years.[1] No details of this reign are mentioned in Revelation 20, but this does not mean the Bible has nothing else to say about the Millennium. Christ's reign will bring the fulfillment of many prophecies that clearly deal with future restoration and blessing.[2] Jesus spoke of a time when "'many will come from the east and the west, and will take their places at the feast with Abraham, Isaac and Jacob in the kingdom of heaven'" (Matt. 8:11; Luke 13:29). Jesus also promised, "'I will not drink again of this fruit of the vine from now on until that day when I drink it anew *with you* in my Father's kingdom'" (Matt. 26:29; Mark 14:25; Luke 22:18). These passages imply a wonderful time of believers having fellowship with Jesus, the apostles, and

---

[1]The sixfold repetition of "thousand years" in Rev. 20:2-7 gives emphasis and suggests that it should be taken literally.

[2]Pss. 2:8; 24:7-8; Isa. 9:7; 11:6-10; 35:1-2; 61:3; Jer. 23:5-6; Ezek. 40 to 48; Dan. 2:44; Hos. 1:10; 3:5; Amos 9:11-15; Mic. 4:1-8; Zech. 8:1-9; Matt. 19:28; Acts 15:16-18; Rev. 2:25-28; 11:15.

the Old Testament saints in the coming Kingdom on earth, where the "fruit of the vine" grows.

OLD TESTAMENT PROPHECIES

The Old Testament focuses primarily on the restoration of Israel, for the prophets were God's messengers to that nation. There would be a remnant: "In that day the remnant of Israel, the survivors of the house of Jacob, . . . will truly rely on the LORD, the Holy One of Israel" (Isa. 10:20). But the prophets did not forget that the promise to Abraham included blessings for "all peoples on earth" (Gen. 12:3).

A KINGDOM ON EARTH

Many passages progressively reveal that these blessings include a kingdom of God on the earth.[3] Daniel saw this Kingdom as a stone that replaced the kingdoms of this world and "became a huge mountain and filled the whole *earth* . . . a kingdom that will never be destroyed" (Dan. 2:35,44).[4] Daniel also saw this Kingdom presented to the Son of Man after the kingdoms of this world had been destroyed (Dan. 7:11-26). That is, Jesus will receive the Kingdom after the Great Tribulation, after God pours out His wrath on the nations (Zeph. 3:8-9). Clearly, the Kingdom does not come as "the result of social reform, but of God's action in judgment."[5] We are to pray for the peace of Jerusalem (Ps. 122:6), but the ultimate peace the psalm looks forward to is a spiritual peace in fellowship with the Lord. That can come in its full-

---

[3]Second Sam. 7:12-16; 1 Chron. 28:5,7; Isa. 9:6-7; Dan. 2:35; 7:13-14; 2 Tim. 4:1; Rev. 11:15.

[4]Cf. Isa. 28:16, "'See, I lay a stone in Zion, a tested stone, a precious cornerstone for a sure foundation.'" See also Ps. 118:22; Isa. 8:14; 17:10; Rom. 9:33; 1 Pet. 2:6-8.

[5]Jack P. Lewis, *The Minor Prophets* (Grand Rapids: Baker Book House, 1966), 52.

ness only through the defeat of the Antichrist and the coming of the Prince of Peace.[6]

Then judgment will be followed by blessing. The "saints of the Most High will receive the kingdom" (Dan. 7:18,22,27). These saints belong to God. They are a "holy seed" (cf. Isa. 6:13).

"The remnant of Israel will do no wrong; they will speak no lies, nor will deceit be found in their mouths. They will eat and lie down and no one will make them afraid." Sing, O Daughter of Zion; shout aloud, O Israel! Be glad and rejoice with all your heart, O Daughter of Jerusalem! The LORD has taken away your punishment, he has turned back your enemy. The LORD, the King of Israel, is with you; never again will you fear any harm. . . . "The LORD your God is with you, he is mighty to save. He will take great delight in you, he will quiet you with his love, he will rejoice over you with singing." . . . "I will give you honor and praise among all the peoples of the earth when I restore your fortunes [your prosperity] before your very eyes," says the LORD (Zeph. 3:13-15,17,20).

ISRAEL'S RETURN

The prophets draw attention to two chief reasons why God will fulfill His promise to return Israel to the Promised Land.[7] One is God's compassion. Isaiah said, "The LORD will have compassion on Jacob; once again he will choose Israel and will settle them in their own land" (Isa. 14:1). The other reason is God's concern for His holy name. His name was profaned among the nations because Israel's being scattered among the nations made them believe God could not deliver His people. But God promised to show the holiness of His great name (Ezek. 20:41; 36:23). This would be done by returning Israel to the land—even while still in unbelief, even while undeserving—

---

[6]Stanley A. Ellisen, *Who Owns the Land?* (Portland, Oreg.: Multnomah Press, 1991), 184-86.

[7]Elmer A. Martens, *God's Design: A Focus on Old Testament Theology* (Grand Rapids: Baker Book House, 1981), 240-42.

because of God's faithfulness. His faithfulness would also be seen in giving them a new heart and a new spirit and in putting His Spirit within them (Ezek. 36:26-27; 37:14). He is a personal God, and He will carry out His will in a consistent way, in line with His "righteous, all-encompassing purpose."[8]

As has been pointed out, these prophecies look beyond the return from Babylon under Zerubbabel. In fact, Zechariah, after that return, prophesied:

"I will strengthen the house of Judah and save the house of Joseph. I will restore them because I have compassion on them. They will be as though I had not rejected them, for I am the LORD their God and I will answer them. . . . I will signal for them and gather them in. Surely I will redeem them; they will be as numerous as before. Though I scatter them among the peoples, yet in distant lands they will remember me. They and their children will survive, and they will return. . . . I will strengthen them in the LORD and in his name they will walk," declares the LORD (Zech. 10:6,8-9,12).

That is, Zechariah spoke of a future scattering (this took place after the destruction of Jerusalem in A.D. 70) as well as a future return to the land.

These prophecies can find complete fulfillment only in a Kingdom on this present earth, not on the new earth, as some hold. Christ will mediate God's kingdom to the world, for He *must* reign (1 Cor. 15:25), which implies time. Then He will hand over the Kingdom to God the Father when the eternal age begins (1 Cor. 15:24-28), for that kind of mediation will not be needed on the new earth.

Many prophecies speak of a restored Israel as God's agents bringing blessings to other peoples. This clearly pictures a real nation and implies conditions in the millennial kingdom rather than on the new earth and

---

[8]R. B. Y. Scott, *The Relevance of the Prophets,* rev. ed. (New York: Macmillan Co., 1968), 158.

in the New Jerusalem. And other prophecies speak of Israel possessing the land in ways that have millennial overtones (Hos. 11:11; 14:4-7; Joel 2:32; 3:1,17-18,20; Amos 9:11-15; Obad. 20-21; Mic. 7:14-20; Zeph. 3:9-20; Zech. 9:10,16; 10:6-8; 14:8-11).

EZEKIEL'S TEMPLE

Ezekiel 40 through 48 pictures Ezekiel's vision of a new temple and a restored ritual of sacrifices and offerings. The land is redivided among the tribes in strips going from west to east across the Holy Land. The central portion for the temple seems to locate the millennial temple in a different spot from that of Solomon's, possibly because its site was contaminated by idolatry. Gentiles who have had children (probably meaning spiritual children and a ministry among the Israelites) will also receive an inheritance among the tribes (Ezek. 47:22-23).

Most premillennialists feel that these prophecies of Ezekiel must be taken literally and that the ritual and the sacrifices described are memorials. Hobart Freeman points out, *"As the Old Testament sacrifices could not expiate sin, but were symbolic of Christ's sacrifice, neither will the sacrifices of the millennium."* Nor does "the individual Israelite himself ever make a sacrifice . . . which would seem to suggest a different purpose in the sacrificial system of the millennial period."[9] "Just as we now observe the Lord's Supper, not as a substitute for his finished work, but as a memorial thereof, so it is held, the observance of the ritual law prophesied by Ezekiel if literally fulfilled would simply be memorial and sacramental."[10] The details given and the distinct separation between

[9]Hobart E. Freeman, *An Introduction to the Old Testament Prophets* (Chicago: Moody Press, 1969), 322-23.

[10]James Oliver Buswell, Jr., *Unfulfilled Prophecies* (Grand Rapids: Zondervan Publishing House, 1937), 82.

the temple and the city (Ezek. 48:8,15) make the literal interpretation logical.[11]

Others, on the basis that the Book of Hebrews treats the Old Testament law and ritual as types and shadows, say that Ezekiel prophesied in terms of the dispensation he was under, but that his prophecies will be fulfilled by the personal presence of Christ, who is himself the fulfillment of the entire sacrificial system (see Heb. 8:13; 9:9–28; 10:1,18). We may not be able to be dogmatic about Ezekiel's temple, though there is nothing against there being "a restored, relocated temple in the midst of the land."[12] Whichever interpretation proves true, we can be sure there will be wonderful fellowship with Jesus throughout the entire Millennium and on into the eternal state.

THE REALITY OF THE COMING KINGDOM

Spiritual fellowship with Christ, however, does not rule out the physical and material realities of a restored land and a restored earth fulfilled in the Millennium. Nor does the fact that all God's promises are fulfilled in Christ "dissolve their meaning into the person of Christ."[13] The coming Kingdom on earth will be real and the physical presence of Jesus will be real. So will the many blessings prophesied in the Bible. The resurrected Jesus was able to eat with His disciples and have fellowship with them. Resurrected be-

---

[11]Paul Lee Tan, *The Interpretation of Prophecy* (Rockville, Md.: Assurance Publishers, 1974), 320–22.

[12]Walter C. Kaiser, Jr., *Toward an Old Testament Theology* (Grand Rapids: Academie Books, 1978), 244.

[13]Robert L. Saucy, *The Case for Progressive Dispensationalism: The Interface between Dispensational and Nondispensational Theology* (Grand Rapids: Zondervan Publishing House, 1993), 32. The idea that the literal prophecies of the future have no meaning because spiritual realities are found in Christ comes from the influence of the Greek philosopher Plato, not from the Bible.

lievers will also have new bodies that will be able to enjoy the blessings of both earth and heaven.

EARTHLY BLESSINGS

Isaiah saw that the promised earthly blessings would be realized in the distant future.

In the last days the mountain of the LORD's temple will be established as chief among the mountains; it will be raised above the hills, and all nations will stream to it. Many peoples will come and say, "Come, let us go up to the mountain of the LORD, to the house of the God of Jacob. He will teach us his ways, so that we may walk in his paths." The law [Heb. *torah*, "instruction"] will go out from Zion, the word of the LORD from Jerusalem. He will judge between the nations and will settle disputes for many peoples. They will beat their swords into plowshares and their spears into pruning hooks. Nation will not take up sword against nation, nor will they train for war anymore (Isa. 2:2-4; Mic. 4:1-3).

Instead, with peace among nations, all the instruments of war will be turned into tools for peace and productivity (Mic. 4:3-4). Everyone will have a place and enjoy God's provisions under his or her own "vine" and "fig tree."

Surely this will be a time for the Prince of Peace to manifest himself, for "the government will be on his shoulders." He will be well equipped, for His name (that is, His nature and character) is "Wonderful Counselor [for in Him is the wisdom of God], Mighty God, Everlasting Father [that is, Ruler of the eternal future], Prince of Peace [for He is our peace]. Of the increase of his government and peace there will be no end. He will reign on David's throne and over his kingdom, establishing and upholding it with justice and righteousness from that time on and forever. The zeal of the LORD Almighty will accomplish this" (Isa. 9:6-7). In other words, God himself will see to it that these prophecies are fulfilled on this present earth.

Isaiah also called God the "Savior of Israel" and prophesied that "Israel will be saved by the LORD with an everlasting salvation," but he went on to give God's own call, a call not limited to Israel: "'Turn to me and be saved, all you ends of the earth; for I am God, and there is no other'" (Isa. 45:15,17,22). God will even use Gentiles to help restore Israel, and they will humbly recognize God's blessings through Israel (Isa. 49:22-23; cf. 60:4-18; Zech. 8:20-23).

Isaiah goes on to say, "You will be called priests of the LORD, you will be named ministers of our God. . . . Instead of their shame my people will receive a double portion, and instead of disgrace they will rejoice in their inheritance; and so they will inherit a double portion in their land, and everlasting joy will be theirs" (Isa. 61:6-7). Then "the nations will see your righteousness, and all kings your glory; you will be called by a new name that the mouth of the LORD will bestow. You will be a crown of splendor in the LORD's hand, a royal diadem in the hand of your God" (Isa. 62:2-3).

God will surely carry out all these objectives for His people, Israel, during the Millennium. Then the prayer of the sons of Korah will find its complete fulfillment: "Love and faithfulness meet together; righteousness and peace kiss each other. Faithfulness springs forth from the earth, and righteousness looks down from heaven. The LORD will indeed give what is good, and our land will yield its harvest. Righteousness goes before him and prepares the way for his steps" (Ps. 85:10-13).

Jeremiah 3:14-18 looks to a future restoration that will include Israel and Judah as one people living in peace and righteousness in the land, but without the ark of the old covenant, and therefore under the new covenant in the millennial age. Though Jeremiah prophesies a return from Babylon after seventy years—which was fulfilled—he also looks ahead to a future return, not just from Babylon, but from all nations (Jer. 29:14). He also sees the Messiah, God's righteous Branch, coming to establish David's throne eternally and to make Jerusalem worthy of the name "The LORD Our Righteousness" (Jer. 33:14-16).

GENTILES' INVOLVEMENT

Amos also saw that the restoration of Israel would involve Gentiles. "'In that day I will restore David's fallen tent. I will repair its broken places, restore its ruins, and build it as it used to be, so that they may possess the remnant of Edom and all the nations that bear my name,' declares the LORD, who will do these things" (Amos 9:11-12). This passage refers to the restoration of David's twelve-tribe kingdom under the Messiah, with His rule over converted nations or peoples who are blessed by Israel and now bear God's name. The remnant of Edom is representative of those who are left of the former enemies of Israel, or of all the peoples of the world who are left after the Tribulation and who come to be possessed by or belong to Israel.[14]

Zephaniah 3:9 confirms this: "'Then will I purify the lips of the peoples, that all of them may call on the name of the LORD and serve him shoulder to shoulder.'"

Surely these great prophecies describe "an unusual order of incomparable splendor on the earth. . . . If these are only figurative and symbolical, then the

---

[14]The Greek Septuagint translation reads, "*So that the remnant of men* [Gk. *anthrōpōn,* "of humankind"] *and all the nations that bear my name may seek the Lord.*" James, the brother of Jesus, in quoting this passage also used "the remnant of men [humankind]" (Acts 15:17). Since the Hebrew was originally written without vowels, the same word (*'dm*) could mean either Edom or humankind (Heb. *'adam*). Many believe later Jews changed *'adam* to *'edom* simply because the Christians drew attention to it in Acts 15:17. The Dead Sea Scrolls give evidence that the Septuagint must have translated an early Hebrew text.

mountain of the divinely inspired Word has labored and brought forth only a mouse of reality."[15]

The disciples also focused on Israel when they asked Jesus just before His ascension, "'Lord, are you at this time going to restore the kingdom to Israel?'" (Acts 1:6). If, as amillennialists and postmillennialists teach, the Church has replaced Israel and there will be no millennial kingdom for Israel on earth, this would have been the perfect place for Jesus to say so. But He did not. He simply said, "'It is not for you to know the times or dates the Father has set by his own authority.'" Therefore, the only question having to do with the restoration of the kingdom of Israel is about when. For Jesus implied that the Father would indeed "restore the kingdom to Israel."

Paul saw in the fullness of the salvation of Israel great riches for the world (Rom. 11:12). God has not rejected His people. Paul loved even those Jews who were his enemies so much that he would have been willing to spend eternity in hell himself if that could have guaranteed their salvation (Rom. 9:3). His "heart's desire and prayer to God for the Israelites" was "that they may be saved" (Rom. 10:1). And he foresaw a time after "the full number of the Gentiles has come in" when "all Israel will be saved" (Rom. 11:25-27).

That Paul is speaking of national Israel is clear by the context, which speaks of those who "are loved on account of the patriarchs" (11:28), and by the fact that Paul draws attention to his own ancestry and tribal affiliation as proof that he is an Israelite (Rom. 11:1). Therefore, in the Millennium, though Israel will become part of the Church (for there will be one flock and one shepherd [John 10:16]), Israel will still be Israel. The Millennium will also see the fulfillment of the specific prophecies that concern the people

---

[15]W. R. White, "Here and Now and Yet to Be," in *Last Things,* ed. H. Leo Eddleman (Grand Rapids: Zondervan Publishing House, 1969), 77.

and nation. This does not mean there will be competition between Israel and the rest of the Church. Each will bless the other, for "God had planned something better for us so that only together with us would they be made perfect" (Heb. 11:40). This perfection of God's purposes for Israel and the Church will find fulfillment as they are together under Jesus Christ, their Lord and King, as He reigns over all the earth during the Millennium.[16]

A RESTORED EARTH

The Millennium will be a time of peace and blessing, with righteousness prevailing everywhere (Isa. 2:2-4; Mic. 4:3-5; Zech. 9:10). The Holy Spirit will do a work of restoration. Even the natural world will reflect the order, perfection, and beauty God intended His creation to have (Isa. 29:17; Joel 2:22-27; Amos 9:13; Zech. 14:8).[17] "The creation itself will be liberated from its bondage to decay and brought into the glorious freedom of the children of God" (Rom. 8:21). The deserts will blossom and the animal world will be changed. This will be a work of creation, for the very natures of the animals will be changed and all conflict will cease (Ps. 72:16; Isa. 11:6-8; 35:1,6,9; 55:13; Ezek. 34:25-27). The present violence and corruption will be gone. "They will neither harm nor destroy on all my holy mountain, for the earth will be full of the knowledge of the LORD as the waters cover the sea" (Isa. 11:9). "'No longer will a man teach his neighbor, or a man his brother, saying, "Know the LORD," because they will all know me, from the least of them to the greatest'" (Jer. 31:34). As the apostle Paul said, "Now we see but a poor reflection as in a mirror; then we shall see face to face. Now I know in

---

[16]Daniel C. Gruber, *My Heart's Desire* (Springfield, Mo.: General Council of the Assemblies of God, Intercultural Ministries Department, 1991), 17.

[17]Pss. 96:11-13; 98:7-9; Isa. 14:7-8; 35:1-2,6-7; 51:3; 55:12-13; Rom. 8:18-23.

part; then I shall know fully, even as I am fully known" (1 Cor. 13:12).

This too will certainly involve the work of the Holy Spirit, for the Spirit is the one who guides "into all truth" (John 16:13). He will continue to be with the transformed believers, "forever" (John 14:16) to energize, empower, equip, and activate us. The people of the restored Israel will also be filled with the Spirit (Ezek. 36:27; 37:14). Joel 2:28-32 shows a continuing outpouring, not just on the Day of Pentecost, not just on Israel, but on "all flesh" (Heb. *kol basar*), which according to Old Testament usage means Gentiles, the nations, or all humankind.[18]

Because of the multitude of Israel and of Gentile believers who are transformed, the Holy Spirit's work in the Millennium will be more powerful and more wonderful than ever (Isa. 35:10; 51:11; Ezek. 11:19; Joel 2:18-32). We have a first installment of this now, but then we shall enjoy a greater fullness in connection with the Lord's return and the restoration of Israel in the land. What worship and praise, what spiritual fervor, what glorious gifts, what holy love, the Spirit will minister through us all! What joy and peace He will bring! No wonder our spirits groan for that day to come (Romans 8:23-24).

BELIEVERS JUDGING AND REIGNING WITH CHRIST

Jesus gave many promises to assure us that He will be continually present with us. "'Because I live, you also will live. On that day you will realize that I am in my Father, and you are in me, and I am in you'" (John 14:19-20). Paul taught that "when Christ, who is [our] life, appears, then [we] also will appear with him in glory" (Col. 3:4). The emphasis is that we will be with Christ.

---

[18]Walter C. Kaiser, Jr., *The Uses of the Old Testament in the New* (Chicago: Moody Press, 1985), 96-100.

A THEOCRACY

The government will be a theocracy, that is, ruled by God.[19] The New Testament focus is on the divine King who is still the God-Man and is now at the right hand of the Father waiting for the time of His coming. The millennial kingdom is Christ's kingdom and He will be personally present. He will restore David's throne and will reign. "He must reign until he has put all his enemies under his feet" (1 Cor. 15:25). This reign of Christ is necessary for Him to fulfill all of God's purpose in creation and redemption.[20] He will right all wrongs. Martyrs and others who were condemned unjustly in this life will be vindicated and blessed.

In His letters to the churches in the Roman province of Asia, Jesus also promised that to those who overcome He "will give the right to sit with" Him on His throne, just as He overcame and sat down with His Father on His throne (Rev. 3:21). Now saints may suffer and must take up their cross. But the Millennium will bring an end to all human suffering and oppression, for all oppressors will have joined the armies of the Antichrist, to be slain by Jesus as He speaks the word when He comes in His glory.

Because "the saints will judge the world" and "we will judge angels" (1 Cor. 6:2–3), and because those seated on thrones are "given authority to judge" (Rev. 20:4), some believe they will spend time in the Millennium reviewing cases and drawing attention to the righteous judgment of God.[21] However, it is not until the Great White Throne that the books are opened and God's righteous decisions declared. It is more likely that the word "judge" is used here in the Old

---

[19]Government by God (Gk. *theos*).

[20]French L. Arrington, *Paul's Aeon Theology in 1 Corinthians* (Washington, D.C.: University Press of America, 1978), 127.

[21]William E. Biederwolf, *The Second Coming Bible* (Grand Rapids: Baker Book House, 1972), 695–96.

Testament sense of "rule" and is parallel to the word "reigned" in the latter part of the verse.

Others suppose that all unbelievers will be killed along with the armies of the nations that gather under the Antichrist at Armageddon. This would mean that only the saints will be present on earth during the Millennium and that their ruling and reigning simply means they will enjoy the privileges of kings and priests who serve God. Then, since believers, with their new bodies, share in Christ's triumph and will never be tempted by Satan again, there would have to be a resurrection of the unbelievers at the end of the Millennium for some to follow Satan when he is released.

There is indication, however, that the final destruction of the Tribulation period applies to the armies of the Antichrist, not to the entire population of the world. The fact that Satan is bound, locked and sealed in the abyss "to keep him from deceiving the nations anymore until the thousand years" are ended (Rev. 20:2–3), clearly indicates that there will be those of the nations of the world still left on earth who could be subject to his temptations if he were present. Zechariah 12:1 through 14:21 deals with the Battle of Armageddon and the defeat of Israel's enemies. All the nations will be gathered against Jerusalem (Zech. 12:3). Then, after they are defeated, "the survivors from all the nations that have attacked Jerusalem will go up year after year to worship the King, the LORD Almighty, and to celebrate the Feast of Tabernacles" (Zech. 14:16). Just how many will be survivors we are not told. There may be millions.

THE FEAST OF TABERNACLES

The requirement to celebrate the Feast of Tabernacles, also called the Feast of Ingathering (Exod. 23:16; 34:22), is significant. In ancient Israel the people gathered in Jerusalem for seven days, living in temporary huts made of branches to remind themselves of the forty years spent in the wilderness. By this they also declared they were just as much dependent on God while living in the Promised Land as they were in the desert when they depended on the manna and the water from the rock. For the survivors of the Tribulation period to celebrate the Feast of Tabernacles, then, means they will be identifying themselves with Israel's history, so that it will become part of their history as people of God. At the same time they will be declaring their dependence on God.

The Feast of Tabernacles also celebrated the conclusion of the summer harvest. The people from all nations coming up in obedience to worship would also be coming in faith, for God does not want any worship except that done in Spirit and in truth. Thus, this will be a final harvest of souls and at least a partial fulfillment of the prophecy that "at the name of Jesus every knee should bow, in heaven and on earth and under the earth, and every tongue confess that Jesus Christ is Lord, to the glory of God the Father" (Phil. 2:10-11).

There will, however, be some resistance to this, for Zechariah goes on to say, "If any of the people of the earth do not go up to Jerusalem to worship the King, the LORD Almighty, they will have no rain" (14:17). Furthermore, in spite of the ideal conditions, there will still be cause for punishment and death. "He who dies at a hundred will be thought a mere youth; he [the sinner] who fails to reach a hundred will be considered accursed" (Isa. 65:20). This implies that during Christ's millennial reign on earth those born to the survivors of the Tribulation will still find it necessary to choose to follow Christ in faith and obedience.

Whatever problems sinners may cause will be dealt with in true righteousness and justice (Isa. 11:3-5). With Satan bound, evil will have no power and believers will enjoy perfect peace. What a joy it will be to live without any fear of violence or evil of any kind. Even though the final overthrow of Satan and the end of evil will not come until after the Millennium at the Great White Throne, believers will not fear. They will know that God's victory over Satan will be final, and they will look forward to sharing in His final triumph.[22]

STUDY QUESTIONS

1. What did Jesus say that shows He looks forward to His kingdom here on earth?

2. What are some of the Old Testament passages that speak of future blessings on this earth?

3. Why do so many people spiritualize Old Testament passages that speak of situations and events that call for a millennial kingdom on this earth?

4. What are the chief reasons for believing God still has a place for Israel in the future Kingdom?

5. How will Gentile believers be involved with Israel in the millennial kingdom?

6. What are the ways Ezekiel's vision of the millennial temple has been interpreted, and which interpretation do you believe fits the whole picture the Bible gives of the Millennium?

7. What kind of an environment can we expect in the Millennium, and how will it be brought about?

8. What kind of government will be exercised in the Millennium, and what will it be like?

9. What is the significance of celebrating the Feast of Tabernacles during the Millennium?

10. How can we best prepare for the Millennium?

---

[22]Philip Mauro suggests that because the phrase "thousand years" occurs six times in Rev. 20, "The millennium, with all its blessings, nevertheless *comes short of perfection. . . .* It is not the new heaven and the new earth. It is not the eternal dwelling place of God and His children." Mauro, *Things Which Soon Must Come to Pass: A Commentary on the Book of Revelation* (Swengel, Pa.: Reiner Publications, 1974), 520.

Chapter Seven

The Final Judgment

The Book of Revelation gives no details of the Millennium, probably because previous prophecies are sufficient. After the thousand years Satan will be released, possibly to bring a final vindication of the justice of God. That is, although people will have experienced the wonderful rule of Christ, they will still follow Satan at their first opportunity. This shows that with or without the knowledge of what Christ's reign is like, unsaved people rebel. In justice God can do nothing but separate them from His blessings forever.

The Bible does not identify those deceived by Satan. Some believe they are people born during the Millennium who do not choose to follow Christ. Others believe they are descendants of people in remote parts of the world who were not destroyed by the plagues of the Tribulation or by the Battle of Armageddon. They are a great number, "like the sand on the seashore" (Rev. 20:8), and they march across the breadth of the earth to surround "the camp of God's people, the city he loves," that is, the earthly Jerusalem.

The nations of the earth who are gathered for this final battle are called Gog and Magog. Although the names are borrowed from Ezekiel 38 and 39, the circumstances described in Revelation are different from those described in Ezekiel. It seems logical therefore

215

that those people described in Revelation are simply a Gog and Magog type of people.

Satan, the great deceiver, also deceives himself into believing he can yet defeat God. But his final attempt will fail. Fire from heaven will devour the entirety of the armies he gathers. There will never be any further rebellion against God and His love.

THE NECESSITY OF JUDGMENT

Someone has pointed out that the world wants to hold on to a "fairy tale attitude" that everything will turn out all right in the end and there will be no judgment. Actually, only those who acknowledge Jesus as the Son of God and live in His perfect love need not fear punishment, having instead confidence on Judgment Day (1 John 4:15-18).

A BIBLICAL EMPHASIS

The Bible from beginning to end has an emphasis on judgment. God first brought judgment on the serpent, the woman, and the man when the latter two ate the forbidden fruit (Gen. 3:14-19). From that point on, judgment by a holy, just, and righteous God is one of the major themes of the Bible. The prophets spoke often of judgment to come. Jesus himself spoke of it frequently and very clearly, though He did speak of different degrees of punishment: "'That servant who knows his master's will and does not get ready or does not do what his master wants will be beaten with many blows. But the one who does not know and does things deserving punishment will be beaten with few blows'" (Luke 12:47-48). Jesus also spoke of judgment in the present: "'Whoever does not believe stands condemned already because he has not believed in the name of God's one and only Son'" (John 3:18; cf. 9:39; 12:31; 16:11). However, this does not rule out future judgment. He speaks of the last day and a future judgment that He has been given authority over (John 5:27,29; 12:48).

Peter, in his second letter, chapter 3, skips over Christ's return and the establishment of His millennial kingdom and goes to the judgments bringing in the new heavens and the new earth in order to point out how much we need a reminder of these things (2 Pet. 3:1-10). Then he emphasizes that the coming end of the present created order of things is one of the greatest incentives to godliness (3:11-18).

It is important for us to keep in mind "the words spoken in the past by the holy prophets and the command given by our Lord and Savior through [the] apostles" (2 Pet. 3:2). They are all part of the one revelation and the one divine plan of redemption. We need this constant reminder of coming judgments, first, because "in the last days scoffers will come, scoffing and following their own evil desires. They will say, 'Where is this "coming" he promised?'" (2 Pet. 3:3-4).

Paul gave a similar warning:

There will be terrible times in the last days. People will be lovers of themselves, lovers of money, boastful, proud, abusive, disobedient to their parents, ungrateful, unholy, without love, unforgiving, slanderous, without self-control, brutal, not lovers of the good, treacherous, rash, conceited, lovers of pleasure rather than lovers of God— having a form of godliness but denying its power . . . while evil men and impostors will go from bad to worse, deceiving and being deceived (2 Tim. 3:1-5,13).

The Spirit clearly says that in later times some will abandon the faith and follow deceiving spirits and things taught by demons. Such teachings come through hypocritical liars, whose consciences have been seared as with a hot iron [that is, branded, being like a criminal's conscience] (1 Tim. 4:1-2).

A MOCKERY OF THE PROMISE

The scoffers focus their mockery on the promise of Christ's coming and say, "'Ever since our fathers died, everything goes on as it has since the beginning of creation'" (2 Pet. 3:4). Their attitude is like that of those in Old Testament times who scoffed at the warnings of judgment on Judah and Jerusalem and thought, "'The Lord will do nothing, either good or bad'" (Zeph. 1:12). They suppose that God will never intervene in this world's affairs and forget that though God "is slow to anger," He is "great in power" and "will not leave the guilty unpunished" (Nah. 1:3). They are something like modern deists who look at God merely as a great First Cause, but refuse to believe He has been present since He set the universe in motion.

Many who call themselves theological liberals hold to this view. Some follow Paul Tillich (1886–1965), who considered God an impersonal "ground of being," and refuse to see the hand of God in human life and history. Consequently, they attempt to explain away miracles and try to make God's promises of healing and the baptism in the Holy Spirit null and void during the present age.

Actually, fallen human nature does not want God to intervene. Sinners have taken God off the throne and put self on the throne. They want to say, "I am the master of my fate. I am the captain of my soul." But they are not the free spirits they think they are, for they are slaves of sin.

A LESSON FROM NOAH'S FLOOD

The scoffers who mock the promise of Christ's coming and who suppose that time itself will go on forever shut their eyes to the fact that God has indeed intervened in the history of humankind. They "deliberately forget that long ago by God's word the heavens existed and the earth was formed out of water and by water. By these waters also the world of that time was deluged and destroyed. By the same word the present heavens and earth are reserved for fire, being kept for the day of judgment and the destruction of ungodly men" (2 Pet. 3:5-7).

God's word brought the heavens into existence. His word also brought the dry land out of the primeval ocean (Gen. 1:9–10), for it was all formed by His word. "Formed" (2 Pet. 3:5) also means "holding together," as in Colossians 1:15–17, where the Bible gives us further insight into the role of Jesus as the living Word of God: "He is the image of the invisible God, the firstborn [highest ruler, Lord] over all creation. For by him all things were created: things in heaven and on earth, visible and invisible, whether thrones or powers or rulers or authorities; all things were created by him and for him. He is before all things, and in him all things hold together." That is, all He would have to do is to remove His hand and the whole universe would fall apart.

By the same word of God (Gen. 6:7,13,17) the inhabited world that came into being as a result of God's creation was flooded with water and destroyed. Thus, God brought an end to the world of that day. Clearly He did intervene after creation.

What the Bible teaches about Noah's flood still escapes the notice of many today. Many modern geologists follow a philosophy of uniformitarianism, which supposes that all processes we now observe in nature have always operated in the same uniform way back through geologic history.[1] They deny any earthly catastrophic interventions, such as the Flood in the past. However, there is no way of proving that the present rates of all processes have always been the same. Moreover, there are evidences of relatively sudden changes in the earth's crust.

The Bible, however, is not concerned about the geologic effects of the Flood. Peter sees it as an evidence that God does judge sin. The world of Noah's day was characterized by two things: corruption and violence (Gen. 6:5,11,13). Except for Noah and his sons, the pattern of humankind's thoughts, inten-

---

[1]Promoted by Sir Charles Lyell (1797–1875), a British geologist.

tions, purposes, and plans was "only evil all the time" (Gen. 6:5). People were not only corrupt, they were actively corrupting their lifestyle more and more. They were not satisfied with the immoral state they were in. They were working at it to make it worse (Gen. 6:12). No wonder God drew the line and said, "'My Spirit will not contend with man [humankind] forever, for he is mortal; his [humankind's] days will be a hundred and twenty years'" (Gen. 6:3). That is, God in His long-suffering and mercy gave humankind 120 years more of grace and then sent the Flood as a judgment on sin.

THE CERTAINTY OF JUDGMENT

The prophets saw a similar limit to God's long-suffering in His dealings with Israel and Judah. When Amos saw visions of locusts and fire as God's judgment on the northern kingdom of Israel, he prayed in humble intercession for the people, and God did not send those judgments. But then God showed Amos a vision of a plumb line (a weight on the end of a string used to see if a wall was perpendicular). If the plumb line showed the wall was leaning out of line, the wall would have to come down. So God was going to hold up His plumb line to Israel, and because of their idolatry and sin, the nation would have to go into exile. God would "spare them no longer" (Amos 7:8,17). That generation was indeed the last generation of the Northern Kingdom. They lived to see the Assyrians destroy Samaria in 722 B.C., and then they were exiled from their land just as God had said.

The Southern Kingdom, Judah, did not learn from this. In the last days of Judah, God told Jeremiah to quit praying, or interceding, for that nation as well (Jer. 7:16; 11:14; 14:11). Even if the greatest intercessors who ever lived, Moses and Samuel, were to stand before God interceding for Judah, He would not change His mind about sending judgment (Jer. 15:1–2). So Jeremiah lived to see the three stages of exile under Nebuchadnezzar (605, 597, and 586 B.C.) as well as the destruction of Jerusalem and the temple (586 B.C.).

Throughout the Bible we see that God sooner or later brings judgment on a sinning people; a sinful world can expect the same. God did promise Noah He would not send another worldwide flood: "'As long as the earth endures, seedtime and harvest, cold and heat, summer and winter, day and night will never cease'" (Gen. 8:22). He also gave the rainbow a new meaning: as a covenant sign indicating that we can indeed expect the uniform processes of nature to continue without further cataclysms while the earth endures. We do not need to be afraid of any natural calamity bringing an end to the total population of the world again. But this does not mean that God will never judge the world again. The present heavens and earth "by the same word" of God that brought about the Flood "are reserved for fire, being kept for the day of judgment and destruction of ungodly men" (2 Pet. 3:7). That judgment refers to what will happen at the Great White Throne.

THE WHITE THRONE JUDGMENT

After Satan is cast into the lake of fire, a huge white throne appears—white because it radiates the holiness, majesty, and glory of God (Rev. 20:11). It is God's final judgment throne. Yet the one who sits on it here must be the glorified King of kings and Lord of lords, our Lord Jesus Christ. Popular Jewish ideas in New Testament times did not conceive of the Messiah as the final Judge of the world, though they did expect Him to share in shattering the pagan world (Ps. 2:8-9). Jesus, however, said, "'The Father judges no one, but has entrusted all judgment to the Son, that all may honor the Son just as they honor the Father'" (John 5:22-23; cf. 5:27).

JESUS THE JUDGE

Paul declared that God "has set a day when he will judge the world with justice by the man he has appointed. He has given proof of this to all men by raising him from the dead" (Acts 17:31). In Romans 2:16 we read also that "God will judge men's secrets through Jesus Christ." Jesus, therefore, will be the Mediator between God and humankind in this final judgment, just as He is now Mediator in our redemption (1 Tim. 2:5) and was also in creation (John 1:3). The fact that Jesus is the final Judge also shows that He shares the majesty of God and that He is more than a Teacher among other teachers, more than a Guide among other guides. Consequently, the other religions of the world have no validity and can lead only to final rejection at the Great White Throne.[2]

THE JUDGMENT OF THE DEAD

Standing before the throne are all the dead, "great and small," that is, regardless of their station in life on earth. (This group does not include those mentioned in Rev. 20:4, for they are already resurrected with new immortal bodies that cannot die or even decay.) They have been resurrected to judgment. Since resurrection is bodily, they will have some sort of body, but it will not be like the resurrection body of believers, for unbelievers can, from their sinful nature, reap only destruction (Gk. *phthoran*, "ruin," "corruption"). They will come out of their graves (Dan. 12:2; John 5:28-29) and be judged by their works (recorded in divinely kept records, undoubted-

---

[2]Willibald Beyschlag, *New Testament Theology,* trans. Neil Buchanan, vol. 2 (Edinburgh, Scotland: T. & T. Clark, 1895), 1919.

ly including their rejection of Christ and allegiance to Satan, as well as all their public and private sins).[3]

The Book of Life will also be opened there, probably as evidence that their names are not in it. That is, Jesus will do more than pass sentence on the wicked. He will provide answers to questions concerning the quality of God's grace, righteousness, justice, care, patience, and love, all against the background of God's wrath against sin and evil. As Charles Ryrie points out, "This judgment does not prove whether Heaven or Hell is to be the final destiny of those being judged; it is a judgment to prove that Hell is the deserved destiny."[4] Then, with the casting of death and hell into the lake of fire, God's righteousness will be finally triumphant, and righteousness and peace will be established forever in the new heavens and the new earth.

Some see the judging according to their works as a contradiction of the Bible's teaching on justification by faith. But since we are saved by grace through faith, justification is a gift by which God looks at us as though we had never sinned. However, God's gifts are truly ours only when we take them and put them into practice. Faith must work, or express itself, through love (Gal. 5:6), and faith is not real unless it is shown through action.

If we really believe, we will care about others, about their needs and especially their sufferings. We will not water down what the Bible teaches "to make it less demanding."[5] Our works then become evidence of the reality of our faith. It is also true that

---

[3]Since these are works, or deeds, done in the present life it is clear that there is no second chance for salvation after death. See John Miley, *Systematic Theology,* vol. 2 (New York: Hunt & Eaton, 1893; repr. Peabody, Mass.: Hendrickson Publishers, 1989), 436-37.

[4]Charles C. Ryrie, *Basic Theology* (Wheaton, Ill.: Victor Books, 1986), 350.

[5]Stephen Travis, *The Jesus Hope* (Downers Grove, Ill.: InterVarsity Press, 1974), 64.

motives are important in the judging of works. Some who have never been found guilty of any crime by human criminal courts may be filled with hate, bitterness, jealousy, or smug, self-centered pride. This will be revealed "on the day when God will judge men's secrets through Jesus Christ" (Rom. 2:16). "'There is nothing concealed that will not be disclosed, or hidden that will not be made known'" (Luke 12:2). "'Men will have to give account on the day of judgment for every careless word they have spoken'" (Matt. 12:36). On that day "every knee will bow before [the Lord] and every tongue will confess to God" and "each one will give an account of *himself* to God" (Rom. 14:11-12).

Some speculate that those who are saved during the Millennium (thus, after the judgment seat of Christ) may also appear at the Great White Throne to receive their rewards. However, the Bible does not say so in any passage.[6] It seems probable that they will receive the fullness of their salvation, including their new bodies, and join the rest of the glorified saints as soon as they are saved and commit themselves to Christ.

OTHER JUDGMENTS

The Bible speaks of other judgments, but without giving details of the time or place. Paul mentioned that the saints (all true believers, for they are dedicated to the worship and service of the Lord) will judge the world and angels, contrasting it to judging in this life (1 Cor. 6:2-3). This may take place during the Millennium.

Some take Matthew 25:31-46, the separation of the people "one from another as a shepherd separates the sheep from the goats" (v. 32), to be a special judgment of the nations at the beginning of the Millennium. It is a judgment of works, recognizing that

---

[6]William E. Biederwolf, *The Second Coming Bible* (Grand Rapids: Baker Book House, 1972), 707.

whatever is done or fails to be done for others is done or fails to be done for Christ. Whatever we do, we are to do as unto the Lord. The word "nations"[7] means peoples, not national states. The acts are acts done by individuals who care for Christ's brothers (and sisters) or who neglect them.[8] The results are an inheritance for those who are the blessed and an eternal fire for those who are not, a fire prepared for the devil and his angels. That is, the final state, not the Millennium, is in view in this picture.

James Oliver Buswell makes an interesting suggestion. Since the scene is "of vast cosmic perspective" it may be that Jesus put both the judgment seat of Christ and the Great White Throne in the one picture for the sake of the lesson that judgment means separation from one another as well as separation from God. Then, just as the Old Testament prophets did not show the time difference between the first and second comings of Christ, Jesus does not indicate the time difference between the two great judgments.[9]

Chapter 7
The Final
Judgment

SERIOUS WARNINGS

Christians must take these judgments seriously. "'If it is hard for the righteous to be saved, what will become of the ungodly and the sinner?'" (1 Peter 4:18).

If we deliberately keep on sinning after we have received the knowledge of the truth, no sacrifice for sins is left,

---

[7]Gk. *ethnos, ethnē* (pl.), has a broad meaning, covering any group of people. God's people are a holy *ethnos* (1 Pet. 2:9). *Ethnē* was often used to mean "Gentiles."

[8]Some hold that the "brothers" are the Jewish people. However, Jesus consistently called His own followers His brothers (Matt. 12:46-50; 28:10; Mark 3:31-35; Luke 8:19-21; John 20:17; Rom. 8:29; Heb. 2:11). His own disciples are the "little flock," the least ones, to whom He is pleased to give the Kingdom (Luke 12:32).

[9]James Oliver Buswell, Jr., *A Systematic Theology of the Christian Religion,* vol. 2 (Grand Rapids: Zondervan Publishing House, 1963), 422-23.

but only a fearful expectation of judgment and of raging fire that will consume the enemies of God. Anyone who rejected the law of Moses died without mercy on the testimony of two or three witnesses. How much more severely do you think a man deserves to be punished who has trampled the Son of God under foot, who has treated as an unholy thing the blood of the covenant that sanctified him, and who has insulted the Spirit of grace? For we know him who said, "It is mine to avenge; I will repay," and again, "The Lord will judge his people." It is a dreadful thing to fall into the hands of the living God (Heb. 10:26-31).

It is possible for those who were once saved to "shrink back" (Heb. 10:39) and be destroyed, though Hebrews encourages us not to throw away our confidence, but to persevere and continue to be one of those who believe and are saved (Heb. 10:35-36,38-39).

STUDY QUESTIONS

1. What are possible reasons why Satan will be released for a short time after the Millennium?

2. Why will it be necessary for God to bring final judgment on unbelievers?

3. Why does the Bible keep reminding us of coming judgments?

4. What lessons does the New Testament draw from the account of Noah's flood?

5. What lessons should we learn from God's judgments on the kingdoms of Israel and Judah?

6. Who will be the judge and who will be judged at the Great White Throne?

7. On what basis will people be judged at the Great White Throne?

8. What other judgments does the Bible indicate will take place?

9. Why does the Bible describe these judgments for us?

Chapter Eight

The Final State of the Wicked

God has never been reluctant to save anyone. He "wants all men to be saved and to come to a knowledge of the truth" (1 Tim. 2:4). He does not want "anyone to perish," but wants "everyone to come to repentance" (2 Pet. 3:9). He has not even prepared a special place for those who are faithless. He simply consigns them to "the eternal fire prepared for the devil and his angels" (Matt. 25:41). Consequently, sinners who do not accept God's offer of salvation and life through Christ are condemned (John 3:18) and, unless they repent, will become objects of God's wrath. He is a God who will do right (Gen. 18:25), and He will deal justly with those who choose to reject His love and go their own way.

GOD'S HOLY WRATH

God is holy. He loves the sinner and reaches out to all of us. But He will pour out His wrath on sin and on everything that is evil, and He will do it in a way that will reveal His justice, power, wisdom, and glory. The Bible uses two words for God's divine anger: *thumos* and *orgē*. *Thumos* is used of specific outpourings of God's wrath (Rev. 14:10,19; 15:7; 16:1,19; 19:15). *Orgē* is used of the wrath that is God's continuing righteous attitude toward sin and evil.[1] Why evil exists, God knows, even though we do not fully under-

---

[1]David Ewert, *And Then Comes the End* (Scottdale, Pa.: Herald Press, 1980), 136–37.

stand. But evil will be finally defeated, and the lake of fire "is the sphere and climax of its final defeat." Therefore we can be sure that God will ultimately overrule evil and fulfill "His own just and righteous" purposes.[2] His wrath must fall on all who "show contempt for the riches of his kindness, tolerance and patience, . . . those who are self-seeking and who reject the truth and follow evil" (Rom. 2:4,8). In fact, God's wrath falls only on unbelievers (Rom. 5:9; 1 Thess. 1:10; cf. 5:9). It is different from the discipline the Lord gives to those He loves.[3] His discipline may be painful, but "it produces a harvest of righteousness and peace for those who have been trained by it" (Heb. 12:5–11; cf. 1 Cor. 11:32). Now is the day of salvation for people, who, because of sin, are by nature the objects of God's wrath. By accepting Christ they will be changed, for God is rich in mercy and His great love has made provision for our salvation (Eph. 2:3–5).

When God's wrath falls on unbelievers, however, it will be too late. The Bible gives no hint that His wrath will bring repentance or draw people to Him. Revelation 9:20–21 specifically states that the rest of humankind who are not killed by the plagues of the trumpet judgments will not repent. The plagues of the bowls of God's wrath will only cause people to curse God (Rev. 16:9,11,21). They effectively cut themselves off from His love.

John the Baptist, in line with the Old Testament prophets, warned of a "coming wrath" (Matt. 3:7), but without seeing the time between the first and second comings of Christ. Jesus and Paul both saw that sinners are already objects of the wrath of God, and judgment may fall on them even in this life (John 3:36; Rom. 1:18 through 3:20; Eph. 2:3; 5:6). But there is also a "coming wrath" (1 Thess. 1:10). It in-

---

[2]Francis J. Hall, *Eschatology* (New York: Longmans, Green & Co., 1922), 217.

[3]William V. Crockett, "Wrath That Endures Forever," *Journal of the Evangelical Theological Society* 34:2 (June 1991): 199.

cludes the wrath poured out during the Tribulation,[4] but it will finally result in eternal punishment in the lake of fire.[5]

THE DESTINY OF THE LOST

DARKNESS

The Bible describes the final destiny of the lost as terrible beyond imagination.[6] It is "outer darkness" for those who choose to love darkness rather than light (John 3:19-20; cf. Matt. 22:13, KJV). In that darkness there will be "weeping and gnashing of teeth." That is, there will be frustration and remorse as the lost continually suffer the wrath of God and as they think of all the sin and wrong in a life that could have been blessed of God but was wasted by their own choices (Matt. 8:12; 22:13; 25:30; Luke 13:28; Rom. 2:8-9; Jude 13).[7]

ETERNAL FIRE

The destiny of the lost is further described as a "fiery furnace" (Matt. 13:42,50) where the fire by its

---

[4]See chap. 4, pp. 124-25.

[5]Ewert, *Then Comes the End,* 137.

[6]Unbelievers do not like the idea of endless torment. Most cults also discard that idea. See Donald G. Bloesch, *Essentials of Evangelical Theology,* vol. 2 (New York: Harper & Row, Publishers, 1979), 219.

[7]Universalists say a good God would not send anyone to hell. Unitarians say there is too much good in every person for God to send anyone to hell. Both ignore the holiness and justice of God. A good earthly father would not give a glass of milk with an ounce of strychnine in it to his children saying, "There is too much good in this milk to throw it out." So our Heavenly Father must cast out those who have refused the only antidote for sin, the blood of Jesus. See Harry Buis, *The Doctrine of Eternal Punishment* (Philadelphia: Presbyterian & Reformed Publishing Co., 1957), 112-22, for a discussion of this. Universalism is dangerous because in effect it denies "the existence of any ultimate risk in the moral life." J. H. Leckie, *The World to Come and Final Destiny,* 2d ed., rev. (Edinburgh, Scotland: T. & T. Clark, 1922), 286.

very nature is unquenchable and never goes out (Mark 9:43; Jude 7). It causes eternal loss, or everlasting destruction (Gk. *olethron,* "destruction," "ruin"; 2 Thess. 1:9), and "the smoke of their torment rises for ever and ever" (Rev. 14:11; cf. 20:10).[8] Jesus called it eternal "punishment" (Gk. *kolasin,* a word used of continual torture; Matt. 25:46). He also used the word *Gehenna* as a term for it (Matt. 5:22,29-30; 10:28;[9] 18:8-9; 23:15,33). *Gehenna* is an Aramaic name for the Valley of Hinnom, a narrow ravine to the west and south of Jerusalem. During the decline of Judah's kingdom, apostate Jews offered their children there in a fiery sacrifice to the Ammonite god Molech (2 Kings 16:3; 21:6; 23:10; Jer. 7:31-32; 32:35). Jews in New Testament times made it a city dump, and a fire was always burning there, so Jesus used it figuratively for the place of final judgment, the lake of fire.[10] Its flames of burning sulfur indicate how painful the fire will be. Surely Jesus would not have warned with such earnestness if there were no such judgment to come.

---

[8]There will be gradations in the intensity of the punishment (Luke 12:47-48), according to their works (Rev. 20:12-13), but no limits as to the time. It will be eternal. Some take "eternal" to mean "age-lasting," but the usage in the New Testament shows it to mean "without end." The same word is used of "eternal life" (Matt. 25:46; John 3:16) and "the eternal God" (Rom. 16:26).

[9]The word "destroy" in 10:28 is the Greek *apolesai,* which speaks of eternal loss, not annihilation. See p. 240.

[10]A heresy spread in the 1920s by Charles H. Pridgeon, *Is Hell Eternal; or Will God's Plan Fail?* 3d ed. (Pittsburgh: Evangelization Society of the Pittsburgh Bible Institute, 1931), identified the fire of 1 Cor. 3:15 with the lake of fire. It suggests that believers who are not holy enough will need to spend some time in the lake of fire. It suggests further that the purpose of the fire is purification and that through it everyone will be saved, including the devil and his demons. This heresy takes the phrase "restitution of all things" (Acts 3:21) out of context, not recognizing that the "all things" include only those things spoken by God's holy prophets. It is hard to see why the Cross would be necessary if the lake of fire could provide another means of salvation.

It will be the place for "the cowardly, the unbeliev-ing, the vile, the murderers, the sexually immoral, those who practice magic arts, the idolaters and all li-ars" (Rev. 21:8). "The cowardly" are mentioned first because they lack the courage and loyalty that are necessary to resist the world, the flesh, and the devil. They include those who join in worshiping the beast and his image. "The unbelieving" are willful unbeliev-ers who reject the truth because they love darkness rather than light. "The vile" are those polluted by the loathsome obscenities of the Babylonian world system (Rev. 17:4–5). "The murderers" include those es-pecially who have killed the martyrs. "The sexually immoral, those who practice magic arts," and "the idolaters" are all part of the false worship that exalts the human and makes people victims of Satan. The "liars" are those who, because they reject Jesus as Lord and Savior, are partakers of the nature of their father the devil, who is "a liar and the father of lies" (John 8:44). These all will be shut out forever from any possibility of entering the New Jerusalem, for they will be "outside" the whole new creation (Rev. 22:15).

The "outer darkness" also indicates they are shut out of the light of God. The faith, hope, and love that remain for us (1 Cor. 13:13) will be forever lacking in that environment.[11] The "rest" we will enjoy will nev-er be available to them, nor will the joy and peace our Lord gives to those who believe. The lake of fire will also be a lonely place, a terrible place, shut off eternally from fellowship with God. Moreover, the wicked's bitterness and gnashing of teeth, as well as

---

[11]A person lacking faith cannot enjoy eternal life in Christ any more than a fish, lacking lungs, can live on dry land. See T. A. Kantonen, *The Christian Hope* (Philadelphia: Muhlenberg Press, 1954), 107. Consequently, there is no hope of final universal sal-vation.

their unchanged fallen nature, will prevent fellowship
with each other.[12]

We can be sure that "sin's punishment will be real
and searching. . . . Infinite love and perfect justice
shall measure the cup each must drink."[13] Only believers will be changed, sinners will not. The gnashing of teeth also indicates frustration caused by the
fact that they will still have the same lusts, the same
desires, the same habits, the same self-centeredness,
the same jealousies, the same bitterness—all with no
opportunity to find satisfaction or relief. Everything
that made them unfit for heaven and unfit for fellowship with God will still be present.[14]

As in life they were hardened by threats of punishment, putting up barriers against the appeal of God's
love and Christ's sacrifice on the cross, so they will
become even harder in the flames of the lake of fire.
Just as the sinners curse God on account of the
plagues of the Tribulation (Rev. 16:21), they may also
curse God when they realize what they could have
had of His blessings—for them forever unattainable.
Because they have rejected God's love they must be
abandoned to the consequences of their own corruption.[15]

---

[12]Millard J. Erickson, *Christian Theology* (Grand Rapids: Baker Book House, 1985), 1235.

[13]Vernon C. Grounds, "The Final State of the Wicked," *Journal of the Evangelical Theological Society* 24:2 (September
1981): 219.

[14]I remember hearing someone tell of a sinner who dreamed
he died and approached heaven. In the dream he saw no walls,
no gates, no barriers, nothing but green pastures and beautiful
fruit trees. But when he walked on the pastures, every blade of
grass was like a sword point. When he tasted the fruit it was
like acid devouring his tongue. When he awoke he understood
the lesson that heaven might be even worse than hell to a person who was not prepared and had not been made a new creation in Christ by the Holy Spirit.

[15]Oliver Chase Quick, *Doctrines of the Creed: Their Basis in
Scripture and Their Meaning Today* (London: Nisbet & Co.,
1938), 257.

Nor will there be any escape from or end to the punishment, for Gehenna, the lake of fire, is a place where "their worm does not die, and the fire is not quenched" (Mark 9:48). What Jesus said of Judas can be applied to everyone who ends up there: "'It would be better for him [or her] if he [or she] had not been born'" (Matt. 26:24).

OTHER VIEWS

UNIVERSALISM (RESTORATIONISM)

Origen (ca. 185-254) taught that the punishment of the wicked will be remedial and everyone eventually will be saved, even Satan and his evil angels.[16] *Misericordes,* who were heirs of Origen, believed all human beings would be saved, but not Satan or demons.[17]

Universalists find hope for the salvation of all humankind in passages like those in Timothy that refer to "God our Savior, who wants all men to be saved and to come to a knowledge of the truth. For there is one God and one mediator between God and men, the man Christ Jesus, who gave himself as a ransom for all men" (1 Tim. 2:3-6). But they point only to God's desire and ignore what Paul goes on to say in the same letter, "The sins of some men are obvious, reaching the place of judgment ahead of them; the sins of others trail behind them. . . . People who want to get rich fall into temptation and a trap and into many foolish and harmful desires that plunge men

---

[16]Origen also thought evil could germinate anew and even in heaven it would be possible to fall into sin and go to hell and there recover. This led to the theory of "an endless alternation of falls and recoveries, of hells and heavens." These ideas were "strongly combatted in his own time by the great body of contemporary fathers, and subsequently by the church." William Greenough Thayer Shedd, *The Doctrine of Endless Punishment* (Minneapolis: Klock & Klock Christian Publishers, 1980; repr. from 1886), 2-4.

[17]Jacques Le Goff, *The Birth of Purgatory,* trans. Arthur Goldhammer (Chicago: University of Chicago Press, 1984), 68.

into ruin and destruction" (1 Tim. 5:24; 6:9). Similarly, Romans 11:32 expresses God's desire to have mercy on all. But Romans also shows the severity of God's judgment. Then Ephesians 1:9-10 speaks of the "mystery" of God's will "which he purposed in Christ, to be put into effect when the times will have reached their fulfillment—to bring all things in heaven and on earth together under one head, even Christ." But Paul goes on to explain that those who are "included in Christ" are those who hear the gospel and believe (Eph. 1:13). Those who are not "in Christ" and whose names are not found written in the Book of Life will be thrown into the lake of fire, which is outside the whole new creation.

Colossians 1:19-20 says, "God was pleased to have all his fullness dwell in him [Jesus], and through him to reconcile to himself all things, whether things on earth or things in heaven, by making peace through his blood, shed on the cross." But Paul goes on to say to the Colossians, "He has reconciled you by Christ's physical body through death to present you holy in his sight, without blemish and free from accusation— *if you continue in your faith,* established and firm, not moved from the hope held out in the gospel" (Col. 1:22-23). People can refuse God's purpose. They can turn away from it even after they are converted and reconciled to God.[18] God does not take away our free will either before or after we are saved.

Universalists take the words of Jesus in Matthew 25:46, Mark 9:44-48, and John 5:29 as figurative. They argue that God's love is infinite, His mercy from everlasting to everlasting, and His grace without limits; therefore, He will restore all things and redemption will be universal.[19] But God's justice is the other

---

[18]Stephen Travis, *I Believe in the Second Coming of Jesus* (Grand Rapids: William B. Eerdmans Publishing Co., 1982), 202-3.

[19]Grounds, "Final State of the Wicked," 212.

side of His love. His love calls for a personal relationship with the believer, who freely loves Him. Consequently, those who choose to reject His love are choosing the broad road that leads to destruction.

Another argument is that God could not make anything in vain, therefore everything must ultimately be redeemed. But those who resist divine grace are already under the wrath of God and will come under the future judgment unless they repent and believe in Jesus (Matt. 3:7; Luke 3:7; John 3:18; 1 Thess. 1:10). God has made us accountable, and our choices have eternal consequences.

Universalists also claim that "eternal" (Gk. *aiōnios*) often means "age-long," just as the Hebrew 'olam often means "indefinite time" rather than "infinite time."[20] However, *aiōnios* in its seventy-one occurrences in the New Testament clearly means "eternal" or "perpetual." Sixty-four times it "describes God or divine facts concerning His work of salvation and everlasting life. . . . Furthermore, in 2 Corinthians 4:18 the term *aiōnios* is over against *proskairos* ('temporal,' 'that which lasts for only a period,' cf. Philemon 15)."[21]

They take 1 Corinthians 15:22, "As in Adam all die, so in Christ all will be made alive," to mean that "all" includes every human being. But Paul was talking to believers and adds, "But each in his own turn: Christ, the firstfruits; then, when he comes, those who belong to him" (1 Cor. 15:23). Thus, "all" means all those who have placed their faith in Jesus and fixed their hope on Him.

Some universalize the promise "We will all be changed—in a flash, in the twinkling of an eye, at the last trumpet. For the trumpet will sound, the dead will be raised imperishable, and we will be changed" (1 Cor. 15:51–52). But "the dead" here are not all the

---

[20]See the section "Annihilationism," on pp. 238–40.

[21]Thoralf Gilbrant, ed., *The Complete Biblical Library,* vol. 11 (Springfield, Mo.: Complete Biblical Library, 1990), 128.

dead, but those who will "inherit the kingdom of God," the ones whose "labor in the Lord is not in vain" (1 Cor. 15:50,58).

Universalists ignore "the hardening effect of obstinate persistence in evil, and the power of the human will to resist the law and reject the love of God."[22] The Bible is clear that sin not only must be forgiven, but also must be repented of and forsaken.[23] "Without holiness no one will see the Lord" (Heb. 12:14).

Universalists ignore the fact that the Bible gives no hint of a second chance for salvation after death. Jesus was clear in Luke 16:26—The "great chasm" makes it impossible to leave hell. Hebrews 9:27 is just as explicit, "Man is destined to die once, and after that to face judgment."

"The nature of hell, the nature of heaven, the sinfulness of sin, the cost of the atonement—all these precipitate a denial of any view of restorationism."[24] Further, many of the warnings of Scripture[25] would have no meaning if every person is to be saved anyway.[26] As William Shedd pointed out, Matthew 25:31-46 shows Jesus "could neither have believed nor expected that all men without exception will eventually be holy and happy."

To threaten with "everlasting punishment" a class of persons described as "goats on the left hand" of the Eternal Judge, while knowing at the same time that this class would ultimately have the same holiness and happiness with those described as "sheep on the right hand" of the

---

[22]Frederic W. Farrar, *Eternal Hope* (London: Macmillan & Co., 1878), xvi.

[23]Even a liberal like Lotan Harold DeWolf admits, "It is hard to see how we can be sure that all will ever turn in repentant faith to God." See his *A Theology of the Living Church,* 2d ed., rev. (New York: Harper & Row, Publishers, 1968), 286.

[24]William W. Stevens, *Doctrines of the Christian Religion* (Nashville: Broadman Press, 1967), 410.

[25]Cf. Mark 9:48; John 17:12; Rom. 9:22-23; Phil. 1:28; 3:19; 2 Thess. 2:3; 1 Tim. 6:9; 2 Pet. 2:3; 3:7,16; Rev. 17:8,11; 20:10.

[26]Leckie, *World to Come,* 286.

Judge, would have been both falsehood and folly. The threatening would have been false. For even a long punishment in the future world would not have justified Christ in teaching that this class of mankind are to experience the same retribution with "the devil and his angels"; for these were understood by the Jews, to whom he spoke, to be hopelessly and eternally lost spirits.[27]

God respects every person as a responsible being. He does not overwhelm people and compel them to be saved in spite of themselves.[28] He invites us to faith, but He also says, "How shall we escape if we ignore such a great salvation?" (Heb. 2:3). The arguments of universalism may appeal to the natural mind, but the New Testament does not uphold them.[29] Only those who serve the living and true God will be rescued by Jesus from the coming wrath (1 Thess. 1:10). No one else and nothing else can do that.

MODIFIED RESTORATIONISM

A modified restorationism emphasizes that God will restore everything (Acts 3:21) and that He is making everything new (Rev. 21:5). It also takes the purpose of the lake of fire to be cleansing and proposes that when believers come before the judgment seat of Christ, those who do not measure up or are not holy enough will be sent to the lake of fire for a time to be purified. Then, when the Antichrist, his false prophet, Satan and his angels, and all the wicked are thrown into the lake of fire (which they say is only "age-lasting"), they too will be purified and ultimately saved and restored to full fellowship with God. Those who hold this view claim it is an incentive to holy living, for the horrible torment of the fire that is the

---

[27]Shedd, *Doctrine of Endless Punishment,* 13–14.
[28]Quick, *Doctrines of the Creed,* 260.
[29]Ewert, *Then Comes the End,* 143.

harvest of sin is almost inconceivable, and who knows how long that age will last.[30]

The restoration spoken of in Acts 3:21, however, is limited in the same verse to what God had "promised long ago through his holy prophets." No prophet promised ultimate restoration of all the wicked. Further, the statement of Revelation 21:5 is made in connection with the new heavens, the new earth, and the New Jerusalem. It in no way implies that the lake of fire will be made new or that those thrown into it will be restored. The fire by its very nature is inextinguishable (Gk. *asbestos*; Matt. 3:12; Mark 9:43; Luke 3:17).

But, some ask, will not the eternal suffering of their friends and relatives spoil the joys of heaven for the believers? It might if God did not wipe away all tears (Rev. 7:17). But, more important, the believers in heaven will understand the exceeding sinfulness of sin and the holiness of God in a new way. Even now, believers have more fellowship with one another than with unsaved friends and relatives. Surely, too, the joys of fellowship with God and Christ and the sharing of their eternal glory will fill our future lives with such blessing that the past will be forgotten.[31]

ANNIHILATIONISM (CONDITIONAL IMMORTALITY)

Annihilationism teaches that the total person goes out of existence and the soul and spirit cease to have any being. Most annihilationists teach that God created Adam and Eve mortal and He later rewarded the righteous with immortality, or they say that no one is immortal except by free grace in Christ and that such grace is not given to unrepentant sinners.[32] Faustus Socinus (1539–1604) promoted this idea during the Reformation. In 1706 Henry Dodwell of Oxford

---

[30]Pridgeon, *Is Hell Eternal?*

[31]Hall, *Eschatology*, 215–16.

[32]Ibid., 228. This was taught by Arnobius (*Disput. c. Gentes*, ii. 15–34).

taught that Christian baptism brought the gift of immortality.

The Scottish writer Henry Drummond (1851-97) taught that conditional immortality is compatible with evangelical faith. That is, those who refuse to repent and believe will not receive immortality.[33] Others teach that God did create Adam and Eve immortal, but He later took away that gift from the wicked.[34] Most rely on passages such as 2 Thessalonians 1:8-9, where Paul says that Jesus "will punish those who do not know God and do not obey the gospel of our Lord Jesus. They will be punished with everlasting destruction and shut out from the presence of the Lord and from the majesty of His power." Annihilationists claim that "destruction" (Gk. *olethron*) means "a total cessation of existence." However, the use of the word "destroy" in 1 Corinthians 3:17, "If anyone destroys God's temple, God will destroy him; for God's temple is sacred, and you are that temple," shows the word does not mean annihilation. No human being could annihilate God's people. They also claim that the word "lost" means "annihilated." But when Jesus sent the Twelve "to the lost sheep of Israel" (Matt. 10:6), He certainly did not mean "the annihilated sheep." They were lost because they were separated from God. Eternal loss means banishment from God's presence forever.

Annihilation, however, would not demonstrate adequately God's hatred for sin, nor does it fit with passages such as Matthew 25:46, where the wicked "will go away to eternal punishment, but the righteous to eternal life." "Eternal" in both cases is the Greek

---

[33]Grounds, "Final State of the Wicked," 214.

[34]See Leckie, *World to Come,* 245-47, for the arguments that the human spirit cannot be destroyed and that "conditionalism implicitly denies the organic unity of the human race."

aiōnion.[35] Therefore, if our life in Christ is eternal and our new bodies immortal and imperishable, not subject to death or decay (1 Cor. 15:42,52–54), then the punishment of the wicked must be eternal, without end (see also Matt. 18:8; 25:41; Mark 3:29; 2 Thess. 1:9; Heb. 6:2; Jude 7).

Nor does the "perish" of John 3:16 (Gk. *apolētai*) mean annihilation or extinction. The same word is often used of sinners who are "lost" (Matt. 10:6; Luke 15:4,6; 19:10; 2 Cor. 4:3), of losing one's reward (Matt. 10:42), and of physical death (Matt. 8:25; 26:52; 27:20; Luke 17:27; Jude 11). The corresponding noun *(apōleia)* refers to eternal loss, eternal ruin, but not loss of existence.[36] Just as eternal life is Christ's life in us by which we share fellowship with Him, so eternal death is the absence of the life of God and eternal separation from Him and His blessings. Believers go to a place prepared for them. The lost go to a place never meant for them, a place prepared for the devil and his angels, a place that is Satan's final doom, his final prison. No wonder Jesus warned sinners so frequently!

Some people treat the subject of eternal punishment carelessly, even frivolously. But it is a very serious matter. Though God will wipe away all tears, as we contemplate this now it ought to bring tears to our eyes and stir us to pray, to witness, to give to home and foreign missions, as we follow Jesus, sharing in His desire to seek and to save the lost (Luke 19:10).

After the final judgment, death and *Hadēs* are thrown into the lake of fire (Rev. 20:14). The lake of fire, which is outside the entire new heavens and earth (cf. Rev. 22:15), will be the only place where

---

[35]In sixty-four of the seventy-two times this word is used in the New Testament it refers to God or to salvation and eternal life. The word also contrasts with *proskairos,* "a little while," or "that which lasts for only a period of time."

[36]Gilbrant, *Complete Biblical Library,* 417–20.

death will exist.[37] As a result, Christ's victory over death as the wages of sin will finally be fully consummated, for "the last enemy to be destroyed is death" (1 Cor. 15:26). As Isaiah foresaw, God "will swallow up death forever" (Isa. 25:8), and in the new heavens and earth "there will be no more death" (Rev. 21:4).

STUDY QUESTIONS

1. For whom was the lake of fire prepared, and why will unbelievers go there?

2. What is the difference in the nature and effects of God's discipline of believers in comparison with His wrath on unbelievers?

3. How can a good God also show wrath?

4. What will the final state of the wicked be like?

5. How does the Bible describe the people who will be in the lake of fire?

6. What are the biblical grounds for believing that the punishment of the lake of fire is eternal and that the purpose of the lake of fire is judgment, not restoration?

7. What are the arguments for and against the doctrine of conditional immortality?

---

[37]Annihilationists teach that after a brief period God will cause a total cessation of their being. Some say human beings were created mortal and immortality is gained only as a reward from God. Others say human beings were created immortal but God by His act deprives them of immortality. There would be little reason for the fire to be "unquenchable" if either were the case. Loraine Boettner, *Immortality* (Philadelphia: Presbyterian & Reformed Publishing Co., 1956), 117–19; Clark H. Pinnock, "The Conditional View," in *Four Views on Hell,* ed. William V. Crockett (Grand Rapids: Zondervan Publishing House, 1992), 135–66; Travis, *I Believe in the Second Coming,* 198.

Chapter Nine

The Final State of the Righteous

Abraham was willing to live in the Promised Land like a stranger, for "he was looking forward to the city with foundations, whose architect and builder is God" (Heb. 11:9-10), a city that already exists in heaven (Gal. 4:26; Heb. 11:16).[1] He was willing to do this because he realized that the New Jerusalem will be more real, more solid, and more beautiful than Canaan's land of milk and honey. It is a city where our relationships will be more wonderful, more exciting, and more glorious than anything we know or experience in this present life on this present earth. Abraham saw in it also a greater security than can be found on the present earth, for he "threw away all earthly security and 'left his own country without knowing where he was going.' Why? because he 'was waiting for the city . . . (Heb. 11:8,10) . . . a kingdom that cannot be shaken.' (Heb. 12:28)."[2] All believers are by faith "children," or heirs, of the same promises

---

[1]David L. Turner, "The New Jerusalem in Revelation 21:1-22:5: Consummation of a Biblical Continuum," in *Dispensationalism, Israel and the Church*, ed. Craig A. Blaising and Darrell L. Bock (Grand Rapids: Zondervan Publishing House, 1992), 273. Some, including Tertullian, Cyprian, Luther, and Calvin, have taught that the heavenly Jerusalem that is our mother (Gal. 4:26) is the Church. Others take it to be heaven itself. See Dale Moody, *The Hope of Glory* (Grand Rapids: William B. Eerdmans Publishing Co., 1964), 265.

[2]Stephen Travis, *The Jesus Hope* (Downers Grove, Ill.: Inter-Varsity Press, 1974), 76.

given to Abraham, and we share in the same hope (Gal. 3:7–9,29).

COMPLETE FULFILLMENT

All the various systems of Christian theology look in some way for the final fulfillment and the consummation of all promised blessings in the new heaven and the new earth with its wonderful, heavenly city, the New Jerusalem. What a contrast this is with the present cities of this world and the Babylon of the Antichrist (Rev. 17:1–18). Some theological systems, however, pay little attention to the future, ultimate consummation of God's kingdom. Luther and Calvin interpreted the New Jerusalem as the Church and did not see it as a literal city at all. But the Church is Christ's body here on earth, and the New Jerusalem is yet to come down to the earth.[3]

Liberation theology as well as feminist theology dilutes and distorts God's promises by seeking to set up social programs, hoping to rescue humanity by "human readjustment of world powers."[4] These theologies ignore the fact that Christ alone is the one who "must reign until he has put all his enemies under his feet" (1 Cor. 15:25). Only obedience to God through faith in Jesus can bring eternal life and real peace.

Humanity's attempts to rescue itself still find death an undefeatable enemy. But Jesus by His mighty power will rob death of its dominion, and death will be destroyed. Jesus can do this because God, who raised Him from the dead, has "seated him at his right hand in the heavenly realms, far above all rule and authority, power and dominion, and every title that can be given, not only in the present age but also in the one to come. And God placed all things under his feet and appointed him to be head over everything

---

[3]Moody, *Hope of Glory*, 265.

[4]Carl F. H. Henry, "Reflections on the Kingdom of God," *Journal of the Evangelical Theological Society* 35:1 (March 1992): 49.

for the church, which is his body, the fullness of him who fills everything in every way" (Eph. 1:19–23). Then when the last enemy death has finally been destroyed, "the Son himself will be made subject to him who put everything under him, so that God may be all in all" (1 Cor. 15:28). The plan of God will have reached its grand and glorious culmination, and we will rejoice forever in the New Jerusalem and in the new heaven and earth.

The Book of Revelation does not give us details describing the new heaven and new earth. Instead it focuses on a beautiful picture of the New Jerusalem that comes from above. This holy city is the final and eternal home and headquarters for all those whose names are written in the Lamb's Book of Life (Rev. 21:27). There will be plenty of room. No one will be homeless there. It is also the dwelling of God (Rev. 21:3). Though God is everywhere, He is able to manifest himself in special ways wherever He chooses. In this age, as in times past, God manifests His presence in a special way in heaven, making heaven the place of His throne. But in the final Kingdom He will transfer His headquarters to the New Jerusalem on the new earth.

This will bring to completion God's plan of having a people for himself. This purpose He revealed to Israel at Sinai. There He said of Israel, "'Now if you obey me fully and keep my covenant, then out of all nations you will be my treasured possession. Although the whole earth is mine, you will be for me a kingdom of priests and a holy nation'" (Exod. 19:5–6). Through the new covenant this was extended to the Church, for "through the gospel the Gentiles are heirs together with Israel, members together of one body, and sharers together in the promise in Christ Jesus" (Eph. 3:6). The Bible also tells all who come to Christ and believe, "You are a chosen people, a royal priesthood, a holy nation, a people belonging to God, that you may declare the praises of him who called you out of darkness into his wonderful light" (1 Pet.

2:9). In other words, all who call the New Jerusalem home will "be his people, and God himself will be with them and be their God" (Rev. 21:3). This is the destiny God in His love has had in mind for humankind from the time of our creation.

THE NEW HEAVEN AND NEW EARTH

Isaiah was the first to foretell God's creation of a new heaven and a new earth. So totally new will they be that "the former things will not be remembered, nor will they come to mind" (Isa. 65:17). But Isaiah, like John, does not give any details about what the new heaven and new earth will be like. The next verse (65:18) begins with a strong adversative (Heb. *ki-'im,* "nevertheless"), bringing a strong contrast. There will indeed be a new heaven and a new earth, *but* the present Jerusalem will also have its fulfillment. The remainder of chapter 65 deals with millennial conditions on the present earth after Christ returns. It does not fit the description of the New Jerusalem given in Revelation 21 and 22 at all.

John saw the New Jerusalem coming down out of heaven from God. This was in connection with his vision of the new heaven and the new earth. Therefore, the New Jerusalem comes down to the new earth, not the present earth, for "the first heaven and the first earth had passed away" (Rev. 21:1).

REPLACEMENT OF THE PRESENT HEAVEN AND EARTH

The passing away of the first earth and heaven refers back to Revelation 20:11, where John "saw a great white throne and him who was seated on it. Earth and sky fled from his presence, and there was no place for them." The simplest meaning of these passages is that the present heaven and earth vanish, disappear, go out of existence, since there is no place for them. That they "fled" indicates they were unfit for God's presence because of past contamination by the sin of humankind and the revolt of the angels who fell. The terminology is like that of Daniel 2:35, where the great image was swept away "without leaving a trace." The image representing the present world system had to be removed in order that the better things of the millennial kingdom could be brought in. Even so, the present heaven and earth are not only transitory, they must be removed so that a new (and better) heaven and earth might be brought into being.

Isaiah prophesied this: "All the stars of the heavens will be dissolved [melted away, rotted away, caused to vanish] and the sky rolled up like a scroll [that is, in sudden, rapid motion]" (Isa. 34:4). "'The heavens will vanish like smoke, the earth will wear out like a garment. . . . But my salvation will last forever, my righteousness will never fail'" (Isa. 51:6). Psalm 102:25–27 declares, "In the beginning you laid the foundations of the earth, and the heavens are the work of your hands. They will perish, but you remain; they will all wear out like a garment. Like clothing you will change them and they will be discarded. But you remain the same, and your years will never end." That is, the present heaven and earth will be replaced by a new, different heaven and earth, just as when one changes clothes and puts on a new set. "Perish" is also used of Jonah's gourd (Jon. 4:10) and of things being destroyed, vanishing, or being blotted out (Ps. 102:26).

Hebrews 1:10–12 bears this out and 12:25–29 quotes Haggai 2:6 and explains that the removing of things that can be shaken means the removing of created things, and adds, "Our God is a consuming fire."

Peter, in describing the final end of the Day of the Lord, says, "The heavens will disappear with a roar; the elements [either elemental substances or, as in Isa. 34:4, the stars and planets] will be destroyed by fire, and the earth and everything in it will be laid

**Chapter 9
The Final
State of the
Righteous**

bare.[5] . . . That day will bring about the destruction of the heavens by fire, and the elements will melt in the heat. But in keeping with his promise we are looking forward to a new heaven and a new earth, the home of righteousness" (2 Pet. 3:10,12-13).

A RENOVATED EARTH?

Some Bible scholars object to the idea of the earth being replaced and teach that the fire Peter describes will simply renovate the surface of the earth. This idea was promoted by Roman Catholic theologian Thomas Aquinas (ca. 1227-74).[6] He took the fire as being purifying rather than destroying. He extended that purifying into the atmospheric heavens fifteen cubits (i.e., 21.88 ft. or 6.67 m.) above the tops of the mountains, but not into the starry heavens, for, he reasoned, they had not been polluted by the sins of humanity. He also reasoned that all alive, both the wicked and the good, would be killed by the fire and then they would be resurrected immediately for a general judgment.[7]

Some today still follow Thomas Aquinas and teach that since the Bible mentions cursing the ground (Gen. 3:17), but never specifically says anything about cursing the planets or the stars, the heavens that will be destroyed include only the atmosphere around the earth, and that the new heaven will sim-

---

[5]Many ancient manuscripts read "will be burned up." It is also possible that a negative was dropped by an early copyist so that the meaning would be "will disappear." The negative is actually found in the Sahidic version translated in upper Egypt about A.D. 200. See Bauer, *A Greek-English Lexicon of the New Testament,* trans. William F. Arndt and F. Wilbur Gingrich (Chicago: University of Chicago Press, 1957), 325.

[6]This became the dominant view of the Roman Church, though Blaise Pascal (1623-62) taught that the present universe would be annihilated. See T. Francis Glasson, *His Appearing and His Kingdom: The Christian Hope in the Light of Its History* (London: Epworth Press, 1953), 182-83.

[7]Ibid., 16.

ply be the atmospheric heavens renewed or renovated along with the earth by fire.[8] David L. Turner says it will be "the old Adamic universe gloriously liberated."[9]

Some take "disappear" (Gk. *paraleusontai*) to mean "pass by," but it is sometimes used of a fast that is past and of time that is past and gone (Acts 27:9; 1 Pet. 4:3). It is also used of the heaven and earth in contrast to God's Word that will never pass away (Matt. 24:35) and of a wild flower that passes away (James 1:10-11). The Septuagintal Greek of Isaiah 26:20 uses it of God's indignation that is passed and gone.

Some take "destroyed" (Gk. *luthēsetai*) to mean "unloosed," "untied," or "broken up into component parts." However, it is also used of tearing down a building and of a ship breaking up (Acts 27:41). Other uses include "repealed," "annulled," "abolished," "destroyed," "brought to an end," "done away with." It would be the New Testament word most likely to be used to describe atomic disintegration. Most in a former generation felt that renovation was a necessary interpretation because science taught that matter could not be destroyed. But atomic science now shows us that matter can be changed completely into energy. When antiparticles, such as positrons, meet corresponding particles, such as electrons, in a flash they are transformed into heat energy.[10] All God would have to do is to let a universe of antimatter drift across the universe we live in, and there would

---

[8]Joseph Pohle, *Eschatology, or the Catholic Doctrine of the Last Things: A Dogmatic Treatise*, English version by Arthur Preuss (Westport, Conn.: Greenwood Press, Publishers, 1971; repr. from 1917), 115.

[9]Turner, "The New Jerusalem," 265; also quoted by Al Truesdale in "Last Things First: The Impact of Eschatology on Ecology," *Perspectives on Science and Christian Faith* 46:2 (June 1994): 116.

[10]Wilbur M. Smith, *The Biblical Doctrine of Heaven* (Chicago: Moody Press, 1968), 229.

be fervent heat and then nothing. Furthermore, the Greek word *tēketai* in 2 Peter 3:12 is a term that always means "to melt or dissolve."

Others object to the annihilation of the present heaven and earth because of passages that seem to say that the present earth will always continue in existence. These include Genesis 49:26 and Habakkuk 3:6, which in the KJV speak of "everlasting" hills. However, the Hebrew is better translated "age-old hills" (NIV), and these "collapse," which seems to mean they are not as "everlasting" as people thought they were.

We read also of "the earth that [God] established forever" (Ps. 78:69; cf. Pss. 104:5; 125:1) and that "remains forever" (Eccles. 1:4). However, Ecclesiastes is simply making a contrast between generations of people that come and go and the earth which is still here. "Forever" (Heb. *lᵉ'olam*) is often used of the distant past (translated "long ago" in Eccles. 1:10) or future where the speaker is not able to see an end, even though there might eventually be one. Some also take Ecclesiastes 1:4 to mean there will always be an earth, even though the present earth will be replaced by a new one.

Still others argue that since (1) the first heaven and earth were created for humankind and (2) we are to "put on the new self" (Gk. *ton kainon anthrōpon*; Eph. 4:24)—without first having to be annihilated— then, by analogy, the first heaven and earth do not need to be annihilated to be created new.[11] However, analogy is a weak argument. The statements in Psalm 102:26; Isaiah 34:4; 51:6; and 2 Peter 3:10-13 are too strong to interpret in any way other than annihilation of the present heaven and earth. It is the new heaven and the new earth that will endure before the Lord (Isa. 66:22).

---

[11]Ibid., 223–27.

A NEW AND DIFFERENT HEAVEN AND EARTH

"New" (Gk. *kainos*) often does mean "previously unknown," "entirely new," even "of a new kind," with the idea of "marvelous" or "unheard of."[12] It is used of the new covenant, which is entirely different from the old covenant given at Sinai (Jer. 31:31; Heb. 8:8). John, in his visions on the island of Patmos, gives details about the new earth that show it will indeed be different from the present earth. Truly, "a wholly new world is to be realised; God the Father is rich enough not to need to copy the present world in the next; He has creative power to set up in it something really new and infinitely higher."[13] Though the old creation was "very good" (Gen. 1:31), the new creation will be even better. Adam was created innocent. As a new creation in Christ the "new self" is "created to be like God in true righteousness and holiness" (Eph. 4:24). Adam was placed in a garden with one tree of life in it. Our final home will be a city with a river of life and trees of life on each side of it (Rev. 22:1-2). God is so good that everything lost in the Fall will be replaced by something better.

There will no longer be any sea (Rev. 21:1). Oceans cover the major part of the present earth, and microorganisms in the sea (especially diatoms) are necessary to replace oxygen and keep the balance in our atmosphere. It seems evident that since our new bodies, like Jesus' glorified body, will be suited to both earth and heaven, we will no longer be dependent on oxygen or a pressurized atmosphere.

---

[12]Walter Bauer, *A Greek-English Lexicon of the New Testament and Other Early Christian Literature*, 2d ed., trans. William F. Arndt and F. Wilbur Gingrich, rev. and augmented by F. Wilbur Gingrich and Frederick W. Danker (Chicago: University of Chicago Press, 1979), 394.

[13]Willibald Beyschlag, *New Testament Theology*, trans. Neil Buchanan, vol. 1 (Edinburgh, Scotland: T. & T. Clark, 1895), 215.

THE NEW JERUSALEM

The new earth will become the site of the New Jerusalem, which will be different entirely from the present Jerusalem, for it will have been built by God. John saw "the Holy City, the new Jerusalem, coming down out of heaven from God, prepared as a bride beautifully dressed for her husband" (Rev. 21:2). "As a bride" is a simile that indicates how beautifully and wonderfully the city is prepared. It does not identify or equate the city with the Church as Christ's bride. Thus, even when one of the angels tells John, "'Come, I will show you the bride, the wife of the Lamb,'" and shows him "the Holy City, Jerusalem" (Rev. 21:9-10), he is still using a simile, just as Jesus did when He cried out, "'O Jerusalem, . . . how often I have longed to gather your children together, as a hen gathers her chicks under her wings, but you were not willing!'" (Luke 13:34), or when He wept over the city (Luke 19:41). Jesus had the people in mind, but that does not mean there was no real city there. Similarly, those who say the New Jerusalem is only the Church and not a real city go too far.[14]

THE CITY'S DIMENSIONS

The city's dimensions (Rev. 21:16) of 1,380 miles (2,220 kilometers) to each side (using the Greek stade *[stadion]* of about 607 feet, which is shorter than the English furlong of 220 yards) would cause it to stretch nearly halfway across the North American continent. Because its height is the same, the city would stretch way beyond the stratosphere into what we think of as outer space. Consequently, many believe this indicates that the new earth will be much larger than the present earth.

Since its width, length, and height are equal, the most probable form is that of a perfect cube, like the inner sanctuary, the Most Holy Place where God man-

---

[14]Turner, "The New Jerusalem," 286-87.

ifested His presence and glory in the Old Testament tabernacle and temple (1 Kings 6:20). This fits the fact that John saw no temple in the city, for the presence and glory of God and Christ fills it all, making the entire city a sanctuary, a Most Holy Place. No longer is there a separation between the holy and the unclean as there was under the Old Testament law, for all is holy and everything unclean has been separated from the new creation and consigned to the lake of fire.

If the city is in the form of a cube, a cubical space one-third of a mile on each side would be available per person for about twenty billion people. Certainly there will be plenty of room for all the saved of all ages.

Others speculate that the city will be in the shape of a step pyramid, with each level having slightly less area than the level below. They picture the river flowing down through the city from one level to another. However, the pyramid shape in Bible times was always connected with idolatrous worship, so it is not so likely that the city would take that form.

Still others speculate that the city will be a cube inside a crystal sphere revolving around the new earth. But the fact that the New Jerusalem comes down from heaven seems to indicate rather that the city comes to rest on the surface of the new earth. Its foundations and open gates would also sustain this conclusion.

All of this suggests the New Jerusalem is brand-new "for those who have the 'new name' and sing 'a new song' in 'a new heaven and a new earth.' Thus the word for 'new' *(kainos)* must mean a newness that is new in a new way."[15]

ISRAEL AND THE CHURCH

From the fact that the names of the twelve tribes of Israel will be written on the gates and the names

---

[15]Moody, *Hope of Glory,* 270.

of the twelve apostles on the twelve foundations it seems clear that both Israel and the Church will be together in the city (Rev. 21:12,14). They will be joined in worship and in sharing the blessings of the presence of God and Christ. No longer will God's people be on earth and God's throne in heaven. The throne will be in the New Jerusalem and will be the headquarters for both the Father and the Son. In this way, the New Jerusalem on the new earth will become the divine headquarters for the new universe.

Paul spoke of God as "the blessed and only Ruler, the King of kings and Lord of lords, who alone is immortal and who lives in unapproachable light, whom no one has seen or can see" (1 Tim. 6:15-16). But He has always wanted fellowship with His people; as Isaiah pointed out, "This is what the high and lofty One says—he who lives forever, whose name is holy: 'I live in a high and holy place, but also with him who is contrite and lowly in spirit, to revive the spirit of the lowly and to revive the heart of the contrite'" (Isa. 57:15). Therefore, in that city there will be no separation from God and His glory.

THE DWELLING OF GOD

John heard a voice from the throne that put it this way: "'Now the dwelling [Gk. *skēne*, "tent," "tabernacle"] of God is with men [Gk. *anthrōpōn*, "humankind"],[16] and he will live with them. They will be his people, and God himself will be with them and be their God. He will wipe every tear from their eyes. There will be no more death or mourning or crying or pain, for the old order of things has passed away'" (Rev. 21:3-4). This will be the complete fulfillment of God's purpose for His people expressed in both the Old and New Testaments (Lev. 26:11-12; Jer. 7:23;

---

[16]"Humankind" here refers to the redeemed, resurrected saints, the godly remnant from both Israel and the nations, for these are the only ones dwelling on the new earth and in the New Jerusalem.

11:4; 30:22; Ezek. 36:28; 37:23,27; Zech. 8:8; Rom. 9:25; 1 Pet. 2:10).

The "dwelling" of God also refers to what the rabbis called the "*shekinah*."[17] It was anticipated by God's glory manifested in the Holy of Holies in the Old Testament tabernacle and temple, as well as in Jesus' incarnation as the Living Word whereby He "became flesh and made his dwelling among us" (John 1:14), a "*dwelling*" that revealed His glory.

Then the One seated on the throne said, "'I am making everything new!'" (Rev. 21:5). There will be no more sin, evil, affliction, hardship, suffering, or fruitless toil.[18] Perhaps even the memory of those things will be eliminated (Isa. 65:17), though certainly the good things God has done will be remembered.

Another thing that is new: "The city does not need the sun or the moon to shine on it, for the glory of God gives it light, and the Lamb is its lamp. . . . On no day will its gates ever be shut, for there will be no night there" (Rev. 21:23,25). The present earth depends on the energy that comes to us from the sun for our food and fuel. But in the new earth God will mediate to us divine light and His own infinite and powerful divine energy directly through Jesus as the "lamp."

The same light will be mediated to all the earth, for "the nations will walk by its light, and the kings of the earth will bring their splendor into it" (Rev. 21:24). Since all the wicked and unbelieving have already been cast into the lake of fire, the "nations" must be the redeemed saints "from every tribe and language and people and nation" who reigned with Christ on the earth during the Millennium (Rev. 5:9–

---

[17]From the Hebrew verb *shakhan*, "to dwell." See Exod. 25:8, "I will dwell among them."

[18]Isa. 35:10 shows a partial fulfillment of this in the Millennium, when "the ransomed of the LORD will return. They will enter Zion with singing; everlasting joy will crown their heads. Gladness and joy will overtake them, and sorrow and sighing will flee away." See also Isa. 65:19.

10). The "kings of the earth" must include the martyrs who also join with them. These nations are people from various parts of the present earth and also include Israel, for even the Old Testament word for nations *(goyim)* sometimes includes Israel (Gen. 25:23; 35:11; Josh. 3:17; Isa. 26:15). They have become the residents of the New Jerusalem, "and whatever glory or honor they had, they will bring into the city and present it all to God, to whom it is due."[19]

THE ETERNAL AGES TO COME

The fact that there will be no night there does not mean, however, that we will be in a timeless eternity. Some take the "we fly away" of Psalm 90:10 to indicate the abolition of time, but Moses was only drawing attention to the transitory nature of human life.[20] Nor does the statement "that there should be time no longer" (Rev. 10:6, KJV) uphold the idea of time being replaced by eternity. The verse is better translated, "There will be no more delay!" (NIV). It refers to the fact that there will be no more delay once the seventh trumpet sounds; the remaining events of the Tribulation will follow in rapid succession.[21]

NOT TIMELESSNESS

A timeless eternity with no before or after, with no past or future, would be like being in a trance. It is also inconsistent to think of time being followed by eternity if eternity is timelessness. How then could it come after time? Eternity, in the Bible, is simply unending, infinite time.[22] No fear of the joy and blessing

---

[19]Stanley M. Horton, *The Ultimate Victory* (Springfield, Mo.: Gospel Publishing House, 1991), 323-24.

[20]G. C. Berkouwer, *The Return of Christ,* trans. James Van Oosterom (Grand Rapids: William B. Eerdmans Publishing Co., 1972), 40-45.

[21]Horton, *Ultimate Victory,* 149.

[22]Hendrikus Berkhof, *Well-Founded Hope* (Richmond, Va.: John Knox Press, 1969), 29.

coming to an end will ever dim the glory we will forever share. We cannot lose any part of the future inheritance that is ours through Jesus Christ. The mention of "gates" implies that the righteous may go in and out. The New Jerusalem will be the capital city of the new heaven and the new earth, and we will serve God and reign as kings for ever and ever (Rev. 22:3–5). "For ever and ever" (Gk. *eis tous aiōnios tōn aiōnōn*, "into the ages of the ages") has the meaning of "unending time," "age after age after age." Therefore, the idea of sequence, of time going on forever, is clearly the meaning. There will be no end to the glory and blessing of those who serve the Lord and share in His reign, His throne, that is, in His royal power and dominion.

DEPENDENCE ON GOD

Nevertheless, we will not be gods. We will still be finite beings, dependent on God for our well-being. This is indicated by the tree of life with its leaves "for the healing [health, well-being] of the nations" (Rev. 22:2).[23] Nevermore will there be any of the effects of the curse that was put on the whole creation because of Adam's sin (Gen. 3:17; Zech. 14:11; Rom. 8:20), nor will a flaming sword keep us from the tree of life (Gen. 3:24).

A GLORIOUS FULFILLMENT

Then we will experience the fullness of what it means to have the Lord as our Good Shepherd providing for everything we need. The glory and honor that the nations now claim for themselves will also become ours in that city, but redeemed from any imperfection and filled with the glory of God. "Nothing impure will ever enter [the city], nor will anyone who does what is shameful or deceitful, but only

---

[23]"Nations" (Gk. *ethnōn*) means "people," rather than nations in the modern sense.

those whose names are written in the Lamb's book of life" (Rev. 21:27).

John, however, does not seem to find human language adequate to express all he saw in the New Jerusalem. Who can imagine pearls big enough for each gate of the city to be made of a single pearl! Who has ever seen gold "like transparent glass" (Rev. 21:21).[24] Gold as we know it today can be pounded out until it is only a few molecules thick and placed on a window as gold leaf. But it is not transparent like glass. It seems the Bible is trying to tell us the new creation will include new substances more beautiful than anything we now know or can imagine.

We are dealing here with the ultimate fulfillment of "what God has prepared for those who love him" (1 Cor. 2:9). Eternally we will share marvelous, loving fellowship with Jesus. The Holy Spirit makes fellowship with Jesus real to us now. But what we will share then will be wonderful beyond our present ability to imagine.

We will also be involved in glorious service to the King of kings (Rev. 22:3), involving exalted kingly activity, not only in the New Jerusalem but throughout the new heaven and earth. And the new heaven and earth will not be a mere copy of the present universe, for God is able to create something completely new and far superior.

Most important, righteousness will be the ultimate issue of the Holy Spirit's work and will characterize this eternal kingdom of our Father. In it the righteous will continue to shine like the sun forever and ever and ever (Matt. 13:43). The Holy Spirit will continue to fill us "to the measure of all the fullness of God" (Eph. 3:19). This implies continuous growth in mind

---

[24]"Street" (Gk. *plateia*) is singular and may indicate a wide street running down through the city in its various levels. Others take the word to be generic, i.e., meaning all the streets of the city will be of pure gold.

and spirit.[25] The apostle Paul, after he had been a Christian for many years, still had a consuming passion to know Christ (Phil. 3:10). Since God is infinite, it is impossible to know all about Him right away.

In a real sense, we will always be disciples, "students," always learning more about the infinite God and His ways—always with an increasing passion to know Him. Those things we do not understand now will be made clear. We will see how in all things God has worked "for the good of those who love him, who have been called according to his purpose" (Rom. 8:28). Then, with eternal joy we will serve and worship God and the Lamb (Rev. 22:3-4). We will share His glory, joy, and peace in supernatural, unending happiness. We will see His face, and His name will be on our foreheads because our lives will show His character and holiness forever. Hallelujah!

STUDY QUESTIONS

1. Abraham's faith was credited to him as righteousness. What was involved in his faith?

2. Toward what goal is God's plan moving?

3. How does the New Jerusalem compare with the Garden of Eden?

4. What are the reasons for believing the new heaven and the new earth will be brand-new rather than merely renovated?

---

[25]Edgar Young Mullins, *The Christian Religion in Its Doctrinal Expression* (Valley Forge, Pa.: Judson Press, 1917), 487-88. Mullins points out that "true moral perfection is not static. . . . It unfolds and expands. . . . Hope is an abiding element of the redeemed life, and this implies endless growth and attainment."

5. What are the reasons for believing the New Jerusalem will be a real city with real walls and gates?

6. What will characterize the people of the city?

7. What does the Bible indicate about the future ages of eternity?

Glossary

Abba. An Aramaic word for "the father" or "O Father."

Allegory. A way of interpreting Scripture by looking for some deeper or "spiritual" meaning behind the literal sense.

Amillennialism. The view that there will be no future reign of Christ on the present earth. Some spiritualize the Millennium and make it represent Christ's present reign in heaven during the entire Church Age. They deny that Revelation 20 refers to a literal period of one thousand years.

Annihilationism. The teaching that the wicked cease to exist at death or after a period in the lake of fire.

Anointing. Refers to an act of dedication to God's service by pouring oil on a person's head. It also refers to the empowering or energizing by the Holy Spirit.

Antichrist. A false Christ who will appear at the end of the Church Age, become a world dictator, and demand worship.

Antisupernaturalism. Denies the existence and reality of the supernatural. It tries to explain everything in terms of natural law.

Apocalyptic. (Gk. *apokalupsis*, "revelation," "disclosure.") The literature that uses rich symbolism to describe the coming kingdom of God and the events leading up to it. The visions of Daniel and Revelation are examples.

Apocrypha. Books written during the period between the Book of Malachi and the birth of Jesus. The Jews did not include them in the Hebrew Bible and all the Protestant reformers rejected them as not being inspired.

Apostasy. A deliberate and total turning away from Christ and His teachings.

Apostle. A "messenger." Two groups are mentioned in the New Testament. The Twelve were especially trained and commissioned by Jesus to be primary witnesses to His resurrection and His teachings and to spread the gospel. They will judge (rule) the twelve tribes of Israel in the millennial kingdom (Luke 22:30). The term is also used of others directly commissioned by Jesus, including Paul, Barnabas, Andronicus, Junia, and James, the Lord's brother.

Archaeology. The scientific study of the remains of a culture and a people. It involves digging up these remains, recording them, and photographing them.

Armageddon. "The mountain of Megiddo," about twenty miles south-southeast of Haifa, the site of the final battle between Christ and the Antichrist (Rev. 16:16).

Atonement. (Heb. *kippurim.*) "The act of reconciliation" to God by covering with a price, the blood of a substitute, so that no punishment is necessary. (Gk. *katallagē*, "reconciliation.")

Blasphemy. Slander, abusive speech that reviles or injures the reputation of persons, or especially such speech directed against God, Jesus Christ, or the Holy Spirit.

Church Age. The period between Jesus' resurrection and His second coming.

Church fathers. Outstanding teachers and leaders of the Church during the first few centuries.

Covenant. A solemn, binding agreement. God's covenants are agreements by which He pledges to bless those who accept the covenant and live under it in faith and obedience.

Daniel's seventieth week. A final "seven," or week, of years which most premillennialists identify with the Great Tribulation at the end of the Church Age.

Demons. Spirit beings, sometimes called evil or unclean spirits, who work under Satan. Some believe they are fallen angels.

Disciple. "Learner," "student." Includes all who seek to learn from Jesus and obey His teachings.

Dispensationalism. A view first popularized by J. N. Darby (1800–1882) and spread by the *Scofield Reference Bible.* It divides God's activity in history into seven dispensations, emphasizes a literal interpretation of prophecy, and holds that God has two plans, one for Israel and one for the Church.

Eschatology. (Gk. *eschatos*, "last.") The study of what happens in the afterlife and what happens at the end of the age and in the final state of both the righteous and the wicked.

Eternal Kingdom. The final state of the saved in the new heavens and the new earth, with the New Jerusalem as their home and headquarters.

Evangelicalism. Affirms the inspiration and authority of the Bible and the truth of its teachings, with emphasis on the need for personal conversion and regeneration by the Holy Spirit.

Existentialism. Based on the teachings of Søren Kierkegaard (1813-55). It emphasizes subjectivity, seeking truth through one's own experience (especially of anxiety, guilt, dread, anguish) rather than by scientific objectivity.

Expiation. The making of full atonement by the Blood.

Faith. Belief in God and Christ expressed in wholehearted, trustful obedience. Biblical faith is always more than believing something is true; it always has God and Jesus Christ as its object.

False prophet. Many false prophets appeared in Bible times and their number will increase in the last days. The final false prophet will accompany the Antichrist (Rev. 16:13; cf. 13:12).

Freudian psychology. The psychoanalytic theories and practices of Sigmund Freud (1856-1939).

Futurist view. The view that everything in the Book of Revelation after chapter 4 takes place in a short period at the end of the Church Age.

Gnosticism. A teaching, beginning in the second century, that salvation comes through special superior knowledge. Some taught that physical matter is evil; most denied the humanity of Christ.

Grace. "Unmerited favor." God's Riches At Christ's Expense; His generosity to humanity.

Hadēs. Greek mythology used it as the name of a grim god as well as a shadowy underworld of departed spirits. In the New Testament it translates the Hebrew $Sh^{e'}ol$ and is always a place of agony (Luke 16:23-24).

Heathen. Pagans; worshipers of false gods.

Hermeneutics. (Gk. *hermēneuō*, "explain," "interpret.") The theory of understanding the meaning of a passage, including analysis of the text, its intentionality, its context, and the customs and culture of the human author.

Historicist view. The view that the events in the Book of Revelation have been gradually fulfilled during the course of church history.

Idealist view. The view that the figures and symbols in the Book of Revelation represent only the ongoing struggle between good and evil, with the ultimate triumph of righteousness.

Imminent. "About to happen," or having the potential of happening at any time.

Incarnation. The act by which the eternal Son of God became a human being without giving up His deity.

Justification. God's act of declaring and accepting a person as righteous in His sight. God pardons sinners who accept Jesus Christ as Lord and Savior and treats them as not guilty—just as if they had never sinned.

Karma. In Hinduism and Buddhism, the force resulting from a person's actions that determines the destiny of the soul in the next life.

Kingdom now theology. A form of postmillennialism that emphasizes making the kingdoms of this world the kingdom of Christ now.

Kingdom of God. The reign, rule, and royal power of God in the believer's heart, in the Church, in the world, and eventually in the millennial kingdom to be ruled on earth by Christ. In the New Testament it is used interchangeably with the "kingdom of heaven."

Liberals. Those who deny the supernatural and redefine Christian teachings and practices in terms of current human philosophies.

Liberation theology. A reactionary theology that interprets the Bible in such a way as to allow a Marxist type of revolution to liberate the poor.

Limbo. (Lat. *limbus*, "border.") According to Roman Catholics, the permanent state of babies who die unbaptized. They are not personally guilty so they do not go to hell, but because of original sin they cannot go to heaven.

Lord. "Master," "owner." A term representing the personal name of God (Yahweh), used of both God the Father and Jesus in the New Testament. However, "Master" in the KJV when applied to Jesus is often used to translate the Greek *didaskalos,* "Teacher."

Manuscripts. Handwritten books. Before A.D. 100 they were scrolls, or rolls; after that they were bound books.

Maranatha. Two words in Aramaic, *"Marana tha,"* meaning "Our Lord, come!" (1 Cor. 16:22).

Marriage Supper of the Lamb. A great celebration of the union of Christ and the Church. It takes place just before Jesus comes in triumph to destroy the armies of the Antichrist and establish the millennial kingdom.

Mass. The Roman Catholic name for the Lord's Supper.

Messiah. From the Hebrew *Mashiach,* "Anointed One."

Mid-Tribulation theory. The theory that the rapture of the Church will occur in the middle of the seven years of the Great Tribulation at the end of the Church Age.

Millennium. From a Latin term meaning "thousand years." It is used to refer to the future reign of Christ on earth.

Mount of Olives. The hill (2,723 feet in elevation) east of Jerusalem's temple area.

Neoorthodoxy. A type of theology associated especially with Karl Barth (1886–1968). It accepts the destructive critical methods of the liberals for the interpretation of the Bible, but teaches the major doctrines of the Reformation and believes that God speaks to people through Scripture (even while holding that Scripture is not inerrant).

Neouniversalism. A trend among some evangelicals to see the possibility of the ultimate salvation of all human beings due to the extravagant love and grace of God.

New Age philosophies. A loosely tied group of teachings based on oriental philosophies with an emphasis on nature worship, often including a smattering of Christian terminology.

Occult. The secret knowledge of supposed supernatural forces or agencies, especially in spiritism, fortune-telling, witchcraft, and astrology. These are dangerous ventures into Satan's territory.

Orthodox. (From the Gk. *orthōs,* "upright," "straight," "correct," "true," and *dokeō,* "think," "believe.") Refers to correct teachings and practices as established by the Church and is used by evangelicals of correct biblical teachings. The eastern churches took the name "orthodox" when the western (Roman Catholic) church split off from them.

Overcomers. "Winners," "victors," all believers who maintain their faith in Jesus Christ (Rom. 8:37; 1 John 5:4).

Parousia. A Greek word meaning "presence," "coming," "arrival." It is used in theology to describe the coming of Jesus at the end of the Church Age.

Pentateuch. The five books of Moses (Genesis through Deuteronomy), called in Hebrew the *Torah*, "Instruction."

Pentecost. "Fiftieth." A name for the harvest feast that occurred fifty days after Passover. On the first Pentecost after the resurrection of Jesus, the Holy Spirit was poured out on 120 believers to empower them.

Pentecostal. The movement that began in 1901 and that emphasizes the restoration of the baptism in the Holy Spirit with the initial outward evidence of speaking in other tongues and the restoration of the gifts of the Holy Spirit.

Pharisees. "Separatists." Members of a strict party that came into existence a century or more before Christ. The Pharisees observed the letter of the written law of Moses and added oral tradition that they claimed had been given to Moses.

Postmillennialism. The teaching that the Millennium is the Church Age or an extension of the Church Age, with Christ ruling but not personally present.

Post-Tribulation theory. The theory that Christian believers will go through the seven-year Great Tribulation at the end of the age. The Rapture is considered identical with Christ's return in glory to destroy the Antichrist and establish the millennial kingdom.

Premillennialism. The teaching that Jesus will personally return at the end of the Church Age and will establish His kingdom on earth for a thousand years. It emphasizes the literal interpretation of the Bible.

Preterist view. The view that the majority of the events in the Book of Revelation refer to the first century and have been already fulfilled.

Pre-Tribulation theory. The theory that the rapture of the Church takes place at the beginning of the Great Tribulation and that the judgment seat of Christ and the Marriage Supper of the Lamb take place in heaven before the Church returns with Jesus to destroy the Antichrist and establish the millennial kingdom.

Providence. God's care and guidance.

Pseudepigrapha. A Greek term meaning "falsely entitled writings." Jewish writings from near the time of Christ not included in the Septuagint. They were attributed to people like Moses and Solomon, who were not their true authors.

Purgatory. (Lat. *purgatus*, "cleansing.") The sphere where Roman Catholics believe the souls of the faithful are purified before entering heaven.

Puritans. A sixteenth-century movement in England that attempted to purify the English church by introducing more Calvinistic reforms, along with a simplicity of worship.

Rapture. The snatching away of all true believers for a meeting with Jesus in the air.

Reconciliation. The bringing of people to God in a restored fellowship.

Redemption. Restoration to fellowship with God through Christ's payment of the penalty for our sins by His death on the cross and the shedding of His blood.

Reformation. The sixteenth-century movement led by Martin Luther that attempted to reform the Roman Catholic Church.

Reincarnation. The belief that when a person dies, the soul leaves the body and enters into another body (a baby, an animal, an insect, or even a god, according to Hinduism).

Religion. A system of belief and a way of worship. The term is also used of human attempts to please God or gods.

Repentance. (Gk. *metanoia*, "a change of mind.") A change of the basic attitudes toward God and Christ, which involves a turning away from sin and a seeking of God's rule and righteousness.

Restorationism. Teaches a second chance for salvation after death.

Revelation. God's disclosure of himself and His will.

Sacramental. Having the character of a religious rite or act of devotion.

Sadducees. They rejected the traditions of the Pharisees and gave their attention to the written Law and the temple. During the time of Jesus, the Jewish high priest and his friends were Sadducees (cf. Matt. 16:1-2; 23:23-34; Acts 23:7-8).

Salvation. Includes all that God has done and will do for the believer in delivering from the power of sin and death and restoring to fellowship, as well as assuring future resurrection and the full inheritance He has promised.

Sanctification. The work of the Holy Spirit that separates believers from sin and evil and dedicates them to the worship and service of God. There is an initial act of sanctification at conversion and a continuing process of sanctification as we cooperate with the Holy Spirit in putting to death wrong desires.

Sanctify. "Separate to God," "make holy."

Sanctuary. A place set apart for God to manifest His presence. The New Testament sanctuary is twofold. Whenever believers gather together they are a sanctuary. The bodies of individual believers are also sanctuaries.

Seal. A mark or impression stamped on something by a signet ring or a small cylinder with an engraved end. It was used to authenticate or identify a document or object. Spiritually it identifies a person as belonging to Christ.

Septuagint. The translation of the Old Testament from Hebrew to Greek made during the two hundred years before Christ. A later tradition said it was done by seventy (or seventy-two) men. As a consequence, it is often referred to by the Roman numerals for seventy, LXX.

Sheʾol. The Hebrew name of the place of the wicked dead, translated *Hadēs* in the Greek New Testament.

Spiritualize. To give a spiritual or "deeper" meaning not in the literal or actual sense of the word or teaching.

Theology. "The study of God." Also used as a general term for the study of all the teachings of the Bible.

Theonomists. (From theonomy, "government by God.") They claim to be working to bring everything under God's government.

Tribulation. (Gk. *thlipsis*, "pressure," "oppression," "affliction," "distress caused by circumstances.") Also used of the Great Tribulation at the end of the Church Age when God's wrath is outpoured just preceding Christ's return in glory.

Types, figures, shadows. Old Testament persons, events, or objects that foreshadow or anticipate New Testament truth, especially as relating to Jesus Christ.

Universalism. The teaching that all human beings, angels, and Satan himself will eventually be saved and enjoy God's love, presence, and blessing forever.

Vision. Sometimes another word for a dream. It is sometimes used of a supernatural appearance that brings divine revelation.

Yahweh (Jehovah). The Hebrew personal name of God formed from the consonants YHWH, also written as JHVH. It speaks of God's being in action as He is with His people. By putting the vowels of the Hebrew title meaning "Lord" with these four consonants (after the eighth century), Jews were reminded to read "Lord" instead of attempting to pronounce this personal name of God. Thus the vowels put with JHVH become "JeHoVaH," in effect a word coined by translators from the personal name and the title.

Zionism. The movement attempting to return Jews to the land God promised them. Political Zionists were instrumental in helping to establish the modern state of Israel.

Selected Bibliography

BOOKS

Adams, Jay E. *The Time Is at Hand.* Philadelphia: Presbyterian & Reformed Publishing Co., 1974.

Allen, R. Earl. *The Hereafter.* Old Tappan, N.J.: Fleming H. Revell Co., 1977.

Allis, Oswald T. *Prophecy and the Church.* Philadelphia: Presbyterian & Reformed Publishing Co., 1945.

Alnor, William M. *Soothsayers of the Second Advent.* Old Tappan, N.J.: Power Books, Fleming H. Revell Co., 1989.

Althaus, D. Paul. *Die Letzten Dinge.* Gutersloh, Germany: C. Bertelsmann, 1926.

Althaus, Paul. *The Theology of Martin Luther.* Translated by Robert C. Schultz. Philadelphia: Fortress Press, 1966.

Anderson, Robert. *The Coming Prince.* Grand Rapids: Kregel Publications, 1957; reprint of the 10th ed.

Arrington, French L. "Dispensationalism." In *Dictionary of Pentecostal and Charismatic Movements.* Edited by Stanley M. Burgess and Gary B. McGee, 247–48. Grand Rapids: Zondervan Publishing House, Regency Reference Library, 1988.

_____. *Paul's Aeon Theology in 1 Corinthians.* Washington, D.C.: University Press of America, 1978.

Assemblies of God. *Where We Stand.* Springfield, Mo.: Gospel Publishing House, 1990.

Bailey, Keith M. *Christ's Coming and His Kingdom.* Harrisburg, Pa.: Christian Publications, 1981.

Ball, Bryan W. *A Great Expectation: Eschatological Thought in English Protestantism to 1660.* Edited by

Selected
Bibliography

Heiko A. Oberman. Vol. 12, *Studies in the History of Christian Thought.* Leiden, Netherlands: E. J. Brill, 1975.

Barnes, Robin Bruce. *Prophecy and Gnosis: Apocalypticism in the Wake of the Lutheran Reformation.* Stanford, Calif.: Stanford University Press, 1988.

Barr, James. *Biblical Words for Time.* 2d ed., rev. Naperville, Ill.: Alec R. Allenson, 1969.

Barrett, Charles Kingsley. *The Holy Spirit and the Gospel Tradition.* London: Society for the Promotion of Christian Knowledge, 1970.

Beasley-Murray, George Raymond. *Jesus and the Future: An Examination of the Criticism of the Eschatological Discourse, Mark 13 with Special Reference to the Little Apocalypse Theory.* London: Macmillan & Co., 1954.

_____. *Jesus and the Last Days: The Interpretation of the Olivet Discourse.* Peabody, Mass.: Hendrickson Publishers, 1993.

Berkhof, Hendrikus. *Well-Founded Hope.* Richmond, Va.: John Knox Press, 1969.

Berkhof, Louis. *The Second Coming of Christ.* Grand Rapids: William B. Eerdmans Publishing Co., 1953.

_____. *Systematic Theology.* 4th ed., rev. Grand Rapids: William B. Eerdmans Publishing Co., 1941.

Berkouwer, G. C. *The Return of Christ.* Translated by James Van Oosterom. Grand Rapids: William B. Eerdmans Publishing Co., 1972.

Beyschlag, Willibald. *New Testament Theology.* Translated by Neil Buchanan. 2 Vols. Edinburgh, Scotland: T. & T. Clark, 1895.

Bickersteth, Edward Henry. *The Holy Spirit: His Person and Work.* Grand Rapids: Kregel Publications, 1959.

Biederwolf, William E. *The Second Coming Bible.* Grand Rapids: Baker Book House, 1972.

Blaising, Craig A., and Darrell L. Bock, eds. *Dispensationalism, Israel and the Church: The Search for Definition.* Grand Rapids: Zondervan Publishing House, 1992.

Bloesch, Donald G. *Essentials of Evangelical Theology.* 2 Vols. New York: Harper & Row, Publishers, 1979.

_____. *A Theology of Word and Spirit.* Downers Grove, Ill.: InterVarsity Press, 1992.

Bloomfield, Arthur E. *A Survey of Bible Prophecy.* Minneapolis: Bethany Fellowship, 1971.

Boettner, Loraine. *Immortality.* Philadelphia: Presbyterian & Reformed Publishing Co., 1956.

_____. *The Millennium.* Philadelphia: Presbyterian & Reformed Publishing Co., 1957.

Boice, James Montgomery. *Foundations of the Christian Faith.* Downers Grove, Ill.: InterVarsity Press, 1986.

Braaten, Carl E. *Eschatology and Ethics.* Minneapolis: Augsburg Publishing House, 1974.

Braaten, Carl E., and Robert W. Jensen, eds. *Christian Dogmatics.* 2 Vols. Philadelphia: Fortress Press, 1984.

Bright, John. *The Kingdom of God.* New York: Abingdon Press, 1953.

Brooks, Keith L. *Prophetic Questions Answered.* Grand Rapids: Zondervan Publishing House, 1941.

Brunner, Emil. *Eternal Hope.* Translated by Harold Knight. Philadelphia: Westminster Press, 1954.

Buchanan, James. *The Office and Work of the Holy Spirit.* London: Banner of Truth Trust, 1966; reprint from 1943.

Buis, Harry. *The Doctrine of Eternal Punishment.* Philadelphia: Presbyterian & Reformed Publishing Co., 1957.

Bultmann, Rudolf. *The Presence of Eternity.* Westport, Conn.: Greenwood Press, Publishers, 1957.

Burrows, Millar. *An Outline of Biblical Theology.* Philadelphia: Westminster Press, 1946.

Buswell, James Oliver, Jr. *A Systematic Theology of the Christian Religion.* Vol. 2. Grand Rapids: Zondervan Publishing House, 1963.

_____. *Unfulfilled Prophecies.* Grand Rapids: Zondervan Publishing House, 1937.

Cadman, W. H. *The Open Heaven: The Revelation of God in the Johannine Sayings of Jesus.* Edited by G. B. Caird. New York: Herder & Herder, 1969.

Caird, George Bradford. *A Commentary on the Revelation of St. John the Divine.* New York: Harper & Row, Publishers, 1966.

Campbell, Donald K., and Jeffrey L. Townsend, eds. *A Case for Premillennialism: A New Consensus.* Chicago: Moody Press, 1992.

Carter, Charles Webb. *The Person and Ministry of the Holy Spirit: A Wesleyan Perspective.* Grand Rapids: Baker Book House, 1974.

Carver, Everett I. *When Jesus Comes Again.* Phillipsburg, N.J.: Presbyterian & Reformed Publishing Co., 1979.

Case, Shirley Jackson. *The Millennial Hope.* Chicago: University of Chicago Press, 1918.

Cauthen, Kenneth. *Systematic Theology.* Lewiston, N.Y.: Edwin Mellen Press, 1986.

Charles, R. H. *A Critical History of the Doctrine of a Future Life: In Israel, in Judaism, and in Christianity.* 2d ed., rev. and enl. London: Adam & Charles Black, 1913.

Childs, James M., Jr. *Christian Anthropology and Ethics.* Philadelphia: Fortress Press, 1978.

Chilton, David. *Paradise Restored: A Biblical Theology of Dominion.* Tyler, Tex.: Reconstruction Press, 1985.

Clarke, William Newton. *An Outline of Christian Theology.* 14th ed. Edinburgh, Scotland: T. & T. Clark, 1905.

Clouse, Robert G., ed. *The Meaning of the Millennium: Four Views.* Downers Grove, Ill.: InterVarsity Press, 1977.

Conyers, A. J. *The Eclipse of Heaven: Rediscovering the Hope of a World Beyond.* Downers Grove, Ill.: InterVarsity Press, 1992.

Corell, Alf. *Consummatum est: Eschatology and the Church in the Gospel of St. John.* Translated by Order of the Holy Paraclete, Whitby. London: Society for the Promotion of Christian Knowledge, 1958.

Crockett, William V., ed. *Four Views on Hell.* Grand Rapids: Zondervan Publishing House, 1992.

Cullmann, Oscar. *Christ and Time.* Rev. ed. Translated by Floyd V. Filson. Philadelphia: Westminster Press, 1964.

_____. *The Immortality of the Soul, or Resurrection of the Dead?* London: Epworth Press, 1958.

Dalton, William J. *Aspects of New Testament Eschatology.* Nedlands, Australia: University of Western Australia Press, 1968.

Denney, James. *Studies in Theology.* London: Hodder & Stoughton, 1895; reprint, Grand Rapids: Baker Book House, 1976.

DeWolf, Lotan Harold. *A Theology of the Living Church.* 2d ed., rev. New York: Harper & Row, Publishers, 1968.

Dunning, H. Ray. *Grace, Faith, and Holiness: A Wesleyan Systematic Theology.* Kansas City, Mo.: Beacon Hill Press, 1988.

Duty, Guy. *Christ's Coming and the World Church.* Minneapolis: Bethany Fellowship, 1971.

_____. *Escape from the Coming Tribulation: How to Be Prepared for the Last Great Crisis of History.* Minneapolis: Bethany Fellowship, 1975.

Eddleman, H. Leo, ed. *Last Things.* Grand Rapids: Zondervan Publishing House, 1969.

Edwards, Jonathan. *The History of Redemption.* [1773]; reprint, Marshallton, Del.: National Foundation for Christian Education, n.d.

Ellis, E. Earle. *Eschatology in Luke.* Philadelphia: Fortress Press, 1972.

Ellisen, Stanley A. *Biography of a Great Planet.* Wheaton, Ill.: Tyndale House Publishers, 1975.

_____. *Who Owns the Land?* Portland, Oreg.: Multnomah Press, 1991.

Erickson, Millard J. *Christian Theology.* Grand Rapids: Baker Book House, 1985.

_____. *Contemporary Options in Eschatology: A Study of the Millennium.* Grand Rapids: Baker Book House, 1977.

_____. *Readings in Christian Theology.* Vol. 3, *The New Life.* Grand Rapids: Baker Book House, 1979.

Ewert, David. *And Then Comes the End.* Scottdale, Pa.: Herald Press, 1980.

**Selected
Bibliography**

Farrar, Frederic W. *Eternal Hope*. London: Macmillan & Co., 1878.

Farris, T. V. *Mighty to Save: A Study in Old Testament Soteriology*. Nashville: Broadman Press, 1993.

Feinberg, Charles L. *Premillennialism or Amillennialism?* 2d ed. Wheaton, Ill.: Van Kampen Press, 1954.

Finger, Thomas N. *Christian Theology: An Eschatological Approach*. Vol. 1. Nashville: Thomas Nelson Publishers, 1985.

Fison, J. E. *The Christian Hope: The Presence and the Parousia*. London: Longmans, Green & Co., 1954.

Frame, James Everett. *A Critical and Exegetical Commentary on the Epistles of St. Paul to the Thessalonians*. International Critical Commentary. Edinburgh, Scotland: T. & T. Clark, 1912.

Freeman, Hobart E. *Exploring Biblical Theology*. Warsaw, Ind.: Faith Ministries & Publications, n.d.

_____. *An Introduction to the Old Testament Prophets*. Chicago: Moody Press, 1969.

Glasson, T. Francis. *His Appearing and His Kingdom: The Christian Hope in the Light of Its History*. London: Epworth Press, 1953.

Gloer, W. Hulitt, ed. *Eschatology and the New Testament*. Peabody, Mass.: Hendrickson Publishers, 1988.

Grenz, Stanley J. *The Millennial Maze*. Downers Grove, Ill.: InterVarsity Press, 1992.

Gruber, Daniel C. *My Heart's Desire*. Springfield, Mo.: General Council of the Assemblies of God, Intercultural Ministries Department, 1991.

Gundry, Robert H. *The Church and the Tribulation*. Grand Rapids: Zondervan Publishing House, 1973.

Guy, H. A. *The New Testament Doctrine of the "Last Things": A Study of Eschatology*. London: Geoffrey Cumberlege, Oxford University Press, 1948.

Hall, Francis J. *Eschatology*. New York: Longmans, Green & Co., 1922.

Hamilton, Floyd. *The Basis of Millennial Faith*. Grand Rapids: William B. Eerdmans Publishing Co., 1942.

Hamilton, Neill Quinn. *The Holy Spirit and Eschatology in Paul.* Scottish Journal of Theology Occasional Papers, No. 6. Edinburgh, Scotland: Oliver & Boyd, 1957.

Hanson, Paul D. *Old Testament Apocalyptic.* Nashville: Abingdon Press, 1987.

Hanson, R. P. C. *The Attractiveness of God: Essays in Christian Doctrine.* Richmond, Va.: John Knox Press, 1973.

Hayes, Zachary. *Visions of the Future: A Study of Christian Eschatology.* Wilmington, Del.: Michael Glazier, 1985.

_____. *What Are They Saying about the End of the World?* New York: Paulist Press, 1983.

Hoekema, Anthony A. *The Bible and the Future.* Grand Rapids: William B. Eerdmans Publishing Co., 1979.

Horton, Stanley M. *The Ultimate Victory.* Springfield, Mo.: Gospel Publishing House, 1991.

_____. *Welcome Back, Jesus.* Springfield, Mo.: Gospel Publishing House, 1967.

_____. *What the Bible Says about the Holy Spirit.* Springfield, Mo.: Gospel Publishing House, 1976.

Hoyt, Herman A. *The End Times.* Chicago: Moody Press, 1969.

Ironside, H. A. *The Lamp of Prophecy.* Grand Rapids: Zondervan Publishing House, 1940.

Jeremias, Joachim. *New Testament Theology.* Translated by John Bowden. New York: Charles Scribner's Sons, 1971.

Johnson, Christopher J., and Marsha G. McGee, eds. *How Different Religions View Death and Afterlife.* Philadelphia: Charles Press, Publishers, 1991.

Kac, Arthur W. *The Messianic Hope: A Divine Solution for the Human Problem.* Grand Rapids: Baker Book House, 1975.

Kaiser, Walter C., Jr. *Toward an Old Testament Theology.* Grand Rapids: Academie Books, 1978.

_____. *The Uses of the Old Testament in the New.* Chicago: Moody Press, 1985.

Kalafian, Michael. *The Prophecy of the Seventy Weeks of the Book of Daniel: A Critical Review of the Prophecy as Viewed by Three Major Theological Interpretations and the Impact of the Book of Daniel on Christology.* Lanham, Md.: University Press of America, 1991.

Kantonen, T. A. *The Christian Hope.* Philadelphia: Muhlenberg Press, 1954.

Kantzer, Kenneth S., and Stanley N. Gundry, eds. *Perspective on Evangelical Theology: Papers for the Thirtieth Annual Meeting of the Evangelical Theological Society.* Grand Rapids: Baker Book House, 1979.

Kay, William K. *Prophecy!* Nottingham, England: Life Streem Publications, 1991.

Kik, J. Marcellus. *An Eschatology of Victory.* Nutley, N.J.: Presbyterian & Reformed Publishing Co., 1971.

Kimball, William R. *The Rapture: A Question of Timing.* Joplin, Mo.: College Press Publishing Co., 1985.

Koch, Klaus. *The Rediscovery of Apocalyptic.* Translated by Margaret Kohl. Naperville, Ill.: Alec R. Allenson, n.d.

Konig, Adrio. *The Eclipse of Christ in Eschatology: Toward a Christ-Centered Approach.* Grand Rapids: William B. Eerdmans Publishing Co., 1989.

Ladd, George Eldon. *The Blessed Hope.* Grand Rapids: William B. Eerdmans Publishing Co., 1956.

_____. *Crucial Questions about the Kingdom of God.* Grand Rapids: William B. Eerdmans Publishing Co., 1952.

_____. *The Gospel of the Kingdom.* Grand Rapids: William B. Eerdmans Publishing Co., 1959.

_____. *The Last Things: An Eschatology for Laymen.* Grand Rapids: William B. Eerdmans Publishing Co., 1978.

Leckie, J. H. *The World to Come and Final Destiny.* 2d ed., rev. Edinburgh, Scotland: T. & T. Clark, 1922.

Le Goff, Jacques. *The Birth of Purgatory.* Translated by Arthur Goldhammer. Chicago: University of Chicago Press, 1984.

Lenski, R. C. H. *The Interpretation of St. Matthew's Gospel.* Minneapolis: Augsburg Publishing House, 1943.

Lewis, Jack P. *The Minor Prophets.* Grand Rapids: Baker Book House, 1966.

Manson, William, G. W. H. Lampe, T. F. Torrance, and W. A. Whitehouse. *Eschatology.* Edinburgh, Scotland: Oliver & Boyd, 1953.

Marcus, Joel, and Marion L. Soards, eds. *Apocalyptic and the New Testament.* Journal for the Study of the New Testament Supplement Series 24. Sheffield, England: Sheffield Academic Press, 1989.

Marsden, George M. *The Evangelical Mind and the New School Presbyterian Experience.* New Haven, Conn.: Yale University Press, 1970.

Marshall, I. H. *Eschatology and the Parables.* London: Theological Students' Fellowship, 1973.

Martens, Elmer A. *God's Design: A Focus on Old Testament Theology.* Grand Rapids: Baker Book House, 1981.

Martyn-Achard, Robert. *From Death to Life: A Study of the Development of the Doctrine of the Resurrection in the Old Testament.* Edinburgh, Scotland: Oliver & Boyd, 1960.

Mauro, Philip. *Things Which Soon Must Come to Pass: A Commentary on the Book of Revelation.* Swengel, Pa.: Reiner Publications, 1974.

Mealy, J. Webb. *After the Thousand Years: Resurrection and Judgment in Revelation 20.* Journal for the Study of the New Testament Supplement Series 70. Sheffield, England: Sheffield Academic Press, 1992.

Miley, John. *Systematic Theology.* Vol. 2. New York: Hunt & Eaton, 1893; reprint, Peabody, Mass.: Hendrickson Publishers, 1989.

Minear, Paul Sevier. *The Christian Hope and the Second Coming.* Philadelphia: Westminster Press, 1954.

_____. *New Testament Apocalyptic.* Nashville: Abingdon Press, 1981.

Moltmann, Jürgen. *Theology of Hope: On the Ground and the Implications of a Christian Eschatology.* Translated by James W. Leitch from the 5th German ed. New York: Harper & Row, Publishers, 1967.

Selected Bibliography

Moody, Dale. *The Hope of Glory.* Grand Rapids: William B. Eerdmans Publishing Co., 1964.

Morris, Leon. *New Testament Theology.* Grand Rapids: Academie Books, 1986.

Mowinckel, Sigmund O. P. *He That Cometh.* Translated by G. W. Anderson. Nashville: Abingdon Press, 1954.

Mullins, Edgar Young. *The Christian Religion in Its Doctrinal Expression.* Valley Forge, Pa.: Judson Press, 1917.

Neil, William. *The Epistle of Paul to the Thessalonians.* The Moffatt New Testament Commentary. London: Hodder & Stoughton, 1950.

Oden, Thomas C. *Agenda for Theology.* San Francisco: Harper & Row, Publishers, 1979.

_____. *Life in the Spirit.* Vol. 3, *Systematic Theology.* San Francisco: Harper, HarperCollins Publications, 1992.

_____. *The Word of Life.* Vol. 2, *Systematic Theology.* San Francisco: Harper, HarperCollins Publications, 1989.

Oesterley, William O. E. *The Doctrine of the Last Things: Jewish and Christian.* London: John Murray, 1908.

O'Meara, Thomas F., and Donald M. Weisser. *Projections: Shaping an American Theology for the Future.* Garden City, N.Y.: Image Books, 1971.

Pache, René. *The Future Life.* Translated by Helen I. Needham. Chicago: Moody Press, 1962.

Papin, Joseph, ed. *The Eschaton: A Community of Love.* Villanova, Pa.: Villanova University Press, 1971.

Pearlman, Myer. *Knowing the Doctrines of the Bible.* Springfield, Mo.: Gospel Publishing House, 1937.

Pentecost, J. Dwight. *Things to Come: A Study in Biblical Eschatology.* Grand Rapids: Zondervan Publishing House, 1958.

_____. *Will Man Survive?* Chicago: Moody Press, 1971.

Pohle, Joseph. *Eschatology, or the Catholic Doctrine of the Last Things: A Dogmatic Treatise.* English version by Arthur Preuss. Westport, Conn.: Greenwood Press, Publishers, 1971; reprint from 1917.

Pridgeon, Charles Hamilton. *Is Hell Eternal, or Will God's Plan Fail?* 3d ed. Pittsburgh: Evangelization Society of the Pittsburgh Bible Institute, 1931.

Quick, Oliver Chase. *Doctrines of the Creed: Their Basis in Scripture and Their Meaning Today.* London: Nisbet & Co., 1938.

Reiter, Richard R., Paul D. Feinberg, Gleason L. Archer, and Douglas J. Moo. *The Rapture: Pre-, Mid-, or Post-Tribulational.* Grand Rapids: Academie Books, 1984.

Ridderbos, Herman. *The Coming of the Kingdom.* Translated by H. de Jongste. Philadelphia: Presbyterian & Reformed Publishing Co., 1962.

_____. *Paul: An Outline of His Theology.* Translated by John R. De Witt. Grand Rapids: William B. Eerdmans Publishing Co., 1975.

Rowley, H. H. *The Relevance of Apocalyptic: A Study of Jewish and Christian Apocalypses from Daniel to the Revelation.* New and rev. ed. New York: Association Press, 1964.

Ryrie, Charles C. *Basic Theology.* Wheaton, Ill.: Victor Books, 1986.

_____. *Biblical Theology of the New Testament.* Chicago: Moody Press, 1959.

Saucy, Robert L. *The Case for Progressive Dispensationalism: The Interface between Dispensational and Nondispensational Theology.* Grand Rapids: Zondervan Publishing House, 1993.

Sauer, Erich. *From Eternity to Eternity.* Grand Rapids: William B. Eerdmans Publishing Co., 1954.

Schlink, M. Basilea. *Lo He Comes.* Rev. ed. London: Faith Press, 1965.

Schwarz, Hans. "Eschatology." In *Christian Dogmatics.* Edited by Carl E. Braaten and Robert W. Jenson, 475–587. 2 Vols. Philadelphia: Fortress Press, 1984.

_____. *On the Way to the Future: A Christian View of Eschatology in the Light of Current Trends in Religion, Philosophy, and Science.* Rev. ed. Minneapolis: Augsburg Publishing House, 1979.

Selected Bibliography

Scott, R. B. Y. *The Relevance of the Prophets.* Rev. ed. New York: Macmillan Co., 1968.

Shank, Robert. *Until: The Coming of Messiah and His Kingdom.* Springfield, Mo.: Westcott Publishers, 1982.

Shedd, William Greenough Thayer. *The Doctrine of Endless Punishment.* New York: Charles Scribner's Sons, 1886; reprint, Minneapolis: Klock & Klock Christian Publishers, 1980.

Simon, Ulrich E. *The End Is Not Yet.* Digswell Place, Welwyn, England: James Nisbet & Co., 1964.

Smith, Wilbur M. *The Biblical Doctrine of Heaven.* Chicago: Moody Press, 1968.

Stevens, William W. *Doctrines of the Christian Religion.* Nashville: Broadman Press, 1967.

Streeter, B. H., A. Clutton-Brock, C. W. Emmet, J. A. Hadfield, and author of "ProChristo et Ecclesia." *Immortality: An Essay in Discovery.* New York: Macmillan Co., 1917.

Strong, Augustus Hopkins. *Outlines of Systematic Theology.* Philadelphia: Judson Press, 1908.

_____. *Systematic Theology.* Philadelphia: Judson Press, 1947.

Sullivan, Clayton. *Rethinking Realized Eschatology.* Macon, Ga.: Mercer University Press, 1988.

Summers, Ray. *The Life Beyond.* Nashville: Broadman Press, 1959.

Swete, Henry Barclay. *Commentary on Mark.* London: Macmillan & Co., 1913; reprint, Grand Rapids: Kregel Publications, 1977.

_____. *The Holy Spirit in the New Testament.* London: Macmillan & Co., 1910; reprint, Grand Rapids: Baker Book House, 1976.

Tan, Paul Lee. *The Interpretation of Prophecy.* Rockville, Md.: Assurance Publishers, 1974.

Thielicke, Helmut. *The Evangelical Faith.* Translated by Geoffrey W. Bromiley. Vol. 1. Grand Rapids: William B. Eerdmans Publishing Co., 1974.

Thiessen, Henry Clarence. *Introductory Lectures in Systematic Theology.* Grand Rapids: William B. Eerdmans Publishing Co., 1949.

Thompson, Clyde H. *Theology of Kerygma: A Study in Primitive Preaching.* Englewood Cliffs, N.J.: Prentice-Hall, 1962.

Travis, Stephen. *I Believe in the Second Coming of Jesus.* Grand Rapids: William B. Eerdmans Publishing Co., 1982.

_____. *The Jesus Hope.* Downers Grove, Ill.: Inter-Varsity Press, 1974.

Van Gemeren, Willem. *The Progress of Redemption: The Story of Salvation from Creation to the New Jerusalem.* Grand Rapids: Academie Books, 1988.

Villafañe, Eldin. *The Liberating Spirit.* Grand Rapids: William B. Eerdmans Publishing Co., 1993.

Volz, Carl A. *Faith and Practice in the Early Church.* Minneapolis: Augsburg Publishing House, 1983.

Vos, Geerhardus. *The Pauline Eschatology.* Grand Rapids: William B. Eerdmans Publishing Co., 1972.

_____. *Redemptive History and Biblical Interpretation: The Shorter Writings of Geerhardus Vos.* Edited by Richard B. Gaffin, Jr. Phillipsburg, N.J.: Presbyterian & Reformed Publishing Co., 1980.

Wainwright, Geoffrey. *Eucharist and Eschatology.* London: Epworth Press, 1971.

Walvoord, John F. *The Blessed Hope and the Tribulation: A Historical and Biblical Study of Posttribulationism.* Grand Rapids: Zondervan Publishing House, 1976.

_____. *Daniel: The Key to Prophetic Revelation.* Chicago: Moody Press, 1971.

_____. *The Holy Spirit.* Grand Rapids: Zondervan Publishing House, 1972; reprint from 1954.

_____. *The Millennial Kingdom.* Findlay, Ohio: Dunham Publishing Co., 1959.

_____. *The Rapture Question.* Findlay, Ohio: Dunham Publishing Co., 1957.

Selected Bibliography

Westermann, Claus. *A Thousand Years and a Day: Our Time in the Old Testament.* Translated by Stanley Rudman. Philadelphia: Muhlenberg Press, 1962.

Williams, Ernest Swing. *Systematic Theology.* Vol. 3. Springfield, Mo.: Gospel Publishing House, 1953.

Williams, J. Rodman. *Renewal Theology.* Vol. 3. Grand Rapids: Zondervan Publishing House, 1992.

Williams, John. *The Holy Spirit: Lord and Life-Giver.* Neptune, N.J.: Loizeaux Brothers, 1980.

Wilson, Dwight J. *Armageddon Now! The Premillennarian Response to Russia and Israel Since 1917.* Grand Rapids: Baker Book House, 1977.

_____. "Eschatology, Pentecostal Perspectives on." In *Dictionary of Pentecostal and Charismatic Movements.* Edited by Stanley M. Burgess and Gary B. McGee, 264–68. Grand Rapids: Zondervan Publishing House, Regency Reference Library, 1988.

Wingren, Gustaf. *Man and the Incarnation.* Translated by Ross MacKenzie. Edinburgh, Scotland: Oliver & Boyd, 1959.

Winklhofer, Alois. *The Coming of His Kingdom: A Theology of the Last Things.* Translated by A. V. Littledale. Freiburg, West Germany: Herder; Montreal: Palm Publishers, 1965.

Wyngaarden, Martin J. *The Future of the Kingdom in Prophecy and Fulfillment.* Grand Rapids: Baker Book House, 1955.

Yates, J. E. *The Spirit and the Kingdom.* London: Society for the Promotion of Christian Knowledge, 1963.

PERIODICALS

Alexander, Ralph H. "A Fresh Look at Ezekiel 38 and 39." *Journal of the Evangelical Theological Society* 17:3 (Summer 1974): 157–69.

Beasley-Murray, George Raymond. "Comments on Craig L. Blumberg's Response to 'The Kingdom of God in the Teaching of Jesus.'" *Journal of the Evangelical Theological Society* 35:1 (March 1992): 37–38.

_____. "The Kingdom of God in the Teaching of Jesus." *Journal of the Evangelical Theological Society* 35:1 (March 1992): 19–30.

Blamires, Henry. "The Eternal Weight of Glory." *Christianity Today* 35:6 (27 May 1991): 30–34.

Block, Daniel I. "Ezekiel's Vision of Death and Afterlife." *Bulletin for Biblical Research* 2 (1992): 113–42.

Blomberg, Craig L. "A Response to G. R. Beasley-Murray on the Kingdom." *Journal of the Evangelical Theological Society* 35:1 (March 1992): 31–36.

Charles, J. Daryl. "An Apocalyptic Tribute to the Lamb (Rev. 5:1–14)." *Journal of the Evangelical Theological Society* 34:4 (December 1991): 461–73.

Crockett, William V. "Wrath That Endures Forever." *Journal of the Evangelical Theological Society* 34:2 (June 1991): 186–202.

Cross, Frank M. "New Directions in the Study of Apocalyptic." *Journal for Theology and the Church* 6 (1969): 157–65.

Crutchfield, Larry V. "The Apostle John and Asia Minor as a Source of Premillennialism in the Early Church Fathers." *Journal of the Evangelical Theological Society* 31:4 (December 1988): 411–27.

Davis, Joe. "The Eschatology of Jürgen Moltmann." *Southwestern Journal of Theology* 36:2 (Spring 1994): 27.

Ebeling, Gerhard. "The Ground of Christian Theology." *Journal for Theology and the Church* 6 (1969): 47–68.

Edgar, Thomas R. "The Meaning of 'Sleep' in 1 Thessalonians 5:10." *Journal of the Evangelical Theological Society* 22:4 (December 1979): 345–49.

Freedman, David Noel. "The Flowering of Apocalyptic." *Journal for Theology and the Church* 6 (1969): 166–74.

Goff, James R., Jr. "Closing Out the Church Age: Pentecostals Face the Twenty-first Century." *Pneuma* 14:1 (Spring 1992): 7–22.

Grenz, Stanley J. "The Deeper Significance of the Millennial Debate." *Southwestern Journal of Theology* 36:2 (Spring 1994): 14–21.

Selected Bibliography

Grounds, Vernon C. "The Final State of the Wicked." *Journal of the Evangelical Theological Society* 24:2 (September 1981): 211–20.

Henry, Carl F. H. "Reflections on the Kingdom of God." *Journal of the Evangelical Theological Society* 35:1 (March 1992): 39–50.

Horne, Charles M. "The Meaning of the Phrase 'And thus all Israel will be saved' (Romans 11:26)." *Journal of the Evangelical Theological Society* 21:4 (December 1978): 329–34.

House, H. Wayne. "Creation and Redemption: A Study of Kingdom Interplay." *Journal of the Evangelical Theological Society* 35:1 (March 1992): 3–18.

Kaiser, Walter C., Jr. "The Davidic Promise and the Inclusion of the Gentiles (Amos 9:9–15 and Acts 15:13–18): A Test Passage for Theological Systems." *Journal of the Evangelical Theological Society* 20:2 (June 1977): 97–111.

Kirkpatrick, William David. "Christian Hope." *Southwestern Journal of Theology* 36:2 (Spring 1994): 39.

LaRondelle, Hans K. "The Biblical Concept of Armageddon." *Journal of the Evangelical Theological Society* 28:1 (March 1985): 21–32.

Mwakitwile, Charles. "The Eschatology of Karl Barth." *Southwestern Journal of Theology* 36:2 (Spring 1994): 25.

Page, Sydney H. T. "Revelation 20 and Pauline Eschatology." *Journal of the Evangelical Theological Society* 23:1 (March 1980): 31–43.

Payne, J. Barton. "The Goal of Daniel's Seventy Weeks." *Journal of the Evangelical Theological Society* 21:2 (June 1978): 97–119.

Saucy, Robert L. "A Rationale for the Future of Israel." *Journal of the Evangelical Theological Society* 28:4 (December 1985): 433–42.

Thomas, Robert L. "A Hermeneutical Ambiguity of Eschatology: The Analogy of Faith." *Journal of the Evangelical Theological Society* 23:1 (March 1980): 45–53.

Wallis, Wilber B. "Eschatology and Social Concern." *Journal of the Evangelical Theological Society* 24:1 (March 1981): 3-9.

_____. "The Problem of an Intermediate Kingdom in 1 Corinthians 15:20-28." *Journal of the Evangelical Theological Society* 18:4 (Fall 1975): 229-42.

Weber, Timothy P. "A Reply to David Rausch's 'Fundamentalism and the Jew.'" *Journal of the Evangelical Theological Society* 24:1 (March 1981): 67-71.

Yamauchi, Edwin. "Meshech, Tubal, and Company: A Review Article." *Journal of the Evangelical Theological Society* 19:3 (Summer 1976): 239-47.

Scripture Index

NEW TESTAMENT

292   *Our Destiny*

Subject Index

Abaddon, 44. *See also* $Sh^{e'}ol$
Abba, 74
Abyss, Satan locked in, 161, 185, 199, 212
Aiōnion, 240
Aiōnios, 235
Allis, Oswald, 172
Amillennialism, 161–63, 168–73, 183–85, 208
  described by Augustine, 169
  among evangelicals, 161
  rise of, 168–69
  spiritualizing of prophecies, 161, 171, 197
Anamenein, 144
Annihilationism, 238–40
Antichrist, 94, 95, 97, 102, 189
  beast, 101, 108, 182
  counterfeit miracles of, 115
  final destiny of, 118
  held back, 111–13
  identified with the Roman Church, 104, 173
  little horn, 97
  man of lawlessness, 109, 114, 131, 132
  mark of, 108, 115–17
  meaning of *anti,* 114
  nature of, 114–16, 118
  ruler to come, 99–100
Apōleia, 240
Apostasia, 110, 131n
Apostles, 12, 16, 127
  judging (ruling) by, 91, 144, 166, 187

Apostles *(cont.)*
  named on the foundations of the New Jerusalem, 253–54
Aquinas, Thomas, 248
Armageddon, 109, 117–18, 212
Arrabōn, 134, 156
Augustine, 59, 86, 137, 169

Babylon
  destroyed by Sennacherib, 95
  fall of, 108, 117
  image in Daniel, 92–96
  Israel's exile in, 25, 36
Barclay, William, 197
Barth, Karl, 179
Beasts, in Daniel's visions, 96–97. *See also* Antichrist
Bēma judgment, 84–85
Book of Life, 223, 234, 245
Bultmann, Rudolf, 178, 180
Buswell, James Oliver, 225

Calvin, John, 137, 244
Catholic. *See* Roman Catholic Church
Chiliasts, 167
Christian responsibility, 33
  ecological, 166
  for good deeds, 13
  political, 13, 181
  to be different from the world, 147, 158–59
  to be disciples always, 259
  to live in readiness for Christ's return, 146, 151

298